CIVIL WAR AND RECONSTRUCTION WRITINGS OF CHARLES NORDHOFF

Civil War and Reconstruction Writings of Charles Nordhoff

Charles Nordhoff

George Bagby

Tall Men Books

ISBN: 9798869320544
E-Book ISBN: 9798869320551
This edition was formatted and prepared for Tall Men Books by
George Bagby in 2024.
Cover graphics by Dora.
This book was edited in Louisiana.
tallmenbooks@gmail.com

Forward

Charles Nordhoff, a German immigrant to America, was a lively and prolific character and writer. Brought by his parents to Cincinnati, Ohio at the tender age of five, he was sent to a publisher for training before leaving home for a career in the Navy in his teens. He travelled the world as a sailor, both in and out of uniform, before starting his career as a journalist in New York City. He wrote copy, and apparently most of his journalism was not signed. Thus, it has become difficult to determine what he wrote through most of his career, although the vast majority was presumably only daily news and of limited interest. He wrote a lengthy study of enduring interest entitled *Communistic Societies of the United States*, in which he documented and evaluated the various utopian experiments proliferating in the North during his early career. He expressed a healthy skepticism reporting on the demise of many an unlikely sect, and this book remains a valuable resource. Nordhoff published several books of travel and adventure, relying on his many sea voyages, his visits to exotic locales in the Pacific Islands, and his eventual fascination and settlement in California, where he died in 1901.

Nordhoff deserves consideration for two main reasons: he is a fair example of a thoughtful supporter of Republican policies during the Civil War and Reconstruction, and he is a valuable eyewitness of events: especially in his mid-war visit to Carolina and his very important tour of the South in 1876, in the mature zenith of his long career, in which he investigated and interviewed concerning the results of Reconstruction.

Nordhoff wrote an editorial in 1860 entitled "Secession is Rebellion: the Union Indissoluble" in which he, presumably, offered support to Lincoln's theory of the perpetual union and the union's existence before the states. This editorial, though mentioned in Nordhoff's bibliographies, remains obscure. Nordhoff's extant work from the period includes an essay proposing reforms of the Democratic machines in the cities, of which New York's Tammany Hall was the most famous. This was the bugbear of the "Muckraker" Republicans, who succeeded Nordhoff and found success on the issue in the next generation. His considered and curious "America for Free Working Men" is a political pamphlet representing Republican talking points on free-labor and thoughts on labor's essential conflicts with slavery. These works well represent the perspectives, unfamiliar after the passage of time, of Lincoln's mainstream middle-class and working-class supporters.

Nordhoff's reliance on Olmstead's legendary claim that the South was made of slaves, aristocrats, and indolent, "po whites" has been rebuffed many times, and Frank Owlsey's *Plain Folk of the Old South* is the indispensable study on Olmstead's claims. We must also note that Nordhoff is in dispute with economists of his own day, such as Thomas Kittell, but these pamphlets are valuable as a study on perspective, and Nordhoff spoke for his party.

Nordhoff's investment in the war effort and his vocal support of Lincoln led him to a wartime visit of Port Royal and Beaufort, South Carolina in 1862. This was the location of various social experiments in free labor using the "contraband" former slaves captured on the Sea Islands: the experimentation made both more convenient and more controversial through the utter helplessness of the blacks and their totally confused legal status at the time. Nordhoff was so impressed by this foreign world and unfamiliar demographic that he he focused his essay on the exotic character of the "contrabands." Completely at the mercy of Bostonian missionaries and "do-gooders" of many capacities and a variety of strange goals, Nordhoff seems confident in good results. In the mean time, Brahmans experimented with wages, welfare, literacy education, and audaciously trying to teach the contraband women make their bread from milled flour and yeast instead of the locally produced cornmeal. Nordhoff's journalism from Port Royal was a topic of great interest to the masses in the North, who had virtually no experience with black Americans outside of major cities, and many of whose states had banned the settlement of blacks in addition to excluding slavery. The surprisingly sanguine attitude about labor, property, and the "contraband rations" given to the Freedmen by the army is surprising, but matches with Nordhoff's liberalism. For a full treatment of Port Royal, look for Roses' excellent *Rehearsal for Reconstruction* (1964).

The most valuable element of this collection is Nordhoff's lengthy and hitherto inaccessible account of a multi-month journey he made through the South in the last year of the Grant Administration. As he mentions, his accounts, presumably published as correspondence in his New York paper, sparked attacks on his politics and character. He defended his Republican pedigree but manfully stood by his testimony, which even then was outrageous to the establishment. He writes of mixed circumstances in regions afflicted with the confusion and pillage of Reconstruction, and is always eager to support the Republican record whenever he can find grounds to do so. Nevertheless, Nordhoff was no lickspittle, and he was never credibly accused of corruption. He was frequently disgusted by the policies and record of the "Carpetbag" regimes, and he expressed his convictions. He was a lifelong critic of the motives and policies of Democrats, and yet had the humanity to appreciate the legitimacy of Southern opposition to Republican policies: the GOP being entirely foreign to the South until the conquest of the War. Nordhoff was an ally of the Greeley campaign of "liberal"

Republicans who opposed Grant's reelection in 1872, and Greeley's platform condemning the self-serving Republican policies in the South and calling for the end of martial law is certainly evident in Nordhoff's criticism.

Nordhoff's work on the Reconstruction South is the most lengthy, best considered, and best informed of these works. After a decade of steady opposition to the radicals in his own party who dominated the Grant administration and were responsible for the vindictive plunder and dysfunction of the Reconstruction regimes, Nordhoff wrote here with realism and judgment. He brought in a wealth of detailed knowledge of the development of the military-backed Republican administrations and their scandals, and he clearly invested himself in researching on location. He recognizes differing qualities and weighs differing judgments on the regions he visits, which also boosts his credibility. His partisanship, pronounced and blinkered in his earlier pieces, is so softened here that he often recognizes the honor of his opponents: the Democrats of the South. Whereas Nordhoff's wartime work are period pieces valuable as journalism, his "Cotton States" is of more permanent value and insight into the most confused period of American history.

Nordhoff's frank and honest partisanship, when it does emerge, makes him easier to judge and also reveals his essentially noble character. His racial opinions were considered very liberal in his day, and remain very interesting for contrast. Nordhoff continues to be regarded as an authority by the historians of the period and a valuable eyewitness and source of interviews.

Nordhoff is a unique and competent voice. This is the first collection of his writings from this period.

George Bagby,
Louisiana, Spring of 2024

Charles Nordhoff

Contents

1

America for Free Working Men!

AMERICA FOR FREE WORKING MEN!

Mechanics, Farmers and Laborers

READ!

HOW SLAVERY INJURES THE FREE WORKING MAN.

THE SLAVE-LABOR SYSTEM

THE

FREE WORKING-MAN'S WORST ENEMY.

1865

What Democratic Leaders think of Slavery.

"Speaking for myself, slavery is to me the most repugnant of all human institutions. No man alive should hold me in slavery; and if it is my business no man, with my consent , shall hold another. Thus I voted in 1851, in Ohio, with my party, which made the new constitution of my own State. I have never defended slavery; nor has my party."

Speech of Hon. S. S. Cox, of Ohio, in the House of Representatives, Jan. 12, 1865.

Mr. Brooks, of New York, in defending slavery, "did not pretend to speak for the democratic party. Indeed, he does not profess to speak for it, but rather as an old line Whig, having now his views independent of all machines of party. During the last session he held that slavery was dead. Gentlemen should not object to his eulogizing the deceased, but by so doing he does not intend, *nor does he if he intends,* commit any democrat to his moral convictions."

Speech of Hon. S. S. Cox, of Ohio, in the House of Representatives, Jan. 12, 1865.

"The democratic party of the free states are neither the advocates nor the apologists for slavery. Democracy and slavery are natural enemies. Impressed with the value of free labor, there is not a democrat in the North who would not resist the establishment of slavery in a free state."

Speech of Hon. William S. Holman, of Indiana, in the House of Representatives, Jan. 13, 1865.

"I have ever believed slavery wrong. The North have always believed it. Hardly one can at present be found who will claim that slavery is now, or has ever been, other than an evil. * * * The South, by rebellion, has absolved the democratic party at the North from all obligation to stand up longer for the defence of its 'corner-stone'. They are now using the very system which this amendment proposes to abolish, for the overthrow of our government, founded on the broad principles of right, justice, and humanity."

     *   *   *   *   *   *   *

"I cannot but conclude, from the best light I can obtain, that the *operation of this measure will be most beneficial to the non-slaveholding white population of the Southern States..* When these poorer laboring classes shall no longer have to contend with and struggle against and be degraded by slave labor, then, and not until then, will they come into the enjoyment of blessings such as are now fully enjoyed by the honest, toiling workingmen of the North.

"When labor shall be free at the South, then will it command and have the respect which is its just due. Then will millions of the white men of the North participate and share in the blessings thus secured. The masses of our native and foreign-born laborers, now toiling in the severer climate of the North, will be invited to enter upon these newly-opened fields, for their industry and occupation. The now hidden resources of the States South will be developed by the brain and muscle of the northern laborer.

"The existence in our country of antagonistic systems of labor has brought upon the nation the terrible calamity of a wasting civil war, with all its desolations. It has cost the country the lives of hundreds of thousands of its best and bravest sons, and had wasted her material resources.

"The say has come when this conflict of labor is to end, and the question is forced upon us by the South. They alone are responsible for it."

Speech of Hon. M. F. Odell, of New York, in the House of Representatives, Jan. 9th, 1865.

"I am opposed to the re-admission into the Union, with the rights of slave property of any State which our triumphant armies have subjected."

Speech of Hon. Elijah Ward, of New York, in the House of Representatives, Jan. 9th, 1865.

"I believe, and have ever believed since I was capable of thought, that it is a great affliction to any country where it prevails; and, so believing, I can never vote for any measure calculated to enlarge its area, or to render more permanent its duration. In some latitudes, and for some agricultural staples, slave labor may be, to the master, the most valuable species of labor, though this I greatly doubt. In others, and particularly in my own State, I am convinced that it is the very dearest species of labor; and in all, as far as national wealth and power and happiness are concerned, I am persuaded it admits of no comparison with the labor of freemen; and above all, disguise it as we may, if the laws of population shall not be changed by Providence, or man's nature shall not be changed, it is an institution, sooner or later, pregnant with fearful peril.

*   *   *   *   *   *   *

"I shall not stop to inquire, as I before intimated, whether the institution has produced the present war or not. However that may be, one thing, in my judgement, is perfectly clear, now that the war is upon us: *that a prosperous and permanent peace cannot be secured if the institution is permitted to survive.*

*   *   *   *   *   *   *

"If suffered to continue, it will never prove a fruitful topic of excitement and dancer to our continuing peace and union. Terminate it, and the imagination of man, I think, is unable to conceive of any other subject which can give rise to fratricidal strife.

*   *   *   *   *   *   *

"I think the honor and good name as well as the interest and safety of the country require, the abolition of slavery throughout our limits."

Speech of Hon. Reverdy Johnson, of Maryland, In the United States Senate, April 5th 1864.

"The question of slavery is rapidly diminishing in importance; whether for good or evil, it is passing away."

Speech of Hon. D. W. Voorhees, of Indiana, in the House of Representatives, Jan. 9th, 1865.

Mr. Yeaman, of Kentucky, justified "anti-slavery measures" by quoting a letter signed by John J. Crittenden, William T. Barry, R. C. Anderson, J. Cabell Breckinridge. G. Robertson. John Rowen and B. W. Patton, all of Kentucky, urging the nomination of Henry Clay to the Presidency, and saying of Clay:

"We apprehend that no mistake could be greater than that which would impute to him the wish to extend the acknowledged evils of slavery; for we are persuaded that no one entertains a stronger sense of its mischiefs that he does, or a more ardent desire, by all prudent and constitutional means, to extirpate it from our land."

Mr. Yeaman added: "Shall a man be told that it is wrong or disgraceful to hold opinions that have been sanctioned by the minds and hearts of such men."

Speech of Hon. George H. Yeaman, of Kentucky, in the House of Representatives, Jan 9th, 1865.

"Slavery is the chief lever by which the rebel leaders have wielded the Southern mind; and for that reason it has lost nearly all the sympathy and support it once maintained."

Speech of Hon. Austin A. King, of Missouri, in the House of Representatives, Jan 13th, 1865.

"At the last session I voted against the proposed amendment, but when the question is again taken, I intend to record my name in the affirmative."

*   *   *   *   *   *   *

"We never can have peace until we in some way dispose of the institution"

Speech of Hon. James S. Rollins, of Missouri, in the House of Representatives, Jan 14th, 1865.

"The democratic party never advocated slavery as a moral institution. That is a question which will not admit of discussion."

New York Leader, (organ of Tammany Hall,) Jan. 7th, 1865.

"The triumphs of our army and navy have put the rebels in such straits that they no longer refuse to listen to propositions of peace; and the plan of getting rid of slavery legally by a constitutional amendment which shall recognise and respect the rights of States, is a democratic measure, suggested by democrats, and it ought to be supported by democrats."

New York Leader, (organ of Tammany Hall,) Jan. 14th, 1865.

How Slavery Injures Free Workingmen.

The slave-labor system gives to the capitalist many unjust advantages over the poor free workman; it gives to a dozen slave-owners, with a thousand slaves, as many votes in the Legislature, and as great a political power in the States as is possessed by five hundred free workingmen; it discourages schools, prevents the formation of villages and towns; and gives to slave mechanics, slave shoemakers, slave blacksmiths, slave carpenters, slave wheelwrights, the labor, and to their wealthy masters the profits, which belong to the free working-man. To quote the words of the governor of a slave state, Governor Cannon, of Delaware, "Slave labor is uncompensated, white labor is compensated; when the two are brought into competition, white labor is crowded out. If capital owns its labor, the avenues to honest livelihood are forever closed to the white."

When a slave commits murder in Virginia, or any of the other Slave States, he is hanged, and his owner is paid for him the price he could have sold him for before the crime was committed. He is paid for the slave out of the treasury of the State; that is to say, *the tax-payers pay the slaveholder for his slave.*

When a farmer's bull does mischief and is killed, does the State pay for the farmer? When a farmer's horse becomes unmanageable and is killed, does the State pay for him? Not at all. It is only the slave, the peculiar property of the rich, for whom the tax-payers are taxed. The poor man's horse or cow may be killed without payment to the owner.

FREE WORKINGMEN, AS SLAVE-GUARDS.

In the Slave States, whether in the city or in the country, a patrol of the white men is kept up at night - for what? To secure the persons and property of free workingmen? Not at all; but *to look after the slaves of the rich*: to prevent the slaves from running away; to keep them from visiting strange plantations; to catch them and bring them back, if they stray into the woods. "An ordinance organizing and establishing patrols for the police of slaves in the Parish Court of St. Landry, in Louisiana," which lies before us, describes minutely the organization of such patrols. "Every free white male person, between the ages 16 and 60," is bound to do patrol duty. The parish (county) is to pay for "all books, blanks, papers, laws, &c., required for the organization of the patrols." Captains of patrols are to see that the enrollment for this duty includes every man; and anyone who neglects or refuses to server, "at any hour of the day or night" which may be appointed are then taken up with defining the powers and duties of the patrols towards the slaves. They have no other duty to perform, as the title, indeed, asserts. They are "patrols for the police of the slaves." They are not to look out for horse-thieves, or to hunt for stolen cattle; it is made no part of their duty to guard the lives and property of the white workingmen of the country. "Every free white male, between 16 and 60,", in the county is required to mount guard over the peculiar property of the few wealthy planters.

Now the parish of St. Landry had, in 1860, according to the census, 10,703 whites and 11,436 slaves. According to the last census there were 3,953,587 slaves, and somewhat less than 400,000 slaveholders in the country - an average of ten slaves to each owner. At the rate the slaves in the parish of St. Laudry would be owned by eleven hundred and forty-three of the 10,703 white (for children and women own slaves as well as men); and *the whole free population of the country was taxed, in time, labor, and money, to care for the property of a little more than a tenth, and those the wealthiest part.*

Do not suppose that the white workingmen of the Slave States have not felt the oppression of this burden. Where they have been permitted, they have complained. Thus, in an address of Mr. Pierpoint, of Virginia, delivered in 1860, he remarked:

"The clerk or mechanic needs no protection of the law; he is one of the sovereign *body guard to protect and keep in subordination the master's slaves.* Yet his income - the labor of his weary hand and aching head, is *taxed two per cent.* To buy arms and erect armories in which to manufacture the munitions of war, *with which to equip himself, to defend the master in his right to his slaves.*"

An address to the working people of Virginia, in 1860, called attention to the fact that "if a bull or a steer of one of our farmers becomes vicious, so as to be public nuisance, he is ordered by the law to be killed, and his loss falls upon his owner, and upon him alone; but if it happens that a slave of one of the Eastern Virginia capitalists becomes vicious and commits crime, he is hanged or transported, and *it is provided by law that his owner shall be paid his assessed value out of the State Treasury*".

The appropriation, by the Virginia Legislature, in 1856, for patrols, and as pay to slave owners for vicious slaves hanged or transported, amounted to over forty thousand dollars! At the same time, every laboring man in the State, with an income above $250 per annum, had to pay a heavy income tax, while the slaves of the rich were almost totally exempted from taxation.

THE FREE LABORER AND THE SLAVE.

The system of bond-labor is *antagonistic to that of free labor*, and breeds in the masters a contempt for the workingman, as well as for his vocation. This is perfectly natural, and indeed unavoidable. *The slave-owner is a competitor in the slave-market against the free workingman.* He lives upon the labor of his slaves, and he regards with dislike the free laborers who come into the market to bid against him and the labor he controls.

This fact is notorious in the South. It has long attracted the attention of free white workingmen there, but they have been too weak to resist the powerful slave-holders. In 1860, Robert C. Tharin, of Alabama, once a law-partner of the notorious William L. Yancey, endeavored to set up a newspaper called the *Non-Slaveholder*, to urge the passage of a law forbidding the employment of slaves except in agricultural labor and as servants. He thus sought to protect free mechanic, and secure them employment. *For this Mr. Tharin was summarily driven from the State.*

Mr. Tharin, exposing the sophistries of William L. Yancey, writes:

"He had seen the rich man's negro 'come in contact' with the poor white blacksmith, the poor white bricklayer, carpenter, wheelright, and agriculturist. *He had seen the preference invariably given to the rich man's negro* in all such pursuits and trades; like me, *he* had hear the *complaints* of the poor white mechanic of the South against the very negro equality the rich planters were rapidly bringing about. These things he had heard and seen in Charleston, New Orleans, Mobile, Montgomery, and Wetumpka

"Have not the planter *for years condemned every mechanic in the South to negro equality?*" explains Mr. Tharin. "I never *envied* planters of Wetumpka, or, indeed, of any part of the South. My *dislike* to them arose from their contemptible meanness, their utter disregard of decency, they supercilious arrogance, and their daily usurpations of powers and privileges at variance with my rights, and the rights of my class."

FREE WORKINGMEN MUST GIVE WAY TO SLAVES.

In 1853 the free mechanics of Concord, Cobarras county, North Carolina, held a meeting, at which they complained that the *wealthy owners of slaves mechanics were in the habit of underbidding them in contracts.*" The free mechanic who led in this movement was driven from the town. A Long Island carpenter removed to a southern town; he was asked for an estimate for certain work in his trade. The person who proposed to have it done demurred at the price, and remarked that *he could do better to BUY a carpenter, let him do the work* and sell him again when it was done. The free carpenter, being a man of sense, packed up his tools and returned to New York, where a rich man cannot *buy* a carpenter and sell him again.

Olmsted related, in his "Texas Journey," that at Austin, the capital of the state, the German mechanics complained that when the labor for building the state capital was given out, many of them came with offers, but *were underbid by the owners of slave-mechanics.* But when the free mechanics had left town, in search of employment elsewhere, the slave owners threw up their contracts, and, having no longer any opposition, obtained new contracts at advanced prices.

In the iron mines and furnaces near the Cumberland river, in Tennessee, before the war, several thousand men found employ-ment, - but almost without an exception they were slaves. One company had a capital of $700,000 - and owned seven hundred slaves. *Of course an equal number of free workermen were rubbed of employment,* and had either to starve, or emigrate to the Free States, as so many thousands have done.

THE "FAT" FOR THE SLAVE, AND THE "LEAN" FOR THE FREE WORKINGMAN.

Printers call that work which is most quickly and easily done, and which is the best paid, "fat;" that which is hard to do and poorly paid, they call "lean." Now, in all mechanical and other labor performed in the Slave States, the slave constantly gets the best, the easiest - the *fat*; the free mechanic or laborer, if he is employed at all, gets only the leavings of the slave, the *lean*. This comes about, because the slave-owner is a wealthy and influential man, who is able to select the lightest tasks for his slave; by this the slave-owner of course makes the greatest profit, and incurs the least expense. But free white workingman must stand aside, or take that task which the slave-owner will not have.

In Virginia, a wealthy slave-owner told Olmsted that he used Hussey's reaper rather than McCormick's, because "it was more readily repaired by the *slave-blacksmith* on the farm." Another planter in Virginia employed a gang of Irishmen in draining some land. But mark the reasons he gave for this use of free labor. "It's dangerous work" (unwholesome), said he; "and *a negro's life is too valuable to be risked at it.* If a negro dies, it is a considerable loss, you know." This slaveholder did not care how many Irishmen died in his malarious ditches. So, too, on the southwestern steamboats, *slaves* are employed to do the *lightest* and *least dangerous labor;* but *Irish and German free workingmen are employed to perform the exhausting and dangerous work.* Thus, on the Alabama river, Olmsted observed that slaves were sent upon the bank to roll down cotton bales but Irishmen were kept below to drag them away. The mate of the boat said, by way of explanation, "The niggers are worth too much to be risked here; *if the Paddies are knocked overboard, or get their backs broke, nobody loses anything.*"

Alfred E. Matthews, of Starke county, Ohio, in his "Journal of his Flight" from Mississippi, in 1861, remarks: "*I have seen free white mechanics obliged to stand aside while their families were suffering for the necessaries of life, when slave mechanics, owned by rich and influential men, could get plenty of work;* and I have heard these same white mechanics breathe the most bitter curses against the institution of slavery and the slave aristocracy." In his journal at Columbus, Mississippi, he writes: "Business is very dull. Many of the free white mechanics have nothing to do, and there is a great deal of suffering amongst them. *Most of what little work is to be done is given to the slave mechanics.* An intelligent carpenter, an acquaintance of one of the persons in the office where I was engaged, came up one day and told his friend that his family were suffering for provisions; he had no money, and could not get work at anything. He assured me this was the case with others of his acquaintance." This was in a town of three thousand five hundred inhabitants.

SLAVES ARE TRAINED TO MECHANICAL PURSUITS.

On a rice plantation in South Carolina the planter showed Mr. Olmsted "shops and sheds at which blacksmiths, carpenters and other mechanics - all slaves - were at work." Of course, *this planter employed no free mechanics.* Indeed, the writer of this pamphlet was told by a wealthy Alabamian in 1860, that *the planters* in his region were *determined to discontinue altogether the employment of free mechanics.* "On my own place," said this person, "I have now slave carpenters, slave blacksmiths, and slave wheelrights, and thus *I am independent of free mechanics.*"

These instances, culled from southern life, show the bearing of the slave system upon the free working population. The planters do not need the assistance of the free laboring class; they despise it, and discourage it. What is the result? Let "mudsill" Hammond, Governor of South Carolina, bear witness. In an address before the South Caroline Institute, some years ago, he said:

"According to the best calculations which, in the absence of statistic facts, can be made, it is believed that of the three hundred thousand white inhabitants of South Carolina there are not less than fifty thousand whose industry, such as it is, is not in the present condition of things, and does not promise hereafter, such a support as every white person in this country is and feels himself entitled to."

In another part of his address he said: "Eighteen or at most nineteen dollars will cover the whole necessary annual cost of a full supply of wholesome and palatable food, purchased in the market," for one person in South Carolina. It would seem, therefore, that so *completely had the slave system robbed the free workingman of the opportunity to make an honest livelihood, the one-sixth of the free white population of South Carolina could not earn the paltry sum of eighteen dollars per annum!* So completely have the slaveholders monopolized the labor market for their slaves!

The bitter hatred of the "free white" in the South for the negro has been often spoken of. Does any one wonder at it, when he considers that these free men feel the wrongs they suffer, but are too ignorant to trace them to their sources? They hate the slaves, but if they were somewhat more intelligent they would hate the slaveholders, who are the authors of all their woes. It is because Mr. Lincoln, himself a southern man, and a son of one of the oppressed and expatriated free workingmen of the South, understanding this, that he will not suffer the re-establishment of the iniquitous class of monopolists of labor, whose hatred for free workingmen has dragged the country into a civil war. He aims, not so much to free the slave, as *to free the workingmen.* He sees, as a stateman, that a system which degrades and discourages free labor, and whose supporters hate and refuse to employ free workingmen, is ruinous to the prosperity of the country, and is necessarily the parent of the constant dissensions , the fruitful source of hatred, jealousies and heart-burnings. He knows as a stateman, that the security of free government rests upon the virtue, intelligence and prosperity of the working class; and that if we desire the perpetuity of our Union and liberties, we must sweep out of the way a system whose constant and necessary tendency is to impoverish and debase the free workingman.

WHY FREE WORKINGMEN HATE THE SLAVES.

They hate the slaves because slavery oppresses them. Turn where he will, the southern *free mechanic and laborer finds the negro slave preferred before him.* The planter has his slave blacksmith, his slave carpenter, his slave wheelwright, his slave engineer, if he needs one. It is now as it was in Marion's day, who said: "These people of Caroline form two classes - the rich and the poor. The poor are generally very poor, because, *not being necessary to the rich, who have slaves to do all their work,* they get no employment from them."

The slaveholders have the political power; they look only to their own interests; and even where they have established manufactures, they have given work by preference to slaves over free men and women. "*We are beginning to manufacture with slaves,*" wrote Governor Hammond of South Carolina, in 1845, to Thomas Clarkson. A writer in the Augusta *Constitutionalist,* quoted approvingly by De Bow, in 1852, said, "for manufacturing in the hot and lower latitudes, slaves are peculiarly qualified, and *the time is approaching when they will be sought as the operative most to be preferred and depended on.* I could name factories in South Carolina, Alabama and

Georgia, where the success of *black* labor has been encouraging." At the Saluda Factory, near Columbia, South Carolina, so long ago as 1851, one hundred and twenty-eight operatives were employed - *all slaves.* "Slaves not sufficiently strong to work in the cotton fields can attend to the looms and spindles," wrote the superintendent of this mill; and he showed how these slaves underworked the free whites:

"Average cost of a slave operative, per annum

....$75

"Average cost of a white operative, at least

....106

"Difference

....$31

"Or over thirty per cent. Saved in the labor alone by using only the weakly and deformed slaves."

Free labor is killed by such unnatural competition. A writer upon manufactures in the South, in 1852, compared the wages paid to operatives in Tennessee with those in Lowell; "In Lowell, labor is paid the fair compensation of eighty cents per day for men, two two dollars per week for women, while in Tennessee the average compensation for labor does not exceed fifty cents per day for men, and one dollar and twenty-five cents per week for women." Another writer dais: "A female operative in the New England cotton factories receives from ten to twelve dollars per month; *this is more than a female slave generally hires for in the southwest."* This was twelve years ago. But he goes on to explain how *the slaveholder,* monopolizing the labor of his slave, has the power to control the labor market and *underbid the free workman under any circumstances.* "It matters nothing to him (the slaveholder) how low others can produce the article; he can produce it lower still, so long as it is the best use he can make of his labor, and so long as that labor is worth keeping." That is to say, a free white mechanic is at the mercy of his neighbor, the capitalist, in a slave state, because, *if the capitalist does not like the price, he can "go and but a carpenter and sell him again when the work is done."* Thus, while it is true that in the long run and on average free labor is always cheaper than slave labor, the capitalist who monopolizes the slave labor is able to *drive out or starve out the free laborer,* over whom he and his slaves have an unfair advantage. The slaveholders used to boast that there were no "strikes" in the South - here we see the reason. The writer we have quoted adds:

"It is a fact that slaves learn blacksmithing, carpentering, boot and shoemaking, and in fact all handicraft trades, with as much facility as white men; and Mr. Deering of Georgia, has employed slaves in his cotton factory for many years with decided success."

FREE WORKINGMEN ARE "PESTS TO SOCIETY".

Olmstead, when he asked in the slave states why the white laboring men where not employed, was told that they were not hired "because you cannot *drive* them as you do a slave" *The aristocratic slave-owner refuses to employ a workman whom he cannot flog and curse.* On a rice plantation in South Carolina he found a *slave engineer,* for whose education in that profession his owner had paid five hundred dollars to a steam-engine builder. This slave machin- ist, an able man, *lived better than any laboring free white man in the district.* His master, who also owned slave blacksmiths, carpenters, and other mechanics, *did not employ a single freeman,* expect an over- seer. But an estate of the same size and value in a free state would have given employment to twenty-five or thirty white mechanics of different trades, not to speak of a large number of free laborers.

By the census of 1850 it appears that the average wages of the female operatives in the Georgia cotton factories were $7.39 per per month; in Massachusetts it was $14.57 per month. New England factory girls were induced by the special offer of high wages to go to Georgia to work in newly-established cotton factories, but they found the position so unpleasant, owing to the general degradation of the laboring class, they were very soon forced to return. Nor shall we wonder at this when we read the following sentiment, which appeared in the Charleston *Standard*, in 1855:

"*A large portion of the mechanical force that migrate to the South are a curse instead of a blessing;* they are generally a *worthless, unprincipled class,* enemies to our peculiar institution (slavery), and formidable barriers to the success of our native mechanics (slave). Not so, however, with another class who migrate southward - we mean that class known as merchants; *they* are generally intelligent and trustworthy, and they seldom fail to discover their true interests. They become slaveholders and landed proprietors; and in ninety-nine cases out of a hundred they are better qualified to become constituents of our institution than a certain class of our native born, who from want of capacity are perfect drones in society, *continually carping about slave competition.* * * * The *mechanics,* the most of them, are *pests to society,* dangerous among the slave population, and ever ready to form combinations against the interests of the slaveholder."

Is it strange that the ignorant, neglected, despised free white workingman of the slave states hates the slave? He feels that the slave injures him in every possible way; the slave robs him of work; the slave deprives him of bread and clothing for his children; the slave gets the easiest tasks, the free laborer the hardest and most dangerous; the slave steps before him whenever he looks for a job, and has the preference everywhere, *because he is the tool of a capitalist whose influence and wealth enable him to grasp* - for his own benefit - whatever might be of advantage to the free mechanic or laborer.

The capitalist, in a slave state, is a man with a hundred black arms, all bare, all eagerly seeking work, all ready to work for less than a free man can support his family decently upon. The capitalist is a hundred-armed workman, with enough social influence to command work for all his hundred arms, *to the exclusion of the honest free mechanic and laborer.* The slave, in the hands of this capitalist, is the most dangerous enemy the free workman can have. Suppose a job of work for twenty mechanics is to be given out in a southern town - twenty free men offer themselves - but a slave-owner comes, with the prestige of great wealth, with his social influence and his political power, and he gets the preference for his twenty slaves, *the profits of whose labor go to make him richer, while his free neighbors grow poorer.* It is not strange that the southern free workingmen resent this monstrous wrong —but it is lamentable that they make the error of hating the tools with which the wrong is done, and not those who use these helpless tools, and the iniquitous system which permits it. It is as though a martyr should abhor only the thumb-screws which torture him, but regard kindly the executioner who applies them; it is as though a western traveller should complain of the scalping knife, but love the Indian savage who uses it.

It is the slave-holder who wrongs the free workingman. It is the slave system which oppresses him. Make the slave free and he is no longer your fatal competitor; take the slaves away from the capitalist, and he has no longer the power to rob you of work and bread. Free the negroes, and you redeem the free white working-class from the domination of the selfish capitalists, and make the blacks themselves harmless to you. It is only while they are slaves that the negroes injure the white working men,

HOW FREE WORKINGMEN ARE OVERTAXED IN SLAVE STATES.

We have shown how the slave-labor system robs the free workingman, the free mechanic and laborer, of employment and bread, and thus keeps him poor and helpless - or drives him into the free states. But the subjection of free workingman condemned by the monopolists of slave labor to idleness and poverty, but his children are held in ignorance; his political rights are cunningly abridged; the products of his labor are force to bear an *unequal* burden of taxation; and he - the non-slaveholding workman - is compelled by the laws to mount guard over the slaves of his wealthy neighbor, or else to pay for such a guard. Thus he is injured in every interest, for the benefit of the slaveholder.

In the free states of the Union a poor man's vote counts as much as his wealthy neighbor's, and the millionaire enjoys no special political privileges over the carpenter who builds his house, or the blacksmith who shoes his horse. We are accustomed to think this a good system, but how is it in the slave states? Take Virginia as an example. There, while in one branch of the Legislature men are represented, in the other *money* and slaves have also a large representation.

So great was this political power of wealth, that before the war *ten thousand white men - slaveholders - in Eastern Virginia* had as much power - as many votes - in the Senate, as forty thousand white men - non-slaveholders - of Western Virginia.

How did the slaveholders, the aristocrats of Eastern Virginia use this power? *They exempted a great part of their peculiar property from taxation,* and laid the burden of taxes upon the free workingmen of the state. They enacted a law by which all slaves under twelve years of age were excepted from taxation altogether - *but they taxed the calves, the colts, the lambs, of the farmers.* They limited the tax upon slaves over twelve years to one dollar and twenty cents per head; but they taxed a trader with a capital of only six hundred dollars, sixty dollars for his year's license, and a heavy duty on his sales afterwards. The slave property of Virginia, before the war, paid about $300,000 per annum taxes - but *if it had been taxed as other property was, according to value, it would have contributed one million three hundred thousand dollars per annum!* The odd million was raised by extra taxes in the earnings of the free laborers.

Not only this - the *products* of slave labor were also exempted from taxation. Tobacco, corn, wheat and oats were not taxed; but the product of free labor, consisting in cattle, hogs, sheep, &c., was heavily taxes; as were *also the earnings of free laboring men,* who were obliged to pay an income tax. It was asserted by Mr. Peirpoint, in 1860, that "upwards of two hundred and thirty million dollars of the Virginia slaveholders' capital in slaves was *exempted from taxation.*"

But while the slave owner was so protected, see how it fared with the free laborer? Every free mechanic, artisan, or laborer of whatever kind, who was in the employment of any person, was obliged, by a special law, to pay an income tax of *one-half of one per cent. If his income did not exceed $250:* of one per cent. If his income was under $500; of one and a half per cent. If it was under $1,000, and two per cent. If he earned over $1000. Our workingmen think the United States income tax onerous; but that, at least, exempts the man who earns less than $600. *The Virginia slaveholders exempted only themselves!* They taxed the poor, but left the rich to pay nothing.

ENORMOUS AND UNUSUAL TAXATION OF FREE WORK-INMEN IN VIRGINIA.

See how this act worked. In Wheeling there were employed in 1859 about 1,500 free men in the iron mills; these earned an average of $400 per annum each. On this they had to pay one per cent. - four dollars - making $6,00 per annum; besides eighty cents poll tax, $1,200 more, total $7,200, drawn from 1,500 free laboring men. Now *this tax was equal to that levied on six thousand slaves.* That is to say, each free workman was taxed four times as heavily as a slave. But take note of this: the owner of the slave was not only very lightly taxed for his property in him; *he paid no income tax at all.* That is to say, the net income from the labor of six thousand slaves might be reckoned by those times at $900,000 per annum. On this the masters, the capitalists, who received this sum, paid not a cent of income-tax! Or, take another example: a foreman in a factory earned $1,100 per annum; he had to pay $22 80 income tax to the State. But a slave-owning capitalist paid no more that that as his tax on nineteen slave; *he trained them to mechanical work* - hired them out in such manner that they threw nineteen free mechanics out of employment - and on the proceeds of the labor of these nineteen slaves, amounting to $5,700 per annum, *he was taxed not a single cent!*

"There are many poor men in this State," said Mr. Pierpoint in 1860, "getting 75, 80, 90, and 100 cents per day, with families to support, who all have to pay, in addition to the income tax, for everything the own on the face of the earth, forty cents on a hundred dollars, while the slaveholder only pays 10 cents on the hundred dollars' worth of slaves!" "The income tax levied by the slaveholders upon the small incomes of free mechanics," Mr. Pierpoint said, "will eat out the very vitals of all the manufacturing energy of the State." Nor were the free mechanics the only sufferers. "The farmer in Western Virginia (not a slaveholder) who 12 years ago paid his tax with 15 dollars, now pays $60, with little increase in actual value." *Only the slaveholders were exempted!*

Thus was slave labor encouraged and free labor made penal in the South. Thus, to use Marion's words, the poor became poorer and the rich richer. Thus free mechanics were driven out of the slave states, taxed out, starved out, until, in 1859, Charleston, one of the chief seaports of the South, had not left so much as a single ship-carpenter. Thus was brought about the unhappy condition of the free workingmen, described by Mr, Tarver, in "DeBow's Industrial Resources of the South and Southwest."

"The acquisition of a respectable position in the scale of wealth appears so difficult that they decline the hopeless pursuit, and many of them settle down into passive idleness, and become the almost passive subjects of all its consequences. An evident deterioration is taking place in this part of the population; the younger portion of it being less educated, less industrious, and in every point of view less respectable than their ancestors."

HOW SLAVES OUT-VOTE FREE WORKINGMEN.

These are the effects of the slave labor system upon the unfortunate free laborers who are subjected to its influence. Bear in mind that it is not only Virginia that the free mechanic and laborer is thus wronged. In Louisiana, in South Carolina, in most of the slave states, slave property is represented and favored in some special manner. In Louisiana the representation, under the old system, was apportioned according to the whole population - free and slave. Thereby it happened that the thousands of free laborers of New Orleans were places at the mercy of a few enormously wealthy slave-owning capitalists in the sparsely settled river parishes; and *a thousand votes of free mechanics had not so much power in the Legislature as two hundred and fifty planters' votes, whose slaves filled up a legislative district.*

South Carolina has always been called the model slave state. Her system was and is the admiration of the slaveholding class. There the free laborer was entirely debarred from influence, totally unrepresented. He could vote - but not for one of his own class; *only a slave owner could serve in the Legislature; only a slave owner could be governor; and the Legislature, composed exclusively of slave owners;* appointed the judges, the magistrates, the senators, the electors for President.

Not only this - the Legislature set apart the state Congressional districts; and it managed this in such manner that the slaveholding interest alone represented in Congress. In the legislative apportionment of the free workingmen of the State were still more outraged. Five-sixths of the white population, residing in those counties where there were but few slaves, had only seventy-eight out of one hundred and twenty-two representatives in the Legislature - a little more than one-half. The Pendleton district, with over twenty-six thousand white inhabitants, but few slaves, sent but seven members; the parishes of St. Philip and St. Michael, with less than nineteen thousand whites, but a heavy slave population, sent eighteen.

Now take notice of the results of this system upon the free workingmen. Governor Seabrook, of South Carolina, said in a message a few years ago:

"Education has been provided by the Legislature *but for one class of the citizens* of the State, which is *the wealthy class.* For the middle and poorer classes of society it has done nothing, since no organized system has been adopted for that purpose. * * * * * Ten years ago twenty thousand adults, besides children, were unable to read or write, in South Carolina. Has our free school system dispelled any of this ignorance? Are there no reasonable fears to be entertained that the number has increased since that period?"

In the Charleston *Standard*, in November, 1855, was advanced by eminent South Carolinians the atrocious doctrine that the State should educate only its capitalists and the officers and overseers who, under the order of the capitalists, should command and direct the laborers. Chancellor Harper, one of the foremost men of the State, said, in a public address printed by De Bow, and received with general approval:

"Would you do a benefit to the horse, or the ox, by giving him a cultivated understanding or fine feelings? So far as the *mere laborer* has the pride, the knowledge, and the aspiration of a free man, he is unfitted for his situation, and must doubly feel its infelicity."

And what was the effect of this system upon the free workingmen of the State? Let Governor Hammond, one of its chief citizens, reply. Fifty thousand, he said, a sixth of the white population of the State, *were unable to earn their living.* He added: "Most of them now follow agricultural pursuits, *in feeble but injurious competition with slave labor.*" And another writer, whose essay on cotton and cotton manufactures at the South is printed by De Bow, remarks that "a degree and extent of poverty and destitution exist in the Southern States among a certain class of people, almost unknown in the manufacturing districts of the North. * * * Boys and girls by thousands, destitute both of employment and the means of education, grow up to ignorance and poverty, and too many of them to vice and crime."

Such are some - but not all - the disabilities under which the free workingman labors, in a State where the slave-labor system prevails. Deprived of employment, left without education, misrepresented in the legislative halls by men whose interests are opposed to his, and before whom he is powerless, the free laborer grows poorer as his wealthy neighbor grows richer; and looking at these things we cease to wonder at the persistent emigration from the eastern slave states, westward, of which Mr. Tarver said, speaking of South Carolina, "That necessity must be strong and urgent which induces *thirty per cent. of the population of a State, in the short space of ten years, to break all the social and individual ties which bind man to the place of his birth, and seek their fortunes in other lands.*"

FREE WORKINGMEN FLY FROM THE SLAVE STATES.

The slave states are the most sparsely popular of the Union; their soil is rich, their climate kindly, they abound in mineral wealth; everything there favors the workingman - yet the workingmen of the free states refuse to go there; and a *constant and large stream of emigration has set for years, from the slave states into the free states.* The free workingmen of the slave states have fled from the oppression and blight of the slave institution, to the part of the Union where all labor is free and paid.

If we take the census report of 1850, we find that the slave states had sent nearly six times as many of their population into free territory as the free states had sent into slave territory. We find that Kentucky had sent on to free soil sixty thousand more persons than all the free states sent into slave soil. Little Maryland had sent more than half as many persons into free territory as all the slave states have sent into slave territory. Virginia had sent sixty thousand more persons into free territory than all the free states had sent upon the slave soil. Kentucky and Tennessee were but little behind the other states we have mentioned.

This shows the course of emigration. But it is even more clearly shown in some interesting tables contained in the last census report - that for 1860. In a table of "Internal Migration" we find that there were in the country, and returned by the census takers, 399,700 persons born in Virginia, but *living in other states;* 344,765 persons born in Tennessee, but living in other states; 272,606 persons born in North Carolina, but living in other states; 137,258 persons born in Maryland, but living in other states; 32,493 persons born in Delaware, but living in other states; 331,904 persons born in Kentucky, but living in other states.

Now it is true that not all these 1,518,726 persons who had migrated from only the border line of slave states were living in the free states, but by far the greater number were. The "course of internal migration" is exhibited in a table of the Census Report. There we find that emigrants from Virginia have removed "chiefly" to Ohio, Missouri, Kentucky, and Indiana; from Kentucky they have removed chiefly to Missouri, Indiana, Illinois and Ohio. From Maryland they have removed chiefly to Ohio, Pennsylvania, Virginia and the District of Columbia. From Delaware they have migrated chiefly to Pennsylvania, Maryland, Ohio and Indiana. From Tennessee they have removed chiefly to Missouri, Arkansas, Texas and Illinois.

But this table shows us a far more remarkable fact. From the southern tier of slave states the migration was chiefly into other slave states, in a western or northwestern direction *towards the free states*. From the border slave states the migration was *chiefly into the free states*, and into that slave states (Missouri) which promised first to become free. But from the free states, which sent forth also a large stream of emigrants, there was *no* emigration to slave states; all, with insignificant exceptions, removed to *other free states*. 399,700 Virginians had removed chiefly to Ohio, Missouri, Kentucky and Indiana; but of 582,512 Pennsylvanians, just across the line, it is recorded that they removed "chiefly" to Ohio, Illinois, Indiana, and Iowa. 331,904 Kentuckians had removed "chiefly" to Missouri, Indiana, Illinois and Ohio; but 593,043 persons born across the river, in free Ohio, had removed chiefly to Indiana, Illinois, Iowa and Missouri. These contrasts hold good of the whole table. From no free state has there been emigration to the slave states; but from every border slave state there has been a very heavy migration to the free states.

Observe, that this course of migration is unusual and unnatural. The tendency, in all the history of the world, has been the other way. Tribes and families have fled from the bleak climate and barren soil of the North to the milder climate and more generous soil of the South. A French writer, the Count de Segur, says: "The human race does not march in that direction; it turns its back to the North; the sun attracts its regards, its desires, and its steps. It is no easy matter to arrest this great current." In other countries all emigration has turned to the Southwards, by an instinctive movement; but with us the horror of slavery, the aversion of the free laborer to come in contact and competition with slave labor, has sufficed to conquer even this strong instinctive tendency.

Bear in mind, too, that the South has lost, by this migration, the best class of her citizens. The indolent masters remained; the slaves remained; those free whites who were too poor and helpless and ignorant either to desire or to be able to remove, remained; but there has been a constant drain of the yeomanry of the border slave states - the forehanded farmers and industrious mechanics, the class whom a state can least afford to lose. These men and their families have helped to fill our northwestern territories and states; and have taken the places of the thousands who removed from the border free states to the northwest. They have faced unwonted winters and harder conditions of life - why? Because *these free workingmen felt slavery to be a curse, a bar to all their efforts.* They were not abolitionists - they brought into the free states with them their curious hatred of the negro, as though it was the slave and not the master who was their oppressor.

SLAVERY EXTERMINATES FREE MECHANICS.

Charles J. Faulkner, of Virginia, said, in 1832, in the legislature of that state: *"Slavery banishes free white labor; it exterminates the mechanic, the artisan, the manufacturer, it deprives them of bread."* And C. C. Clay, of Alabama, not less eminent in the South than Mr. Faulkner, said a few year ago: "Our wealthier planters, with greater means and no more skill, are buying out their poorer neighbors, extending their plantations and adding to their force. The wealthy few, who are able to live on smaller profits, and to give their blasted fields some rest, are thus pushing off the many who are merely independent. Thus *the white population has decreased, and the slave increased*, almost *pari passu* in several counties of our state. In 1825 Madison county cast about three thousand votes; now she cannot cast more than two thousand three hundred. In travelling that county one will discover numerous *farm-house, once the abode of industrious and intelligent freemen, now occupied by slaves*, or tenantless, deserted, and dilapidated. He will see the moss growing on the mouldering walls of once thrifty villages, and will find 'one only master grasps the whole domain,' that once furnished happy homes for a dozen white families."

Thus southern men, themselves slaveholders, bear witness to the causes which lead to the great and constant migration of the most valuable class of citizens from the slave to the free states. The agriculturist and the mechanic alike, the blacksmith, the carpenter, the farmer, all are "pushed off," to use the expressive phrase of Mr. Clay, to make way for the masters and their slaves.

SLAVERY SHUTS THE SOUTH AGAINST GERMANS AND IRISHMEN.

If a considerable part of the white workingmen of the slave states have migrated to the free states, it is equally true that of the thousands of German, Irish and other workingmen who have, with their families, sought our shores, the southern states has received but an insignificant fraction.

To the industry and thrift of this part of our population a large share of our prosperity and wealth is owing; without the help of their strong arms, the free states, though thriving and populous, and receiving increase from the South, must have advanced much more slowly than they have. This fact has been generally recognized amongst us. Indeed, in the western states special inducements have been held out to immigrants, so strongly have the people there felt the need for their labor and the advantage of their presence. Consider, then, what has been the loss of the South, which has utterly failed to attract this class, while at the same time it was drained to a considerable extent of its own free working class.

If we compare free states with slave states, we find that while South Carolina had in 1860 but 9,986 foreign born citizens. Massachusetts had 260,114; Virginia had but 35,058 foreigners, but Pennsyslania , but her neighbor, had 430,505; Georgia, the empire state of the South, had but 11,671, but New York had 998,640; Mississippi had only 8,558, but Illinois had 324,643, Tennessee had 21,226, and Kentucky 59,799; but Ohio had 328,254, and Indiana 118,184. Little Rhode Island, with an insignificant territory and a dense population of 133 to the square mile, had attracted 37,394 foreign emigrants; but North Carolina, with a milder and more varied climate, a fertile soil, ready access by sea, and the advantage of a profitable fishery and several other special pursuits, not to speak of an immensely greater territory, had been able to attract to her borders but 3,299 foreign emigrants.

Nor must we fail to notice that in those states where slavery languished or had but a slender hold, emigrants at once increased in numbers. Maryland had 77,536, nearly seven times as many as Georgia; Delaware had 9,165, nearly three times as many as North Carolina; and Missouri had 160,541, as many within fifteen thousand as all the slave states east of the Mississippi, except Maryland and Delaware. That is to say, Missouri, which was in the popular belief certain to become a free state before many years, was able to attract to her soil nearly as many emigrants as Kentucky, Tennessee, Mississippi, Alabama, Georgia, North and South Carolina and Virginia together! Still, slavery told against Missouri when compared with the free states. With a milder climate, immensely greater mineral resources and a nearer and cheaper access to great markets, Missouri had attracted bit 13.59 per cent. Of foreigners, while Iowa has 15.71 per cent., Minnesota 33.78 per cent., and Wisconsin 35.69 per cent.

The census report shows that of the foreign born population the free states have received over eighty-six and one-half per cent., and the slave states less than fourteen. It shows the States which have received the smallest percentage of this accretion to be North Carolina, Arkansas, Mississippi, Georgia, and South Carolina - *all slave states.* And it shows also the singular fact, that while eight foreign emigrants have settled in the free states to one in the slave states, the number of slaves - if we add the insignificant number of free colored - gives just one to over eight of our population.

FREE WORKINGMEN KEPT OUT OF THE FINEST PART OF THE UNION.

Is it no matter to workingmen that they are thus driven out and kept out of the largest, most fertile, and pleasantest part of the Union by the slave-labor system, which there robs them of work, and attacks their rights? In the mild climate of the border slave states, the seasons are longer, the productions more varied; trades which can be pursued in the North during only eight or none months, may be carried on there all the year round; food is or ought to be cheaper; the workingman and his family need fewer and less costly clothes; in many ways the conditions of life are easier, for the mechanic and laborer as well as the farmer, than in the colder North. *But that great region the slavemasters closed against the free working men,* and preserved for themselves and their slaves.

The climate is not too hot in any of those states for white men and women to labor in the fields. Governor Hammond, of South Carolina, said: "The steady heat of our summers is not so prostrating as the short, but sudden and frequent heats of northern summers." White men work on the levee in New Orleans in mid-summer, and have the severest labor put upon them at that. He who writes this rolled cotton and sugar upon the levee of New Orleans in the month of July, and screwed cotton in Mobile Bay in August. Dr. Cartwright, the great apostle of slavery, rightly remarked: "*Here in New Orleans the large part of the drudgery - work requiring exposure to the sun, as railroad making, street paving, dray driving, ditching, and building is performed by white people.*" This severe labor was put upon the free white workingmen; the slave-owners reserved the light tasks for their slaves.

In Alabama, by the census in 1850, sixty-seven thousand, in Mississippi, fifty-five thousand, in Texas forty-seven thousand *white men, non-slaveholders, labored in the fields,* and took no hurt. Cotton was cultivated in Texas, before the war, with perfect success, by white men; the Germans managed even to raise more pounds to the acre, pick it cleaner, and to get a higher price for it, than the neighboring planters. Olmsted mentions an American in Texas who would not employ slave labor, and who, with white men as his help, "produced more bales to the hand than any planter around him."

The mortality reports of the census show that the southern states are not peculiarly unhealthful. In Alabama, the deaths, per cent., were less than in Connecticut; in Georgia they are 1.23 per cent., in New York, 1.22; in South Carolina they are 1.44 per cent., in Massachusetts, 1.76, which is precisely the same as Louisiana, notoriously, till General Butler cleaned New Orleans and drove out the yellow fever, the most sickly state of the South.

Nothing, therefore, has kept free workingmen out of these states - nearer to the great markets of the world, having more abundant mineral wealth, and in every way more favorably situated than the cold Northeast and the far away Northwest - except the fatal competition of the slaveowners. To avoid that, millions of workingmen, native and foreign born, have removed to the northwest, until at last the tide of emigration has even trenched upon the inhospitable desert, and has spread beyond the extreme limits of arable land, and far beyond the profitable reach of markets. The Northwestern farmer has burned his corn because he could not afford to send it to the distant seaboard - *was it no loss to him that slavery kept him out of the fertile fields of Virginia and North Carolina?*

Even had slavery remained in full vigor, the time had come when free labor, seeking new outlets and greater opportunities, would have pressed hardly upon it. If slavery is swept away, free workingmen will hereafter have opportunity in the South, and to all that great region a boundless future of wealth and prosperity opens up. The abandoned farms, the mouldering villages, the empty cottages, will once more be filled with the busy and cheerful hum of the labor of freemen.

Their cunning will repair the waste of unskillful slave labor; their ingenious toil will redeem the barren fields of Virginia and other southern states. The tide of emigration, sweeping in that direction, may repeat in the South the marvellous results which it has accomplished during the last twenty-five years in the North-west; Virginia will be another Minnesota, North Carolina a new Iowa, and in Tennessee will be repeated the story of Ohio.

HOW TO LESSEN THE BURDEN OF TAXATION

When a man falls into debt, and is anxious to free himself of it, what does he do? He works harder, and lives more frugally. He tries to make a dollar more per week, and live on a dollar less. In that way he may hope to get clear of debt. Well, as with a man, so it is with a nation: we have incurred a great debt; and hence-forth, we must, as a people, live more economically, and use, to better advantage, our property and our strength. We can no longer afford to exhaust our soil, by "artless" methods of culture; we can no longer afford to employ half a dozen men to do one man's work; we can no longer afford to use poor tools, to do with a hoe the work of a plough, to reap by hand instead of by steam, to work by main strength and stupidity, instead of intelligently.

It is not enough that one part of the country shall do its best – the resources of all parts must be fully developed. It is not fair to the working men of the free states, that they shall pay heavier taxes, in order that slaveholders may indulge their fancy for dull, plodding, unskilled slave labor. It is not fair that we of the North should bear a heavy burden, more than our proper share of the common debt, when, by the use of proper means, by throwing the Southern states open to free labor, and to skilled labor, its resources can be rapidly developed to the point where those states will be as populous, and as wealthy, as the free states.

If we can discover a way to make the whole country populous, and to make the whole nation prosperous, the weight of taxation will be much lightened; increased numbers and increased wealth will enable us to bear, without suffering, burdens under which we might sink if these elements of strength were lacking.

WE CANNOT AFFORD SLAVERY.

We cannot afford to omit measures which will add to our ability to pay taxes. There was a time when we might live after a slipshod fashion, but hereafter it is important to every man in the country, and especially to the workingmen and their families, that the natural resources of the whole country shall be wisely and effectively developed. It is easy to show that the Southern states have enormous and inexhaustible wealth of iron, coal, copper, and many other things; but if that mineral wealth is to remain, in future as in the past, in the bowels of the earth; if Virginia, with the richest coal and iron deposits, is hereafter, as heretofore, to buy both coal and iron in Pennsylvania; if Tennessee, abounding in minerals, is to continue to be cursed with a slave-labor system, which forbids the development of her greatest sources of wealth; if we do not use the only means in our power, or any one's power, to bring out that wealth, and thus add enormously to the general wealth of the country – which can only be done by extirpating slave-labor, and substituting free labor in its place – why then, we may as well reconcile ourselves – we free working men of the North- to paying perpetually much the heaviest share of the national taxation.

A shrewd foreign traveller once remarked that the slave-labor system was such a costly economical blunder, that no European nation could afford it; only a country having no debt, and scarcely any expenses, could indulge in it. The time has come when we, too, can no longer afford it. *If the working men of the free states wish to lift from their backs some portion of the heavy burden of taxation, they must insist that the southern states shall be thrown open to free labor,* in order that this vast region shall be enabled to yield an equal share of the national revenue. It cannot do this till it is equally wealthy; but, as we shall proceed to show, the slave labor system made it poorer instead of richer, for many years.

How are we to equalize the burden? By making Virginia as populous and wealthy as Pennsylvania, Kentucky as Ohio, Tennessee and Georgia as New York, South Carolina as Massachusetts, Mississippi as Iowa. The Lynchburg *Virginian* wrote some years ago:

"The coal fields of Virginia are the most expensive in the world; and the coal is of the best and purest quality; her iron deposits are altogether inexhaustible, and in many instances so pure that it is malleable in its primitive state; and many of these deposits are in the vicinity of extensive coal fields. She has, too, very extensive deposits of copper, lead, and gypsum. Her rivers are numerous and bold, generally with fall enough for extensive water power."

VIRGINIA AND PENNSYLVANIA COMPARED

But these coal and iron and copper and lead deposits of Virginia, greater than those of Pennsylvania, and lying in a finer climate, are almost untouched. And because they are so, the whole industry of the state had suffered. The census of 1850 gave the following values to agricultural lands in the adjoining States of Pennsylvania and Virginia:

	In Virginia	In Penn'a
Number of acres of improved land in farms	10,380,135	8,626,619
Number unimproved	15,792,172	6,294,728

Cash value of farms in Virginia, *eight* dollars; in Pennsylvania, *twenty-five* dollars per acre.

Does any one need to be told which state is able to pay and will pay the largest amount of revenue to the government? Is it not easy to see that, with the same policy in Virginia which was prevailed in Pennsylvania, that state would in a very few years be as populous, as wealthy, and as great a source of revenue, as her neighbor? And is it not to the interest of every free workingman, every tax-payer, that this should be brought about?

The Southern states, if we include Missouri and Kentucky, have an area of 851,508 square miles; the free states have an area of only 612,597 square miles. The South has a milder climate, short winters, a far more fertile soil, immensely greater mineral wealth, more abundant natural water communications with the sea, than the North. Yet in 1850, by the census, the total values of the real and personal property of the free states was $1,161,081,000 *greater* that that of the real and personal property of the South, *including three millions of slaves.* But in 1860, according to the census of that year, the total value of the real and personal property in the free states was $2,657,165,268 *greater* than that of the South. The wealth of the free states, excluding the territories, was in 1860, in round numbers, nine thousand two hundred and eighty-seven millions; that of the slave states, including Missouri, six thousand six hundred and thirty millions, also including the slaves!

Now if, by wise measures, by encouraging the mechanic arts, fostering free schools, developing, mineral resources, and, in short, treating the South as we treated the Northwest, we can make it increase as rapidly, after the war, in free population, and in wealth, as the Northwest has, we may expect this difference to disappear in a very few years; we may expect the South to become as prosperous and as wealthy, in a few years, as the North is. In that case *it will contribute a revenue to the government greater than the whole North does at this time. That is to say, we can double our revenue without increasing our taxation, or we can raise the same revenue with half the taxes.*

But to do that we must do away with the wasteful and ruinous system of slave-labor which has made sterile the lands of the South, driven out her mechanics and artisans, made poor her people, and decreased her wealth. We cannot afford to waste anything; but Olmsted wrote to a Texan friend as the fruit of "a large class of observations:"

"The natural elements of wealth in the soil of Texas will have been more exhausted in ten years, and with them the rewards offered by Providence to labor will have been more lessened than without slavery would have been the case in two hundred. After two hundred years' occupation of similar soils by a free laboring community. I have seen no such evidence of exhaustion as in Texas I have after ten years of slavery."

TESTIMONY OF SLAVEHOLDERS.

In 1959 Charleston had not a single ship-carpenter. In 1859 Governor Wise, of Virginia, said to his people:

"Commerce has long ago spread her sails, and sailed away from you. You have not, as yet, dug more coal than enough to warm yourself at your own hearths; you have set no tilt-hammer of Vulcan to strike blows worthy of gods in your own iron foundries; you have not yet spun more that coarse cotton enough, in the way of manufacture, to clothe your own slaves. *You have no commerce, no mining, no manufactures.* You have relied alone on the single power of agriculture, and *such agriculture!* Your sedge-patches outshine the sun. Your inattention to your only source of wealth has seared the very bosom of mother earth. Instead of having to feed cattle on a thousand hills, you have had to chase the stump-tailed deer through the sedge-patches to procure a tough beefsteak. The present condition of things has existed too long in Virginia."

Thomas Marshall, another slaveholder, said:
"Slavery is ruinous to the whites; it retards improvement *roots out an industrious population, banishes the yeomanry of the country; deprives the spinner, the weaver, the smiths, the shoemaker, the carpenter, of employment and support.*"

In little more than ten years Wisconsin lands became worth on an average nine dollars and fifty-four cents per acre; but after two hundred and fifty years those of Virginia, with all her natural advantages, were worth but eight dollars and twenty-seven cents per acre. Virginia, free, might have had as rapid an increase as Massachusetts; she would have had in 1850, that id to day, a population of 7,751,324 whites, instead of 894,800. Consider what would have been her wealth, with such an enormous population. Consider what would have been her ability, with her minerals, her water-power, her grain fields and her seacoast, to contribute to the national revenue.

If we want to lighten the burden of taxation, we must give the South the same opportunity for growth and increase which has made in the West and Northwest so populous and rich in the last twenty-five years. But to do that, we must encourage free labor there – for it is the free workingman who makes the land rich – and the free man will not and cannot toil in competition with the slave.

THE WASTEFULNESS OF SLAVE LABOR.

The slave-labor system exhausts the soil, wastes its products and contributes less - a very great deal less – to the national wealth , than the more skilful and intelligent free labor. The slave workman cannot be trusted with machinery; he cannot be trusted with the best tools; he must have – so the slaveholders themselves have said – the coarsest, rudest tools; anything else he breaks. Now every workingman knows that with heavy, rough tools, he cannot accomplish as much as another man can with light, well-made, handy tools. Every working man knows that it makes a world of difference what sort of plough, what sort of an axe, what sort of a plane, what sort of a hammer he uses. He wants the best; he knows that it pays him to have the best; and he knows, too, that if he can make a machine saw, or plane, or mortice, or do anything else for him, that is so much gained – so much more money made in a given time. But the slave laborer cannot be trusted with any of these helps. It is a wonder that with *a system which thus prevents the use of the best tools and machinery, the South is poor?*

It is a fact, proved by the census, that *labor in Massachusetts is four times as productive as in South Carolina.* The average value of the product *per head* of the cotton factories of Massachusetts was in 1855, $725 – ten times greater than the average value of the products of labor in South Carolina. The State of Massachusetts, with the help of skilled and industrious free labor, sent annually into the commerce of the world, *values greater than that of the entire cotton crop of the South!* Such is the enormous difference between slave labor and free labor.

Mr. Guthrie, in his report on the finances, in 1854-5, prepared a table from the census report, showing the average value of products per head in the different States. A comparison of some of the Free States with some of the Slave States, will show how much more productive is free labor than slave labor. In Massachusetts, with a bleak climate and a sterile soil, the average product per head of the population is valued at $166 60; in South Carolina but $56 91; in New York, $111 94; in Georgia, the Empire State of the South, $61 45; in Pennsylvania, $99 30; in Virginia, $59 42; in Ohio, $75 82; in Arkansas, $52 04; and in North Carolina, $49 38.

SLAVERY LOWERS THE VALUE OF LAND.

But this is not all; slave labor not only produces far less, and thus adds less to the taxable wealth of the community; it at the same time wastes and ruins the substance of the country. It ruins the soil. The cotton planters were continually removing westward, with their slaves, to new lands; AND Olmstead reports that in Texas even, recently settled as it is, he already found the two curses of the planter – worn out and abandoned plantations and "poor whites". In North Carolina, six bushels of wheat to the acre is counted a fair crop. Compare Virginia and Pennsylvania, and we find, by the census report, that the actual crops per acre of corn were, in *Virginia eighteen,* and in *Pennsylvania thirty-six* bushels; of tobacco, in Virginia – whose speciality is tobacco – 630 pounds per acre, in Pennsylvania 730 pounds, Under the slave-labor system of the South, according to Mr. Gregg, an accredited writer of the southern side, South Carolina had, before the war, one hundred and twenty-five thousand *white* persons "who ought to work and who do not or who are so employed as to be wholly unproductive to the State."

Does anyone imagine that it is not the slave system, but the climate, which is to blame for this enormous and ruinous waste of labor and of the natural resources of the South? In Virginia, whenever, before the war, free labor got the upper hand, and slavery was driven out, there productions were at once largely increased. The Charleston *Standard* remarked, in 1857, "The Virginia journalists have frequently borne witness to the fact that in many districts where large estates have been divided and sold to small farmers, the land is turning odd from three to six times as much produce as it did a few years ago." In Cahill, Mason, Brooke, and Tyler counties, Virginia, which had before the war, a free laboring population, with slaves but one in fifteen to the freemen, but no advantages of towns in or near them, land was worth, in 1855, $7 75 per acre. In Southampton, Surrey, James Town, and New Kent counties, in the same state, where the slave population was as 1 to 2, the *land was worth but half as much*, $4 50 per acre. In Fairfax county the slave population was much reduced within the last twenty-five years; free laboring men took the places of the slave laborers; and the County Commissioners reported officially:

"In appearance, the county is co changed, in many parts, that a traveller, who passed over it tens years ago, would not now recognize it. Thousands and thousands of acres had been cultivated in Tobacco, by the former proprietors, would not pay the cost, and were abandoned as worthless, and became covered with a wilderness of pines. These lands have been purchased by *northern emigrants*; the large tracts divided and subdivided, and cleared of pines; and neat farm-houses and barns, with smiling fields of grain and grass, in the season, salute the delighted gaze of the beholder. Ten years ago, it was a mooted question whether Fairfax lands could be made productive; and, if so, would they pay the cost? This problem has been satisfactorily solved by many, and, in consequence of the above altered state of things, *school-houses and churches have doubled in number*."

That is to say, slavery makes a rich country poor, free labor makes a poor country rich; slave labor – improvident, wasteful, unskillful – rots out the heart of the land, and finally, leaves the soil when it can no longer make a living thing from it: free labor comes in, and, in ten years, restores the soil, and works it at so great a profit that the face of the county is changed, and "churches and schools are doubled." *But mark! until slave labor is driven out, free labor will not come in.* The two systems cannot work together. Which, then, shall we protect – the slavemaster, who impoverishes the country, or the free laborer who enriches it?

The Wheeling *Intelligencer,* the published in a slave state spoke out on this question, some ten years ago, in the following words:

"The present great and pressing want of our state, like that of the whole United States, is cultivation and improvement, not enlargement and annexation, and the obvious and the only mode of a rapid growth of our state or city is such a change of public policy as shall invite to our aid and co operation our Caucasian cousins, the intelligent, moral, and industrious artizans, mechanics, miners, manufacturers, and commercial men of Europe and the northern states, to share our taxation, develop our resources, and make ours a *white man's country,* with all the energy, education, love of order, of freedom, and of order characteristic of the Anglo-Saxon race. The history of the world, and especially of the States of this Union, shows most conclusively that *public prosperity bears an almost mathematical proportion to the degree of freedom enjoyed by all the inhabitants of the state.* Men will always work better for cash than for the lash. The free laborer will produce and save as much, and consume and waste as little as he can. The slave, on the contrary, will produce and save as little, and consume and waste as much as possible. Hence states and counties filled with the former class must necessarily flourish and increase in population, arts, manufactures, wealth, and education, because they are animated and incited by all the vigor of the will, while states filled with the latter class must exhibit comparative stagnation, because it is the universal law of nature that force and fear end in ruin and decay."

EFFECTS OF FREE AND SLAVE LABOR CONTRASTED.

In the newly settled free states we find villages, towns, churches, schools, and other conveniences of civilization springing up in the immediate track of the settlers; in the slave states, on the contrary, these are to a great extent lacking. The free working-man of Iowa, or Minnesota, may count upon being able to send his children to good schools, to attend church with his family, to enjoy the profits of a sale in an adjacent village for all the "small truck" of his farm, if he is a farmer; or if he is a mechanic, to obtain em-ployment, through the gathering of the population in villages and towns, to afford him a comfortable living. In the slave states, on the contrary, even in the oldest settled of them, towns and villages are few and far apart; the small farmer can find no sale for his chickens, eggs, vegetables or fruits; the free mechanic is restricted to the few cities where alone he can find employment; all inducements to any methods of mechanical labor, or of farming, not practised in cities or upon great slave plantations, are lacking.

So few are the towns, even in the long settled states of Georgia and South Carolina, that a large part of the railroad stations are numbered - as station 1, station 2, station 14; and where, as at Millen, and other points, a name is given, there is, in most cases, no town or village, but only a dépôt for cotton.

SLAVERY LEAVES NO CHANCE FOR SMALL FARMERS.

Of course, in such a country, with such a state of affairs, the small farmer, and the country carpenter, blacksmith, wheel-wright, &c., have no chance to live. The small farmer, with us in the free states, carries his chickens, eggs, feathers, turkeys, pigs, apples, and other minor produce to the "store", in the next village, and with this produce often clothes his family, and keeps up the supply of tea, coffee and sugar, while the staple of his farm, his grain or cattle, go to pay the cost of labor, and other expenses, and to form the balance of profit, which laid by, makes him yearly a more comfortable and independent man. But in the slave states, this small farmer is surrounded by great plantations; no town or village is near him where he can sell the profitable "small truck"; he must neglect this important source of profit for the man of few acres; he toils away in the cotton field, and *his wife toils with him*; and they are no better off at the year's end than at the beginning.

Moreover, he does not enjoy the intellectual benefit of a weekly visit to a town or village; his children have no school provided for them; he and his wife cannot often go to church. He is deprived, too, of the numberless conveniences which the numerous villages and towns, even in the most recently settled free states, afford to the farmer there. If he needs the services of a carpenter, or tailor, or blacksmith, or wagon maker, of any mechanic, the farmer of the slave state must either set out on a long journey over bad roads, for fifty or sixty miles – or he must do without. In South Carolina, to this day, the country people are obliged, in this way, to make their own rude, heavy, inconvenient wagons, often without a tire on the wheels, which are not unfrequently of solid wood. They must make their own ill-fitting harness; they must build their own rude cabins; no mason, or plasterer, or carpenter, or skilled mechanics are found – *but they are slaves.*

There is thus , in the condition of society which is created by the slave labor system, *no room, and no encouragement for the free mechanic and the small farmer,* who make up the bulk of our population in the free states, and whose industry, and thrift and intelligence make the country prosperous and happy.

Does any one ask why this is so? Why has slavery this singular and disastrous effect? Because the wealthy own slaves, and "do not need the services of the free workingmen," to quote once more the words of Marion. The rich planter living upon his estate, owns his slave mechanics, goes North or to Europe when he wants to amuse himself, and has no interest in the social advancement of the county in which he happens to be settled. *What should he care for school? His children have tutors at home, or go to northern colleges.* Why should he seek the form or elevate society around him? When he wants "company" he goes to Charleston, or Savannah, or Mobile, or New Orleans, or New York. Why should he buy the small farmer's "truck"? *His own slave raise all he wants.* Why should he employ free mechanics? He prefers to *buy* a carpenter and sell him again when the work is done. Moreover, he would not help to support the village store, if there was one – for *he buys his supplies at wholesale in the great city.* He does not need the village tailor, for his clothes are made in New York. His wife does not employ the village milliner, for she get her dresses from New Orleans, or New York, or Paris.

In short, the planter has no interest in the country where he happens to own soil, except to raise as much cotton off the land as possible; he spends the proceeds away from home.

WHY THE SLAVE STATES LACK CAPITAL.

But with this, there has been a singular complaint amongst the planters, which meets one in almost every essay printed by DeBow; a complaint of a lack of capital. "The south needs capital" was the constant cry. "Our tanneries will not succeed, because of our limited capital," says a writer on the resources of Georgia. "For the last twenty years, floating capital, to the amount of $500,000 per annum has left Charleston, and gone out of the state" complained Governor Hammond, in a famous essay on Southern Industry.

"Ninety millions of capital," he says in another place, "has been drained out of South Carolina in twenty years;" and another writer, urging the establishment of manufactories in the south, admits that "we have not the capital to spare". *We do not hear such complaints in the free states.* Our workmen are not idle, our mines are not undeveloped, our manufactories are not stopped for want of capital.

But they would be, if the manufacturer – or mine owner – had not only to buy his machinery, *but also his workmen.* No company, however wealthy, could afford to run a mill in Lowell, or work a coal mine in Pennsylvania, or keep up a furnace in Pittsburgh, if they had to provide means, not only to pay for its machinery, but to buy also its working men and women. All the industry of the free states would come to a stand still if this system should suddenly be forced upon us. No wonder the manufacturing industry of the South was never set going "for lack of capital."

But this same mischief has injured the South in other ways. Look for instance, at this: Take two men, both farmers; let one remove to Texas, the other to Iowa; let each have his land purchased; and have five thousand dollars over. Each needs a carpenter to build a comfortable house for him. The Iowan gives notice in the newspapers – which are glad to print such intelligence – that carpenters can get higher wages in his neighborhood than farther East; and he readily gets the services of an enterprising young mechanic. But the Texan? He must *buy his carpenter;* he must pay probably two thousand dollars for the man. He has but three thousand left – the Iowan has spent only the wages of a carpenter while he needed him.

That done, each requires three laborers to clear and cultivate the new land. The Iowan advertises, offers good wages, and gets his men without trouble; *the Texan must pay off his remaining three thousand dollars for three slaves.* He has now all his money invested – the Iowan, however, has yet the greater part of his in hand. He is able to purchase the best implements – but the Texan must manage without or run in debt. He is able to contribute to the building of a school and church; but the Texan, in the first place, has no money left for such purposes; and in the next place, the children of his slaves must not be educated. *Therefore, his own children have no school or church.* The Iowan, having still say two thousand dollars in hand, may set up a friend, in a mill, or a store – and both will be supported by the laboring population which he has gathered about him, who are earning wages and will purchase clothing and pro-visions. But the Texan has no money to loan for such enterprises; and if he has, they could not succeed, for his slaves have no wages to spend, and gets his supplies at wholesale, from his factor in New Orleans or Shreveport.

Let any one, farmer or laboring man, answer, who is the most comfortable, whose children have the best chance to grow up intelligent, who has the most money at commands, the Texan slave owner, or the Iowan farmer? who builds up around him the most quickly, a thriving community? who gives employment to free mechanics? whose skill and capital is most productive of wealth and progress, and happiness, to the neighborhood?

We see by this instance, how it is that in the South they always "lacked capital". The Texan emptied his purse before he got fairly started; the Iowan has money in hand when his farm was thoroughly furnished. The Texan was condemned by the slave system to live in solitude – the Iowan at once, and necessarily, gath-ered a little company about him, of workingmen, and mechanics, and their families, and if he selected his farm, he saw within a year a little village spring up near him, with its schools, church, stores, and proper supply of mechanics of different kinds.

Mechanics and laboring men, remember, that the slave system leaves no room for you! It shuts you out! The Southern planter does not need you; he cannot bear your independent ways; he "buys a carpenter when he wants one". He and his fellow planters have, for half a century, shut up, against you and your families, the finest part of the Union; *while slavery lasts you can gain no foothold there, for every slaveholder is your enemy;* your children can have no schools there; you can have none of the conveniences of life; you cannot even get employment. But do away with the slave system, make all labor free, take away from the rich planter his fatal monopoly, let every man who works be paid wages according to his ability and let every employer pay just wages to his workmen, and you can safely go to the South, and take with you the society, the schools, the churches, the frequent villages and towns, all the conveniences of civilization, which the slave labor system has not.

Slavery is the free workingman's worst enemy; let this truth be spread abroad amongst you, free workingmen of the North and South! Then, for your own sakes, and for the sake of your children, *whom you do not wish to grow up in the overcrowded North,* let slavery die. In the South, if slavery is abolished, *the wages of the mechanics and laboring men must for many years to come be very high.* The whole vast region is almost without skilled labor; free mechanics have been driven from it. *A region greater than all the free states, as healthful, with a finer climate, more abundant mineral resources, cheaper lands and a richer soil, lies open before you and your families.* You have only to possess it, and with your skill and energy subdue it. Then you will not feel the hard struggle which severe climate, and tenement houses, and lack of employment, and the oppression caused by an overcrowded labor market, subjected you to in the North. *But you can never enter that land of the ease and plenty; without first striking down your fatal enemy, slavery!*

50 | CHARLES NORDHOFF

2

The Misgovernment of New York: A Remedy Suggested

Great cities are, so far, the curse and the puzzle of our civilization. Neither here nor in Europe has any ruler discovered how to rule them. Napoleon made Paris convenient, but bankrupt ; and it is scarcely worth while to Hausmanize a city, if it is to be bombarded just when it is completed. London is less expensively but almost as badly misgoverned as New York. In the United States, the great cities are, almost without exception, the prey of jobbers ; and it is curious that the most of these city plunderers work by means of Irishmen. The Irish emigrants to our shores display an extraordinary aptitude for misgoverning cities, which deserves the attention of some scientific investigator. They have two traits which go far to account for the success of their leaders in this bad business: they, in common with some other foreigners, though to a greater extent, attach great importance to government employment. An Irishman, just landed in New York, will sweep the streets for the city government for less money than he will take to serve a private citizen in a more agreeable employment. An American is, until he turns loafer, averse to accepting minor service under the government, because it is of uncertain duration, and he counts it no particular honor. For an Irishman, the uncertainty has perhaps a charm, and his self-importance is swelled by the character of his paymaster. Secondly, the Irish, more readily than any other people amongst us, accept charity. They count it, as a rule, no disgrace to have a patron, and their leaders know very well how to use this weakness. Thus, a notorious and successful New York politician, who was asked what were the means by which he ruled a large part of the city, replied, " I spend almost all my time in helping the poorer sort of people. If a woman has a son out of employment, she sends him to me ; if a man newly landed needs work, he is brought to me; if any one is in want he comes to me, and I try to get him a place." Now "a place" meant, in this man's vocabulary, a place where he would be paid by the city or county government, well paid for light work, and of course he voted for the man who helped him. If this benevolence had been legitimate, if it had been practised at private cost, and not at the expense of the city, it would have been laudable; but in this case it answered precisely to Sydney Smith's definition of charity, which consisted in A borrowing a sovereign of B, to give to C. B was here the body of tax-payers of the city of New York.

But such as our cities are, they must be ruled. We cannot change the conditions of the problem. The population of a great city must continue, for a long time at least, to consist, partly, of the very rich and the very poor; of idle, luxurious, over-cultivated, poor, ignorant, and vicious people, together with a great mass of hard-working, poorly accommodated, struggling, honest men and women, living from hand to mouth. Given such a population, in which there is a large proportion of foreigners, unaccustomed to equal civil and political rights, and yet possessing both; given universal suffrage; — how can we obtain efficient and tolerably honest government for our great cities? This is the real and important question.

Why should a million of people living in streets on Manhattan Island be more exposed to misgovernment than an equal number scattered over one of our Western States? Not because they are less intelligent, for they are not; or less energetic, for they are not. Not even because they are much more vicious, for there is no reason to believe that they are so. If the poorer part of the population of New York were as depraved, vicious, or lawless as it is a bad fashion to represent them, Fifth Avenue would have been "gutted," to use a street phrase, long ago.

The city differs from the country in these, among other respects : —

1st. Fewer of its people own real estate.

2d. A great proportion of them live in crowded tenements, which is not the case in the country of course.

3d. A far greater proportion of them live from hand to mouth, and lay by little or nothing.

4th. The distinctions between wealth and poverty are far more marked in the city than in the country; and

5th. The relations between the wealthy and the poor or humble citizens are less intimate; and not only less intimate, but, what is of extreme importance, of a different kind altogether. In the country rich and poor usually worship in the same church. In the large cities, — notably in New York, — a wealthy congregation usually builds a fine church for itself, and a mission chapel a mile off for the poor its hired or volunteer missionary can gather together. In the country, the sick or destitute are relieved by individual care and benevolence; in the city, a hired distributer of alms investigates the case, and doles out assistance. In the country, you help a man by finding work for him; in the city, you "give him a dollar and let him go." In New York the public schools form now almost the only common meeting-ground for the rich and poor; and these are vigorously threatened by the Roman Catholic influence.

It is plain, then, that the relations existing between the different classes of society, in city and country, are very different. Not only do they live much, farther apart in the city, but when they come into contact their attitude towards each other is very different. But one of the most experienced city missionaries of New York is reported to have said that charity is almost always a curse; that to give money or the means of living to the poor has been, in the majority of cases known to him, to make them paupers, at least gravely to impair their efficiency; and that when he had once supplied a measure of coal, or any other indispensable means of life, he found, almost always, that he was called upon to repeat the gift year after year. If this is true, how demoralizing must be the whole attitude of the rich towards the poor in a great city like New York, where Tweed was praised last winter, because he gave out of his ill-gotten millions a few thousands to those of his followers who chose to call themselves "poor."

But this, too, we cannot prevent. The busy city merchant has not time to administer his own charities; he gives freely, but it is only money; he cannot give time.

Again, the city differs from the country in this, that its government has much more intimate relations to the comfort and convenience of the people. A large part of the duty of the city government concerns internal improvements, — always and everywhere a fertile source of corruption. Gas, street pavements, sewers, railroads, docks, parks, all these the city government builds or controls, and each becomes a means of robbery and corruption the moment the machinery of the city government is ill arranged.

That is to say, it is far more necessary that a city charter should be perfect, than that the constitution of a rural county should be so. Every point of difference between city and country makes against the city; makes the evil of a badly framed charter greater, more powerful for mischief, less efficient for good, and more effective for robbery, and, what is worse, for corrupting public morals and debauching public opinion.

Mill rightly reckons it one of the first merits of a good system of government, that it trains the people. "The first question," he says, " in respect to any political institutions, is how far they tend to foster in the members of the community the various desirable qualities, moral and intellectual; the government which does this the best has every likelihood of being the best in other respects, since it is in these qualities, so far as they exist in the people, that all possibility of goodness in the practical operations of government depends. "We may consider, then, as one criterion of the goodness of a government, the degree in which it tends to increase the sum of good qualities in the governed, collectively and individually." Of course he does not mean that any one shall be made virtuous by act of Congress, or that an ordinance of the common council can create public spirit. But government ought to be so framed that it shall not hinder the exercise of public spirit; that it shall leave free play for the faculties of men; and that it shall not make the citizen in-active, by making efficient action for the public good hopeless. It is with public very much as with private affairs: Convince a man that no effort of his can better his private fortunes, and you make him an idler and skulk; persuade the mass of citizens that their action, however determined, cannot abolish public evils or reform abuses, and you crush public spirit.

Now the great and radical fault of the charters which New York has had is that they did just this. They have crushed the public spirit of the city, by taking the government out of the hands of the people, and by making it needlessly cumbrous and complicated. It is not necessary here to describe the older charters of New York; none of them were intended to institute a government directly responsible to the people. The evils under which the city suffers grew up mainly under the last charter, which was superseded by the present one in the spring of 1870. Under this charter and its amendments, —

I. The city, which includes the whole territory of the county, was saddled with two distinct governments, which necessitated two separate sets of accounts, two sets of officers, those of the city and those of the county; and left one of these bodies, the Board of Supervisors, entirely irresponsible to the Mayor.

II. As though this had not been bad enough, it was next arranged that the Supervisors should be what is called a "nonpartisan" board; composed, that is to say, in nearly equal numbers, of men of both political parties. This of course completed their independence, and made jobbing their natural and inevitable business. For the Supervisors were thus as independent of party control, and as well guarded against the interference of politicians and of public or party opinion on both sides, as they were irresponsible to the Mayor.

III. Next, many of the most important functions of the city government were given into the hands of commissions, hoards, also non-partisan, and usually appointed by the Governor, or, worse yet, by the Legislature.

The story of these non-partisan commissions runs in a uniform course. When first created, they were zealous and efficient. Generally in about a year the useful men were driven to resign, and in their places at once appeared the worst class of politicians, and thenceforth the commission or board became a mere machine for corruption and political intrigue. While, for instance, Mr. Jackson S. Schultz, one of the most public-spirited as well as one of the ablest citizens of New York, remained at the head of the Board of Health, that commission did good work. But his health broke down under the strain, not of his legitimate duties, but of the pressure and worry of the viler sort of politicians; he resigned in disgust; and the board has ever since been a mere political machine. Had Mr. Schultz been sole head of the Sanitary Department, responsible only to the Mayor, he would have been ten times as efficient, and would not have resigned; for every strong man likes power.

IV. Next, the Comptroller, the city's secretary of the treasury, was elected, and for a longer or different term of office than the Mayor. This made him also an independent officer. This was in accordance with one of the political superstitions of the State of New York, in which people of both parties imagine that, unless the head of the treasury were independent of the chief executive officer, the two would inevitably combine to plan a burglary of the treasury vaults. It must appear odd to such people that the President and his Secretary of the Treasury have never, in a single instance, since the days of Washington, gone off between two days with the treasury balance.

V. The judges and the prosecuting officers were elected, which has proved a blunder everywhere.

VI. What was equally mischievous, the citizens were obliged to elect also a sheriff, school trustees, and a number of other petty officers.

VII. Finally, as though to declare in the most plain and positive terms that the citizens of New York would elect only rogues to office, the State Legislature assumed to declare, not only how much money the two governments of the city should spend, but for what the expenditures should he made.

This system, which grew up gradually, had two leading ideas, — to destroy party government in the city (by "nonpartisan " boards), and to give the Legislature at Albany all real power over the city. It was, of course, a device of the Republican politicians, who then ruled the State, and who, silly creatures as most of them are, imagined that they could thus, if not reduce, at least make of little consequence the Democratic majority of the city. But the results, which were clearly foreseen and foretold by wise men, were:

1. To demoralize and corrupt the State government, which, called upon to decide in matters of which most of its members were necessarily ignorant, — how can a member from St. Lawrence County know what the local needs of New York City are? — had to decide ignorantly, which is but the preliminary step to deciding corruptly.

2. To give the State, finally, to the Democrats, who might have kept it for fifty years, if they had not been even more ignorant and corrupt than the Republicans. It is one of the most certain signs of the utter corruption and demoralization of the Democratic leaders, that they had not spirit, wisdom, and self-control enough to use rightly their great opportunity in New York. We shall see what they did.

The folly of obliging the people to decide at the polls upon the fitness for office of a great number of persons, lies at the bottom of almost all the misgovernment from which we suffer, not only in the cities, but in the States. It is a darling device of the political jobbers, and a most successful one; for, under the hollow pretence that thus the people have greater power, they are able to crush public spirit, to disgust decent and conscientious citizens with politics, to arrange their "slates," to mix the rascals judiciously with a few honest men wherever public sentiment imperatively demands that much, and to force their stocked cards upon the people. When Smith wants Jones to vote for a Democratic Federal administration, he asks him to vote for the Democratic candidate for the Presidency, — that is all. The Presidential candidate involves all. The Federal administration controls, taxes, and makes happy or unhappy forty millions of people, excluding Indians untaxed; its officers are appointed in every State, in every county, and in almost every township ; its treasury draws more than four hundred millions from the people every year; its laws are the supreme law of the whole Union. Yet, when Smith is called upon to vote upon all these questions and interests, he votes for precisely two persons, the President, and the member of Congress from his district. It is not difficult for Smith, if he is a conscientious or intelligent voter, to discover all about these two men before election day, and to decide which two of the four presented to his suffrage by the two parties are the fittest. The press helps him; discussion of their character, fitness, responsibility, is general and unintermitted during the canvass; they live in glass houses; whatever in their past conduct or history bears upon their capacity for the places they seek is exposed to public view, and no citizen need vote in ignorance. As voting is, on the whole, a pleasant exercise of power, when one can know for whom one is voting, the Presidential and Congressional vote is always full.

But suppose, at the Presidential election, the citizens were asked to vote for President, member of Congress, judge of the Supreme Court, Secretary of the Treasury, Postmaster-General, Attorney-General, Secretary of State, Secretary of the Interior, Collector of Customs, Collector and Assessor of Internal Revenue, Postmaster, and perhaps a dozen other Federal officers, all nominated on the party tickets, how long would it be before only those who hoped to gain something from the election, and those whom they could persuade or influence, would be the only ones to vote? Would it not be an insult to a citizen of intelligence to ask him to decide upon the merits and capacity and honesty of such a number of men? Would he not give up the undertaking in despair, and stay away from the polls, — as half, and the best half, of New York City does now, on the day of a municipal election?

If, then, the citizens of New York seem to the rest of the country to lack public spirit, here is one reason for it. No thoughtful man, feeling the responsibility of his act, and desirous to do right, or, at least, to vote intelligently, can go to the polls, at a municipal election in New York, — and this holds true of almost every other large American city, — without disgust with himself, and with the system which, by compelling him, if he votes at all, to support a number of persons of whose character and fitness he cannot inform himself, makes him a dummy in the hands of the swindling politicians who nominate ; and makes reform hopeless.

Nor, when the election is over, does the result tend towards good government, even if a certain proportion of honest men should chance to be chosen. For the result is only a jumble; the people, or such of them as have chosen to vote, have exercised their authority in a manner which does not give them a responsible government. A number of men have been put into office, all holding place from the same supreme authority, the people, and all therefore equals. There is no responsible head, no one man to whom the people may look, upon whom they may call for honesty or efficiency; authority and responsibility have been divided out in dribbles; and when a wrong is exposed, when inefficiency is censured, the blame falls upon no single head; and thus the first step towards reform, the impaling of the offender, is made impossible by this vicious system; and the citizen, be he never so public-spirited, after going from one officer to another, trying in vain to fix upon some one the guilt of a misdeed, at last gives up in despair.

What is thus true of the city of New York is no less true of the State, and of many other States. In most of the States of the Union demagogues have persuaded the people that they are wise enough to choose a number of public officers, and that this is the most democratic way, the way in which the people can exercise the most control over their affairs. But in fact it is the way in which the caucus and the reign of political jobbers is perpetuated; in which the people stultify themselves and resign all real control over their affairs to a secret, unofficial, and self-seeking council of political managers; and in which able and honest men, who cannot be the creatures of such a conspiracy, are almost inevitably driven out of political life.

The demoralization of our State governments, which is so general that it has excited very just alarm, will never be cured until public opinion, rightly instructed, demands a change in the State constitutions, which shall restore power to the people by giving them in the State, as they have in the Federal government, a single responsible head, to whom alone they may look for the remedy of grievances, and upon whose head the whole power of public opinion may be brought to bear.

The present Constitution of the State of New York (and in most of the other States it is the same) leaves the Governor of the great Empire State a mere figure-head, almost without authority, except to veto bills, to pardon criminals, and to appoint militia officers. No matter how great or able a man he may chance to be, he can have no broad or proper influence upon the policy of the State, because he has no power over his subordinates, the " State officers." "Would he make the prisons better? The prison inspectors are his equals, elected as he is by the people, and independent of him. "Would he improve the management of the canals? The canal officers are chosen by the people, and are not responsible to him. And so to the end of the chapter. Not only this, but with an ingenious and almost droll determination to break down power and responsibility, some of these officers are chosen at an election different from that at which the people choose a Governor; and it has happened that nearly the whole State administration has been of opposite politics from their helpless chief. Can a situation be imagined more deplorable for an able and honest man ; or more, welcome to a trickster, a weakling, or a cheat?

It results of course that a man of brains no longer cares to be Governor of New York; or if he seeks the place, it is only as a stepping-stone to a snug seat in the United States Senate, or as a candidate for the Presidency. It results that, instead of Clinton, Wright, or Seward, New York is promised Oakey Hall for its next Governor, and has Hoffman at present; neither Tweed nor Sweeney caring for such empty honors.

But if the executive has been deprived of the necessary power and responsibility in the city, as in the State, of New York, the legislative body, the Common Council, has been no less deprived of all the functions the exercise of which could give it importance. Whatever legislation for the city has real importance was transferred to Albany by the Republicans, and has been kept there by the Democrats. If a horse-railroad company wants to use one of the city's streets for its private purposes, it applies to the State Legislature. If a gas company wants a charter, it goes to Albany. Whatever concerns the health, the comfort, the convenience, or the burdens of the citizens, or the usefulness of the port, the State legislature is called upon to provide. Even the budget of expenses and the bill of appropriations were carried to Albany under the Republicans, — usually by a very drunken and demoralized Democratic crowd, — in the last days of the session, were laid in secret before a legislative committee, and passed in a great hurry in the last tumultuous hours of the session. The Democrats, in the new Tweed charter, no more trusted New York than their opponents. They also laid their budget before the Legislature, but in a lump. Tweed demanded twenty-two millions, and leave to do what he and his associates chose to do with the money; and he got both. Suppose the President should demand of Congress four hundred millions, and should say, "You must authorize me to use this as I choose, without giving account to you," — what would the people say? But suppose he should add, "I want leave, besides, to increase at my own will the public debt." But that is substantially what Tweed has asked and got, under the

name of "consolidating" the floating debt which the extravagance
and robbery of his crew had created.

To the Common Council under the old charter was left a good
deal of the minor administrative business, with which no legisla-
tive body can interfere without doing mischief. It granted licenses,
authorized street stands, protected the apple-women, bribed the
reporters, made out large printing bills ; and the rest of its time was
spent in jobbing, as was perfectly natural, for Satan finds some labor
still for idle hands to do. People cry out that such men as the Astors,
the Dodges, the Taylors, and Phelpses, the great and rich mer-
chants, will not be seen in the Common Council. But why should
they ? They are men of brains, accustomed to the management
and control of important affairs, and impatient of trifling. Give the
Common Council of New York the power and responsibility which
a legislative body ought to have, let it hold the purse-strings of the
city, as Congress holds the purse-strings of the nation, and the best
citizens will seek a place on its benches ; if no other reason impels
them there, the instinct of self-protection will imperatively do so;
and, once there, under such circumstances, and feeling themselves
able to exercise a real control over the city's affairs, they would like
it, — for all men like power.

The city charter described above was that repealed eighteen
months ago. That which has been substituted for it, and under
which New York now lies helpless, was a most ingenious con-
trivance of the Tammany leaders. They had long cried out against
the system under which so many of the city's affairs were carried to
Albany; they were pledged, not only to a new charter, but to a new
system. They pretended that their differences with the Republicans
were not trivial, but fundamental and radical. But the Democratic
leaders, in New York, had profited corruptly by the system which
they cried down. It is indeed true that they had not only profited
by it, they had been corrupted by it. Moreover, the Tammany

leaders hate and fear the people, as all corruptionists do; and it was not in their desires to give New York a sound and popular charter. They contrived an act which most carefully perpetuates the power of the Tammany ring, makes the people helpless, fribbles away responsibility, and almost destroys the very hope of reform. The recent exposure of monstrous robberies of the Tammany ring, made in the *"Times"* of New York, stirred the city as no other event has stirred it since the bombardment of Fort Sumter. Disgust gave place to rage, fear, and hatred, in the great body of citizens. But the ring laughed at the fury of their victims, as well they might ; for under the new charter, scarcely anything short of a revolution can help New York. To the threat to oust the ring, by abolishing the charter, the Tammany organ replied that Governor Hoffman is sure to veto the repealing bill. Mr. Hoffman has been so obedient a tool of Tammany, and of the leaders of the ring, that it is probable he would do this. There is one way to make a break in the city ring ; the Common Council has, by the charter (section 29), the power to impeach the Mayor, and bring him to trial in the full court of common pleas of the city; and the court may declare his office vacant. But even this would do but little good. See how the charter guards the power of the ring at every point: to remove the Mayor by impeachment would yet leave untouched the heads of the departments, that is to say, Tweed, Sweeney, Connolly, and their partners. For section 107 of the charter declares that the appointing power shall be exercised only by the " Mayor elected to that office, and not by an acting Mayor"; and it adds that "in the event of the death, resignation, or removal of such elected Mayor, such power shall devolve on, and be exercised by, the Comptroller. And it is further provided that when a new appointment of one of the Heads of Departments is made, it shall be, not for the remainder of the term of the officer removed, but for the full term of his office under the charter. What this means we shall now see.

The Mayor who is elected is, under the new charter, to hold his office for two years. But he is to appoint, and Mayor Hall accordingly appointed, four Police Commissioners, to hold office for eight years. Five Commissioners of Charities and Correction, to hold for five years. One Commissioner of Public Works, to hold for four years. Tweed was appointed to this place. Five Fire Commissioners, to hold for five years. Four Commissioners of Health, to hold for five years. Five Commissioners of Parks, to hold for five years. Sweeney is the head of these. One of Buildings, to hold for five years. Five of Docks, to hold for five years. The Comptroller and Corporation Counsel were elective, and hold for four years.

That is to say, even if the Mayor were impeached and removed, his companions in crime would go on just the same; and they could only be impeached, not removed, by a new elected Mayor. Any one can see that this is not responsible government. The people cannot, at a single election, make a clean sweep of the whole city government : they can only elect a new Mayor. The Mayor's subordinates are beyond their power and beyond the power of a new Mayor, except by a tedious process of impeachment.

But this is not all. The new charter fixes the number of one house of the Common Council at only fifteen persons; and the assistant aldermen number only one for every assembly district. These small houses are easily manageable; and, moreover, the charter takes care to limit their powers very precisely and narrowly, and leaves a great deal of power over the city, especially that over the expenditures, to the State Legislature, where it rested before. The Legislature of 1871 adopted forty-seven laws relating exclusively to the city of New York, many of them needless and mischievous, and most of them relating to matters on which the Common Council was the proper body to act. Among these was the "Two-per-cent

Act," which limited the city taxes to two per cent on the assessed valuation, and gave the sum to be thus raised in a lump to Tweed, Sweeney, Hall, and Connolly, to spend as they chose, — an unheard-of authorization to misappropriate and misuse the money of the tax-payers.

But by one of these acts of the State Legislature the charter is so amended as to give the Mayor the appointment of the Comptroller for five years; and the following astounding provision is added: "The Mayor, the Comptroller, the Commissioner of Public Works, and the President of the Department of Public Parks " — their names are Oakey Hall, Connolly, Sweeney, and Tweed — shall meet on the 1st of December, every year, and "make and agree upon an estimate of the various sums of money which, in their discretion, will be required to defray all the various expenses necessary for conducting the various boards, commissions, and departments, whether executive, judicial, legislative, or administrative, of the city government, and also for paying the interest on the city debt, and the principal of such debt falling due, and for providing for charitable and other objects, and thereupon fix and determine the amount of all such estimates, which amount, when so established by said Mayor, Comptroller, Commissioners of Public Works, and President of the Department of Public Parks," — that is to say, by Hall, Connolly, Tweed, and Sweeney, — "by the concurring vote of all present, shall thereby become appropriated"; and the Board of Supervisors are "directed" to cause such sums to be "raised and collected upon the estates, real and personal, subject to taxation within the said city and county of New York." Suppose the President and three of his Cabinet should thus assume to determine, in a private meeting, how much should be raised annually for the expenditures of the Federal government, and for what the money should be spent, — what would the people say! But here is a monstrous power, given

specially into the hands of four men, who, as the "*New York Times*"
has asserted, and as everybody believes, have been for years engaged
in the most enormous and shameless acts of robbery.

This is the Democratic plan of governing New York. It is,
briefly, to deprive the people of all power, and to give the chief
robbers unlimited and self-perpetuating power.

If any proof is needed that a State Legislature is as unfit to
legislate for the local affairs of a city as Congress for the local
affairs of a State, here it is. What could be more monstrous, more
unjust, more destructive of good government, more dangerous to
the rights of property, than for a State Legislature coolly to hand
the property of the great city of New York over to four exposed and
convicted corruptionists, to do with it what they choose to do in a
secret meeting?

Popular government is, as Mr. Lincoln happily phrased it, "
government of the people, by the people, and for the people." There
are, it is said, Americans who do not think it the best kind of gov-
ernment; but probably no American out of an insane asylum imag-
ines any other kind of government possible here just now. I believe
it to be the only form of government which can produce good and
lastingly good results, and therefore in the long run the cheapest. It
requires patience and a certain amount of faith in the observer; and
if any one expects perfection from it, he will be disappointed. But
it is, on the whole, the cheapest and the least mischievous form of
government yet contrived by men, and it is this because it works
according to natural laws; because — if it is really popular and not
a sham, if the machinery is so arranged that the people do actually
control — it enables them to have just as good a government as they
want. No community has a right to more than this ; nor is any man
wise and just enough successfully to impose upon a community, for
any length of time, a government better than they desire.

The great evil of all the charters under which New York has suffered is that they have limited the power of the people over their own concerns. New York City government has not really been popular. It has never made the people responsible to themselves. It has cut them off from political education; and to a great extent this has, of late, been purposely done, either by Republican politicians anxious to make of no account the Democratic majority of the city, or by Democratic politicians eager to job and rob; and both have been assisted by a multitude of rich men, who had no faith in what they call "the populace," but, on the contrary, a great terror of their poorer fellow-citizens. Now there is nothing more absurd or less reasonable than this dread. The mass of the people of New York are poor, own no property, and live from hand to mouth; most of the poorer sort in New York are wretchedly lodged; yet they are, in the main, a law-respecting, peaceable, orderly people. In the riot of 1863, the most serious New York has seen, there is the strongest evidence for the assertion that the actual rioters never numbered one thousand men; with these were an inconsiderable number of women and street boys, who stole, and occasionally set fire to an abandoned shop or warehouse. But the people of New York, though their fears had been artfully appealed to for weeks, had no part in the disturbance. One proof of the good character of the population of the city is seen in the ease with which disturbances are put down, and this in face of the fact that a riotous body has always full sway for days to organize, and is quietly allowed to gather on its own publicly appointed day, and to obstruct the streets, and badger the police, for hours, before it is dispersed.

To say, then, that the city is unfit for popular government, is nonsense. Moreover, almost every conceivable device to rule it without the direct and effective action of the people has now been tried. There remains only this one plain, square, honest, simple way, which Democratic and Republican hack-politicians alike abhor, because it would, within five years, and probably within three, put an end to jobbing and inefficiency, and give the city a reasonably honest and useful government, in which the best citizens would be able and proud to take a part.

If it is asked, what is the precise machinery of such a system as I urge, I must reply that it is not my duty to plan a new city charter. But look all over the country, and ascertain what form of constitution has, on the whole, given the most satisfaction, and best fulfilled all the conditions of (1) interesting the people in the government; (2) giving them complete power over their rulers, and thus enabling them, whenever they wished, by a single effort, to change these; (3) consequently securing, generally, efficiency and honesty in the rulers; (4) giving these abundant power to preserve the peace and secure obedience to the laws ; and (5) thus securing to the people as good a government as at any period they want. Better they have no right to.

The Constitution of the United States is that organic law which, better than any other, fulfils all these conditions. Now what are the prominent features of the machinery it provides?

1. One responsible head, the President, who appoints all his subordinates, and to whom alone the people look for the enforcement of the laws, for the preservation of order, and for the exercise of economy and the practise of honesty in all the departments of the administration.

2. A judiciary appointed for life.

3. A legislature which holds the purse-strings, and determines how much money shall be spent and for what purposes.

Now, there is in all this nothing which could not be applied to the government of a State or a city, just as well as to the government of the whole country. If New York is to have efficient and economical government, its charter must accord with the Federal Constitution in these three great points. First of all, it must give the city a Mayor, elected by the whole people, for a short term (I should prefer one year), who should appoint, but for his own term of office only, all his subordinates, including the Comptroller, and who would thus be directly and solely responsible to the inhabitants of the city for the good conduct of these officers. It must provide a city judiciary to be appointed by the Mayor for life, or good behavior. It must provide a Common Council which shall have all legislative power over every interest which is purely municipal, and, above everything else, over the appropriations of the city government.

It is not important that this city legislature should have two houses; and there are some good reasons why a single house would be better. But this ought to be numerous. It should contain at least one hundred and probably one hundred and fifty members. That would so subdivide the city into small districts, as to give every part of the population a chance to be represented by men known to them; and it would be a check upon corruption, if any such check were needed.

Further, the charter should prohibit to this legislature the exercise of any administrative or executive functions whatever. This has been one of the most fertile sources of corruption and misgovernment in the city, as it is wherever the organic law does not prohibit to the legislature such functions. Moreover, the charter should prohibit the passage of special laws, or the granting of particular privileges. Whatever a legislature may do usefully, it may do, even in a city, by general enactments, giving equal privileges to all. It would remain, to define the limits of the municipal government; to declare, carefully, what belongs to the city, what to the State, and what perhaps to the Federal government. And here I am conscious is an undertaking of no little difficulty. I would begin by giving to the Governor the appointment of the sheriff. That officer is, properly, the lieutenant of the Governor, in a county. He is, properly, a part of the State and not of the local or municipal administration.

He is the custodian of the peace of the county. It is his duty, on the order of the Governor, or without if the case is urgent, to suppress unlawful assemblages, to quell riots and affrays, and to arrest and commit to jail, if need be, those engaged in the disturbance of the public order. For a breach of the peace, crime, or misdemeanor, committed in his presence, he may arrest without a warrant. It shows to what an extent the government of the city and State of New York have fallen into disorder, that the sheriff was not even heard of on the day of the Orange riot. The Mayor surrendered to the mob; and the Governor, who originally agreed with the Mayor, when he changed his mind took the affair into his own hands, issued all the orders himself, and of course, as is the custom with men of that kind, suffered the mob to gather in force and obstruct the streets for hours, during which the business and comfort of an important part of the city were disturbed, before he chose to disperse the rioters. If he had resolutely ordered the police to keep the streets clear and unobstructed from early dawn, no mob could have collected, and the troops need not have fired. No one would have been killed; but the infuriated Roman Catholic Irish would have been still more angry with the Governor than they now are.

In preventing or quelling disturbances of the peace, the sheriff acts under the orders of the Governor, who is commander-in-chief in the State, and sworn to protect the peace and maintain order. He should, therefore, be a State officer, appointed by the Governor, and responsible to him.

Over every matter which concerns the city specially of course the city government ought to rule. Thus the appropriations for the city government, — how can the people of the whole State, assembled by their delegates at Albany, know how much the city of New York ought to spend, or for what? As reasonably might the Congress at Washington assume to decide upon the necessary expenses of the different State governments. So, too, with the corporations which exist alone in the city, and for the convenience of its people, such as street railroads and gas companies. Is it not absurd that when a company wants to lay rails and run cars in streets which are the property of the inhabitants of New York, and for which these have paid, the company should get a charter at Albany? The streets of the city are the property of the citizens; and if New York had possessed a proper charter, if the rights of its people had not been shamefully invaded by the State, a way would have been discovered long ago to make the city railroad companies keep in thorough repair the streets they use, if not all the streets; to make the gas companies light free of charge the streets which they also occupy, and at will break up; and thus to effect an important saving to the tax-payers.

The public schools, the police, the Fire Department, the Water Department, etc., would, of course, under such a charter, be under the charge each of a single head appointed by the Mayor, removable by him at his own will, and going out of office with him at the expiration of his term. Each head of a department would name his subordinates, as is the custom now in the Federal administration. It would belong to the Common Council to scrutinize their acts and accounts; and the people would hold the Mayor responsible for every shortcoming.

Under such a system of direct responsibility, the Mayor's life would be made intolerable if the streets were dirty, if the schools were mismanaged, or if the police were inefficient ; and he might even, with such a goad as this, by and by succeed in abolishing in our cities the absurdity of ringing the bells when a fire is discovered, and even denoting, as they do in New York, by regulated and published signals, to the noble fraternity of thieves and pickpockets, where precisely a house or shop is on fire. Surely nothing is more ridiculous, even in China, than to hire bell-ringers to point out to the idlers and criminals of a great city where a fire is raging; the fire-telegraph having already informed the firemen, the only persons who have a right to this information, or who can usefully appear at a fire.

As it is the State government which would grant such or any city charter, it would do wisely to prohibit to the municipality certain things. It should, for instance, forbid it to hold real estate, except so far as this is needed for the public offices, the school and engine houses, the parks and pleasure-grounds. Markets and docks are well managed only by private hands ; the example of the English docks, which are owned by companies, shows that this is perfectly safe; and the city legislature may always provide by general rules against their mismanagement. As to markets, no one pretends that a city ought to provide accommodations for the sale of dry-goods, clothing, flour, or molasses; and there is no good reason why it should undertake this service for the venders of meat and vegetables. Governments have never done this work well; and they can safely leave it to private enterprise, under proper and general sanitary regulations.

Finally, under such a charter, decentralization might be possible, by confiding to the citizens in subdivisions certain duties which experience might show could be better done thus than by the general administration. I am not prepared to say how far this might be carried ; but it is a fact that for some years the only clean streets in New York, at all seasons, were two or three which were kept clean by the private enterprise of their inhabitants. In Chinese cities the residents of a street are made to keep the peace within their bounds, and are held responsible for good order ; and as our cities increase in size, we may discover the need of providing by decentralization for their better government, and, what is of extreme importance, for the political education of the mass of the people.

In conclusion, it remains to ask what effect such a charter as has been suggested would have upon the government of a great city like New York.

1 . It would let in daylight. It is not improbable that at the first election under such a charter, the old corruptionists would be returned to office. It is possible that the worst demagogue in New York would be chosen Mayor. But what then? He and his followers could scarcely steal more than the Tweed-Connolly gang have stolen in the last year. But they would have to rob in the light of day. The Council would have to make the appropriations publicly and after a discussion which would fix public attention upon the result. It might appropriate many millions more than were needed, but it could not do this secretly; and at the next election their conduct would be punished, and the people, clearly instructed by the press and by public speakers, and alarmed by self-interest, would surely put new men in office.

2. It would do away with such expedients as the Citizens' Association committees, which, under the present system, stand between the people and good government, and serve to discourage and make more helpless the good citizens. The present iniquitous charter of New York could not have been adopted, had not the manager of the Citizens' Association, Nathaniel Sands, at the last moment, agreed to take office under Tweed and Sweeney, and put the whole influence of the reform society which he controlled at the service of these men. Sands is Tax Commissioner; his son and his assistants hold office under the ring; and the city is bound hand and foot, because its most eminent citizens trusted Sands, instead of trusting the people.

3. Having the prospect before them of a reform by appeal to the people, and being able to hold one man, the Mayor, responsible for abuses, and a body of residents of the city, the Council, for extravagant appropriations, good citizens would no longer be tempted to lend their names, as they do now, to bolster up a rotten government, in the futile hope of being thus able to control and check corruption. At present some of the most honorable citizens of New

York hold office under the ring. They do so, undoubtedly, because they see no other way to check extravagance and misrule. But their efforts are vain ; and it is with them as it is in all such cases; their character is lent to the ring, and serves to bolster up corrupt men and keep them in power; but they have little influence themselves. It is the same kind of mistake which Mr. Seward made when he remained in President Johnson's Cabinet. He could not control the President, but he ruined himself.

4. It would give a real interest to city politics. At present the editors are as unable to decide upon the worthy candidates for the numerous elective city offices as the citizens. Most of the New York daily papers employ a special person, whose duty it is to inform the editor of the changes in city politics, to advise him of the character of the men nominated, and in fact to decide the course of the paper towards the municipal candidates. These persons are mere reporters ; not uncommonly they hold office under the ring ; and their chief work is to darken counsel by words without meaning.

5. It would, by confining the duty of the citizen to the election of two persons, a Mayor and a councilman, disable the political jobbers, whose success depends upon their ability to nominate a long ticket, of men little known, and whom no citizen not devoted to local politics — no honest voter, that is to say — can hope to know much about.

6. It would educate the people, would give the best citizens a lively interest in the city politics ; would make a city election intelligible and easily understood, not only by the humblest citizen, but, what is of more importance, by the conductors of the press, who are now either silent, because a municipal election in New York is a riddle to every honest man, or allow their papers to be used by friends of the candidates.

7. It would restore party government in the city, and thus make the minority vigilant in discovering and denouncing dishonesty and inefficiency, for which the majority alone would be responsible.

8. It would open the door to many reforms and new expedients in government, which now have no chance. For instance, it might be found useful to try some system of minority representation; though, if the Council were a numerous body, this would hardly be necessary.

9. It would lead the wealthy citizens to interest themselves in the political education of their poorer neighbors. Why, for instance, should not the owner of a tenement-house, in presenting his monthly or quarterly bills to the occupants, make out an account of so much for rent, and so much added as the tenant's share of the general taxation? Such an exhibit would lead the inconsiderate poor to think, and to vote intelligently.

I have endeavored to outline the only possible system under which (as I believe) our cities can purify their governments. Its sole merit is not that it will absolutely and at once cure the present evils, — only a political quack would venture to promise such a cure, — but that under it the people could have just as good a government as they wanted; and that they would be undergoing, constantly, a course of political education. Of course, the political hacks, of both parties, will oppose such a system. Its adoption would ruin them. Unfortunately a great many good and honest people will also oppose it, because they dread the immediate result, and have little faith in the future. And yet it will be adopted; because it is the only just and right system, and because almost every other possible device has been tried, and in vain.

3

The Freedmen of South Carolina

Some Account of their Appearance, Character, and Peculiar Customs

Port Royal, March 20, 1863.

As the ship steams up to her anchorage in the broad bay of Port Royal, she passes numerous men-of-war launches and cutters, propelled by the regular and lusty strokes of black oarsmen neatly dressed in Scotch caps, substantial pea-jackets, and blue flannel shirts and trowsers.

The anchor is scarcely down when the Provost-Marshal's boat — the little "tug" Relief — puffs alongside, and peering curiously down on her deck you notice as many black faces as white among her crew.

If you are permitted to land by this steamer, you may see, as I saw, during the passage to the long wharf, a shining black face suddenly popping up from the dog-hole, which is called "forecastle" on ship-board, a pair of black hands rapidly turning over the well-thumbed pages of a primer; and if you have interest to watch further, you will see a black South-Carolinian learning to read. I must warn you, that in looking on at this process, you commit a grave offence against the whole "Southern Confederacy while if you should rashly venture to help Sam in his lesson of the day, you become guilty of a crime held infamous in Sam's native State, and convicted of which, fifty miles from Hilton Head, you would share the fate of burglars and murderers.

If some heavily-laden steamship such as the *Arago* should chance to be unloading at the wharf, you will see four or five hundred stout black fellows working like beavers, rolling casks and barrels, moving boxes, and carrying burdens of all kinds.

If, after dinner, you ride out to General Drayton's plantation, you may see the camp-ground of the First regiment of South-Carolina volunteers. General Drayton was the leading rebel in this region — the commander of that force " born insensible to fear," which ran away from Du Font's shells — and his "place" was fitly assigned by General Hunter for the camp of the " First Loyal South-Carolinas."

By the time you have seen all this, you begin to lose faith in the person who assured you that the negroes of Port Royal are an idle, dissolute, worthless set of creatures, who are supported at an enormous expense by an abolition government, etc., etc. You see, on the contrary, that black men are usefully employed in the navy, in the army, and as laborers by the Quartermaster's Department. When you have' looked around a little farther, you will find that in yet other useful work not only black men, but black women and children, are busily and profitably engaged.

There are at this time within our lines in South-Carolina about twelve thousand colored people, as absolutely free men and women as the same population of whites in any military department where martial law is strictly enforced. A census of the freedmen has just been taken, but the returns are not yet all at hand. According to a census taken on the first of May, 1862, there were then in South-Carolina, on the plantations within our lines nine thousand and fifty. To this number have been added since, five hundred refugees from Santee; five hundred from St. Simon's Island, and about four hundred from other parts. There are besides, according to the more recent census, one thousand seven hundred and eighty freed people living in Beaufort.

I must repeat that these people are absolutely and entirely free. No attempt is made to control them, either by special laws, or by any coercion, other than that to which all men and women submit in a civilized state. If I should add that, nevertheless, they have murdered no white men, have injured no white women or children; that they have burned no houses, destroyed no property; that crimes against the person are almost unknown, crimes against property not more frequent than in any equal population of ignorant whites; that the only murder committed by a black man since the islands have been ours was an act for the exact parallel of which a Congressman, now a general in the Union armies, was held justified by a jury, and by a large part of the public, especially in the slave States — if I should add all this, I am aware that my story would seem to many ignorant persons as absurd and impossible as a wise public once thought Bruce's or M. Bu Chaillu's. But I should nevertheless have told the simple truth.

The planters have always persuaded us that their four millions of slaves were a dangerous class; and the precautions they took and their evident apprehensions in regard to this population prove that they were in earnest. As slaves then, they were dangerous to the community, so every slaveholder told you: as free men they have proved themselves peaceable, law-abiding and useful. As slaves, special laws, cruel punishments and disgraceful guards were required — in the opinion of the slaveholders — to keep them from murder and rapine; but our experience in these Sea Islands shows that as freemen these same people are so harmless, so kind, so ready to submit to all laws and to all proper guidance, so averse from violence, that in all parts of the island ladies are stationed as teachers, and move about among them unguarded, unarmed and unharmed. The recent order of General Hunter, drafting all ablebodied blacks into the army, is enforced by black soldiers, squads of whom are sent over the islands to pick up conscripts. A new broom sweeps clean: the negro soldiers are zealous — sometimes they display more zeal than discretion. At St. Helena their search for recruits was conducted somewhat rudely. It is reported that they took an old man of seventy and several boys under age. They entered the school- houses and the churches where schools are assembled. They frightened the children, many of whom ran home, seeing fierce-looking armed men rushing in among them with bayonets fixed. They searched under the old-fashioned pews for fugitives. In one place a black soldier even drew a sabre to compel a man to go along with him. I was on the island two or three days afterward, and saw a number of the teachers and superintendents, but I heard not the slightest complaint of even chance incivility, from the ladies, who were entirely defenceless in their lonely little country schools.

The South Carolina freedmen are not paupers. They receive no support of any kind from the Government, nor charity from any source. They have done almost all the work in the Quartermaster's Department; they have, besides this, raised on the plantations, during the past year of freedom, sufficient food to supply themselves. In the season they have sold garden vegetables, melons, etc., to the troops to a considerable amount; they have furnished a full regiment, and more, of soldiers; and besides this, they have raised, gathered, ginned and packed seventy-five thousand pounds of Sea Island cotton, which will presently come to market.

I have before me papers from which the following figures are drawn. Of the nine thousand and fifty freed people of color on the island on the first of May, 1862, three thousand six hundred and nineteen were children "under quarter hands," as it is called — that is to say, under twelve years of age, and unfit to work. There were six hundred and ninety-three infirm and old. There remained four' thousand seven hundred and thirty -eight men, women and youth, *all of whom are workers.* Of these, three hundred and nine were returned as mechanics and house-servants, unused to work in the fields. The remainder were all laborers, fit and willing for all kinds of unskilled work.

If you consider these figures for a moment, you will see the immense importance to the rebels of their slave population. For a time of war, when the whole energies of a great region must be used only to feed great armies, no doubt four millions of people trained to labor as the slaves of the Southern States have been, are equal to six millions of any other population. As you ride through the islands you will find this thought frequently recurring to your mind. It is just now the time when the fields are made ready for corn and cotton. The able-bodied men have been drawn away to work in the Quartermaster's Department and to serve in the army; but the field work does not therefore stop. On every side you see women, and boys and girls, working with their heavy, ungainly but effective hoes, preparing the ground. It is found that the women are in fact more persevering in their industry than the men. Their earnings are, on the average, quite as great as those of the men who work in the fields. This is shown by the labor books. But I must add that it is not the opinion of some among the black men. Harry, a smart fellow, who manages a plantation on St. Helena's Island, said to me:

"De men's nearly all gone, now, sir, and so de work don't go on; for, you see, de women don't work well when de men's gone."

"But," said I, "Harry, the women *do* work; I see them on every hand, busy in the field."

"Yes, sir, dey work" was his reply, "but dey don't work like men. After all, sir, one good-fornuffin man's worth two smart women any day."

Have you not heard some such opinions from ignorant men in the North?

I hope I have made it plain that the freedmen of South-Carolina are not a burden to any one. On the contrary, they have been of great service to us. If the rebels had been able to carry off all the negroes with them, they would have very seriously embarrassed our operations in the Department of the South, By the Quartermaster alone about one thousand able-bodied blacks are employed. They receive five dollars per month and a soldier's ration.

To have brought white laborers from the North to perform this severe but necessary work would have cost a great sum in the first place for transportation, and at least double the amount now paid in wages. Colored mechanics employed by the military authorities are paid eight dollars per month and a soldier's ration. Some, the most capable, receive as much as twelve to fifteen dollars per month.

There is no cause to fear that the conscription will bring suffering or want on the freed people of this region. General Hunter's order takes away from his home and puts into the public service, either as laborer in the Quartermaster's Department, or as soldier, *every able-bodied man of the 'population.* But the wants of those who remain behind are so few, and, as I have shown, the women are to so great a degree accustomed to dig and hoe, plant and harvest, that the culture of the soil, their chief dependence, cannot be injuriously affected.

While slaves, the only food these negroes on the Sea Islands of Carolina received from their masters was one peck of Indian corn per week. On a very few plantations the masters gave in addition, during the season when the field-work was most exhausting, a little bacon twice or thrice in the week. Fresh meat they tasted, probably, once or twice in the year, as at Christmas and on Independence-day. An old woman said: "My missus she bery mean woman, bery mean woman, indeed — she kill a cow once in t'ree year !"

They ground their peck of corn in small mills turned by hand, after the day's work was done. They bad no other allowance of food from their masters except a little salt. But in every cabin I found a scoop-net, and every cove and inlet abounds in mullet and other fish. Oysters are also abundant; and you hear pigs squealing and hens cackling around all the "quarters." The last they raise to sell, and not to eat.

Insufficient nourishment and untimely work has affected the health of these people. I am told by physicians here, that scrofulous diseases are commoner than among a similar population in the free States, and rupture is also more frequent. The recruiting officer will not find an equal proportion of able-bodied men for the army here as with a like population in the North, but for fieldwork even those unfit for arms are still able. They understand very well, themselves, that they have not had a fair chance in this way. The women tell you that they will raise stronger children now that they are not worked so hard, for it was the custom here to extort field-work from pregnant women up to the very day when their children were born, and when the child was two weeks old the poor mother was again sent to work with her hoe. I noticed in most of the large cotton-fields, single palmetto-trees, of considerable size, dotted like sentinels, at regular intervals, over the field; it was easy to see that they had been planted there for a purpose, and on asking, I was told by the people that under these trees the mothers left their young babies, in charge of some old crone, while they were busy with the hoe, and hither they came to suckle the little ones at appointed hours. It was, I think, the only labor or time-saving arrangement I saw on these islands, contrived by slaveholders, and that saved time and labor only for their profit.

Aunt Phillis, an old woman on one of the Pope plantations, speaking one day of the changes she noticed since the flight of the masters, remarked:

"De chillen what's born sence de Yankees cum, dey's fat, dey's big and hearty. Dey an't like dem in de old time. De chillen born in de old time, dey poor tings, dey lean, han like buzzard — you know buzzard, massa? Dem chillen lean jest like buzzard."

"For why," she continued, "dey used to make we work, work WORK, so poor moder hab nuffin to gib her child — child starve 'fore it born — dat's what make 'em lean, like buzzard."

For a people living under a patriarchal system, they display a singular dislike to the patriarchs. I find the testimony universal, that the masters were "mean." All were not cruel, but all were hard task-masters, so their former subjects say.

"Dej's all mean alike," said one man, when closely questioned. Now there was, one Fripps, a planter on one of the islands, of whom the blacks habitually speak as "good Mr. Fripps." "Come now, Sam," said the questioner, "there was good Mr. Fripps, he could not have been mean."

"Yes, sah, he bad to his people same as any of 'em."

"Why do you call him good Mr. Fripps, then?"

"Oh I" said Sam, " dat no tell he good to we; call him good' 'cause he good Metodis' man — he sing and pray loud on Sundys."

I heard no words of hatred toward the masters; but the expression of horror which overspread many of their faces, particularly among the women, at a suggestion, soberly made, that "old massa" might presently come back, was painful to me — and surely disgraceful to the runaway patriarchs.

"Suppose, if we get to Charleston, we catch your master," said one of our company, to a woman at Pope's, "shall we bring him here?"

" Oh ! don't, massa, don't bring him here; we no want to see him nebber more," shouted a chorus of women.

"But what shall we do with him?"

"Do what you please," said the chorus.

"Shall we hang him ?"

"If you want, massa" — somewhat thoughtfully.

"But shall we bring him here and hang him?"

Chorus — much excited and shriller than ever — " No, no, don't fetch him here, we no want to see him nebber more again!"

Aunt Phillis told how her master built his new house only the year before the rebellion, and "sarve him right, he no get good of it. Suppose he good to we he no run away, he stay in his house. But he mean man, he run away now, he nebber come back."

She dwells much upon the fact that her master had paid much money for the house, "great deal of money, much as twenty thousand dollar." I asked: "Where did your master get so much money ?" At this the old woman rose in her bed — she was sick, and my friends were paying her a visit of kindness — and with some excitement exclaimed:

"Whar he git he money? Whar he git he money? Is dat what you ask — whar he got he money? I show you, massa." Pushing up her sleeve, she showed a gaunt, skinny, black arm, and tapping it energetically with her fore-finger, exclaimed: "You see dat, massa? Dat's whar he got he money — out o' dat black skin he got he money."

I have set down as nearly as I can the rude jargon in which they speak. The tones of the voice are impossible to give, and they give a wonderful force to such a conversation, as that above related. They are highly dramatic, and present a narrative in the conversational form, which makes it extremely difficult to follow their rapid and thick utterance. I found it impossible to understand all they said, when speaking with those who had been fieldhands. They have a curious accent, something like that of a Frenchman speaking English poorly; but, in addition, they have numerous contractions, inversions of form, and cant phrases, which make the unaccustomed listener's task more difficult. "I go shum," was a puzzler to me, often occurring, till I learned that "shum" is simply a contraction for "see him," and the whole phrase means generally, "I will go and see about it."

Men like the Harry whom I have mentioned, who have been accustomed to work about the house — Harry had been his master's manager — speak plainly enough; and as the children learn to read in the schools, they also will come gradually to speak correctly. There are already signs of improvement in this respect. It is very desirable that the rising generation should be taught to speak the language correctly. The jargon of the old people is really, in many cases, a barrier to intercourse, and gave me, unconsciously, some-times the feeling that I was speaking with foreigners.

Port Royal, March 25, 1863.

My first visit was to Hilton Head Island, and here I noticed but very few mulattoes. Nearly all the people are pure black. On St. Helena and other Islands the proportion of yellow people is greater, but on Port Royal Island they form a considerable part of the population, especially in Beaufort. There are no statistics to show the number of each complexion. I was told that among the documents found when our forces took possession were a great number of records or manifests of shipments of slaves made from Hilton Head, in years past, with a descriptive list of each "chattel and those who examined these lists found that the greater number of those sold away were of the mixed blood. Thus the planters and overseers profitably rid themselves of the evidences of their vice and guilt.

In Miss Kennedy's school, at Beaufort, I saw a child perfectly beautiful and charming — a little girl, some six or seven years old, by complexion a clear brunette, with slightly "wavy " hair, regular, almost classic features, and the most graceful motions. It was a child that any one might be proud of, but its father had taken no thought of this little one when he fled from the terror of the "Yankees," unless, perhaps, he thought bitterly of the thousands of dollars she would have brought him in a few years, exposed on the auction-block.

I suppose it was mere chance that in the schools I visited I found the best scholars to be among the pure blacks. My tests were by no means sufficient to found a theory on ; and I heard no one generalizing in the matter. The little child mentioned above, though evidently bright, was certainly behind her class-mates with her reading and spelling ; but then pretty children are scarcely ever good students. In her class, the boy who outspelled every body, in my hearing, and who was equal to every hard word given out, was as black as night, and in features and gesture a regular "Jim Crow." In almost all the schools you .find children with blue eyes and light hair— oftenest yellow. One boy I saw in Miss Town's school on St. Helena's, who had the square head, the "shock" of hair, and much of the expression of Robert Toombs, of Georgia.

The children in the schools are of all sizes and ages. Generally, in one corner of the room you will find half a dozen or a dozen girls nearly grown; and from that they range down to little urchins of four and five years. The larger girls I always found dressed with neatness and propriety; the mass of the school, however, is clad in a curious and inexhaustible variety of rags, of all shades and materials. On Sunday, children and parents come to church in better clothing, and many of the women have finery, and even wear hoops. The rags seemed to me clean, which is the main point; but they hung upon the little fellows in the oddest ways imaginable; and some of the materials were of the most curious. I think it was Captain Hooper who described to me a boy he met going to school in the morning, clad in a shirt of Brussels, and a pair of trowsers of ingrain carpet. You see, they use what comes to hand.

Their conduct in the schools is satisfactory to the teachers. They are restless, as all children are; for my part, with doors and windows open, and the warm sunlight shining in upon the busy company of spellers and readers, I wondered that they could be kept in at all. The attendance is regular, the parents being anxious that their children shall learn. I heard no complaints from teachers; and I am sure that these ladies would find it difficult to manage, in a New-England or Western country school, such big boys as I saw sitting submissive under their rule. They take great delight in singing, which is very properly a part of the daily routine. They have fine voices, and an excellent ear for time ; and some of the larger boys roar a deep bass. Besides the songs which have been introduced by the teachers, they have their own, of which the melodies are always quaint, and often full of music. "Roll, Jordan, Roll," has a glorious swing. The words mostly tell of death, and the happier life beyond; and in fact, all the songs I heard, even among the boatmen and other grown people, related to Scripture stories and religious sentiment.

One song, sung with peculiar force and unction, had for refrain an aspiration for liberty which not even the masters, probably, ventured to check. I remember but two lines:

> *"I'll follow Jesus's ways, No man can hinder me !*
>
> *I'll do what Jesus says,*
>
> *No man can hinder me"*

The first stanza of another clings to me, as curious a bit of folk-song as I ever met:

"Old massa Death,

He's a very little man,

He goes from door to door ; , '

He kills some souls.

And he woundeth some.

Good Lord, remember me ;

Good Lord, remember me ;

Remember me as the years roll round,

Good Lord, remember me."

I trust the teachers will gather up and preserve not only the words but the melodies which are thus sung. They will quickly disappear; and some of them are eminently worth preserving.

The people remain for the most part in their old homes. Some have removed to Beaufort, where there is a considerable demand for servants and other laborers; and on Hilton Head Island the necessities of the Quartermaster's Department, which employs there alone some six hundred men, have brought many families down to the fort. Outside of its limits General Mitchel caused a village to be laid out, where there are now upwards of a hundred houses; and on General Drayton's place another is growing up from the same demand. General Mitchel's village was unfortunately laid out on too contracted a scale. The plot of ground assigned to each cottage is not large enough to furnish support to the owners, as it is desirable, for the present, at least, that it should — the women being quite capable and ready to cultivate the ground. It seemed to me, too, that the site chosen was the least fertile I saw. I am afraid some city-bred surveyor was engaged to do the work, more used to measuring mother earth by the inch than by the rood. However, the people are contented and industrious; I saw the women and children in every "lot," planting sweet potatoes, and preparing the ground for corn. I observed that wood-ashes are used as manure.

"Ef only de Yankees whips 'em," said an old woman to me, "I'se happy." There is a degree of uncertainty about their position and about their future which is doubtless a clog upon their enterprise — yet it does not affect them greatly.

Not only have the greater number of the people remained on their old plantations, but they still live in their old quarters, they continue to work in their old "tasks," they display the same strong local attachment which Mr. Sewell noticed as characteristic of the black freedmen in the British West-Indies. It is known throughout the Department that General Hunter never refuses a negro the necessary pass to take him to the North; but not a dozen applications have been made since our occupation began — and of the halfdozen blacks who have ventured from here to the Northern States, several have returned.

This attachment to their old homes is very strong, but they love liberty even more than home, as they have shown in numerous instances. Some months ago all the negroes on a plantation within the enemy's lines, seventy-six in number, fled in one night, in an old scow, and landed next morning on Port Royal Island. Their master had told them that when they had gathered his crop he meant to remove them a little farther back, where the Yankees could not get at them, to sell, them to Cuba. The very next night 12 men, women and children packed up, put their bundles into a scow, and drifted down into our lines. Negroes frequently come here from the interior. Not long since ten fellows, who belonged nearly a hundred miles inland from Hilton Head, were sent as spies, to report on the situation and defences of a region they were familiar with. They were gone a number of days on their hazardous undertaking, and brought General Hunter what he considered a satisfactory and accurate report. But they brought back also their wives and children.

When our forces evacuated Edisto Island, last year, sixteen hundred blacks left their homes and all their property, rather than run the risk of falling again into the hands of their masters. These people had their corn and cotton growing finely; they were a happy and prosperous community, living where they had always lived. They were given their choice, to remain or to become exiles, leaving all their property behind. Not a man or woman remained. They preferred to lose every thing else, in order to assure their liberty. It is very plain, that to produce that "invasion of black laborers in the free States," of which some foolish and wicked persons at the North speak so often, we have only to maintain slavery in the South. If by any chance the region here in our possession could be once more declared slave soil, not a negro would remain here — all would fly to New York. But while they can be free here, not one desires to go North.

I am ashamed to say that the love of liberty, felt and shown by these people, constantly surprised me. We who have not been slaves do not appreciate the horrors of that state, nor will you ever know the endurance and ardor of that love of liberty which God has planted in the breasts of all men and women, till you see it shining out in the faces of these ignorant and abused fellow-men; till you learn how it has made brave the hearts of their most timid women, how it has nerved them to face every danger, to suffer every loss, to sacrifice every feeling, that they may secure freedom.

The results of emancipation in the West-Indies proved long ago that the negro, free, is not that fatal lover of idleness which the master always proclaimed him. On these Sea Islands the freedmen have shown themselves industrious and willing workers, and that without the slightest compulsion. Many have even shown enterprise, which was not to be expected of them, from their antecedents. Last summer, Barnwell and Hall Islands were evacuated by our troops. When the pickets were removed, the blacks were also taken to Port Royal Island. They left their crops of com, potatoes and cotton, standing. They discovered presently that the rebels did not take possession; and emboldened by this, petitioned for permission to return and care for their crops. Leave was granted, but they were warned that no guards would protect them, that it was at their own risk they ventured back. This independent colony returned, tended and harvested their corn and cotton without the guidance of a superintendent, and for months without the slightest encouragement or pay; and I saw cotton of their raising in the gin-house at Beaufort. These two islands lie very near Port Royal Island, and doubtless they felt tolerably secure from capture in the fact that flight was easy, and a refuge near at hand.

The old plantation lines are preserved in the administration of affairs, and thus the circumstances of the people are but little changed, except in the great matter that they were slaves and are now free. The system of administration which has been adopted is probably as good as could be contrived. It has the great merit that it interferes very little with the people, but leaves them almost altogether to their own guidance, and regards them as self-supporting men and women.

The islands in our possession are divided into four districts. The first embraces Port Royal and Cat and Cane Islands; the second comprises St. Helena's, Ladies', Wassa, Coosaw, Dathaw, and Morgan islands; the third consists of Hilton Head and Pinckney Islands; the fourth, Paris Island. The first division, of which Mr. H. G. Judd is General Superintendent, has sixty plantations, which are arranged in twenty-three districts, each of which has a local superintendent. The second, Richard Soule, Jr., General Superintendent, has twenty-five districts, comprising eighty-two plantations. The third. Rev. Thomas D. Howard, General Superintendent, has four districts. The fourth, Paris Island, of which Mrs. F. D. Gage is General Superintendent, has two districts.

The duties of the superintendents are necessarily general. They form a kind of local magistracy, to whom disputes are referred; but they also take charge of the plantations, keep the accounts, apportion the land according to rules laid down, look after Government property, and exercise such supervision as is found necessary. The local superintendents make semi-monthly reports to the general superintendent, and they meet frequently for consultation and to compare experiences.

The people "are made responsible for planting and cultivating sufficient corn and potatoes for their own subsistence." This is the groundwork. To enable them to do this, each family has an allotment of ground, at the rate of two acres for each working hand, and five sixteenths of an acre (one task and one quarter task) for each child. The superintendents make the allotments in such manner that there shall be no waste land. The "task" is a quarter of an acre; and the old plantations are all marked off by peculiar ridges, so that the labor of allotting ground is not great.

The land is held to belong to the Government, and to pay for its use and for the use of the cattle necessary to its cultivation each community or plantation is obliged to till as. much land as will support the cattle, with an acre for the superintendent, an acre and a half for the plantation ploughman, and an acre for every infirm or disabled person. It will be seen that each community is thus at once made self supporting, and takes care of its own paupers.

It was thought well not to intermit altogether the cultivation of cotton, and accordingly, at the commencement of the season of 1862, the people agreed to undertake, in addition to their own allotments, each a certain space of cotton land. For labor on these they are paid at the rate of twenty-five! cents for the day's work, the nature and extent of which is strictly defined. That is to say, they are paid not by the day, but for the amount of work, each performs. In addition to this, they are paid two and a half cents per pound for the cotton each raises and picks. Such of them, if any, as do not choose to work in the cotton fields, are required to pay two dollars per month rent for the houses and lands they occupy. There are some additional expenses necessary before the cotton is ready for market, as for assorting, bagging, ginning, moating and packing, the whole cost of which is three cents per pound.

Under this system a cotton crop has been raised by free labor, and is now nearly ready for market. This crop amounts to seventy-five thousand pounds, worth now in this market at least one dollar per pound. If the amount does not seem great, we must remember the circumstances under which it was raised. Concisely stated, the drawbacks on successful culture were as follows:

First. It was not determined to grow cotton till the season was far advanced; and the superintendents did not enter on their labors till two months after the usual time for commencing to prepare the ground. The consequences were, hasty and insufficient preparation and late maturity, which gave the caterpillar, cut-worm and frost a chance to injure the crop.

Second. A farther delay was caused by the time required to organize labor and to gain the confidence of the people; and all through the season the superintendents not only had no money to pay the workmen, but they actually had no authority to make any definite arrangements or conclude on terms. They had to ask the people to trust to them, that it would be "all right." "We had to run our face in the most shameless manner," said one to me. Finally, after the ground was prepared and the cotton planted, which is the heaviest of the work, the laborers were paid one dollar per acre, which is only about half what the work is fairly worth.

Third. All the able-bodied men were withdrawn from the plantations, to be used by the Quartermaster, etc. This kept back the work and greatly lessened, of course, the area planted and the quantity raised. That is to say, the women, children, and old and infirm people, raised nearly the whole of this crop.

Fourth. The work was done with old and broken tools, there being no fresh supply at hand.

Fifth. The crop was put in so late that an early frost found one half the cotton still in the field, not mature enough for picking.

I have described above the system in which society is carried on in these islands. Strict orders forbid the issue of rations to any who have become destitute by their own act or fault. During the past year there have come to our lines some fifteen hundred refugees; besides these, sixteen hundred people were brought from Edisto when our forces evacuated that island. All these were destitute by no fault of theirs, and to these, of course, rations were issued for a time. Here I must explain that a "contraband" ration is, by no means, a soldiers ration, as the following will show: One hundred rations for the refugees consist of seventy-five pounds hard bread, one gallon of molasses, four pounds of soap and three pounds of salt. They receive, in addition, three ounces of bacon each per day; but this is not permanently incorporated in the ration. Any one who knows what a soldier's ration is, will see the great difference between the two.

You will now ask, How does this system work? I asked what punishments or penalties were provided for refractory or utterly indolent and improvident negroes? To this I got no definite reply, and found the reason to be that not enough of such cases had arisen so far to necessitate the formation of a code. We have none amongst. -us either at the North — our laws take no account of the idle and improvident; society leaves them to their reward. Even so it seems to be among these people. Here was another instance, and only one of a hundred, where it was brought home to me that these freedmen are men and women as we are, and that the problem of forming them into useful members of society is divested of most, if not all, its difficulties the moment we make this the first principle ruling our plans. "He that will not work, neither let him eat" — that is the whole law needed.

It remains to describe more particularly the customs, peculiarities and mode of life of these freedmen, and this I hope to do in another letter.

Port Royal, April 3, 1863.

I come now to speak more particularly of the people — their customs, mode of life and appearance.

They are not a good-looking people. I did not see the soldiers, who are, of course, the flower of the population; they were in Florida. But I saw those employed as laborers on the docks, as well as those remaining on the plantations.

In the schools I was struck with the singular shape of many heads. Some seemed to me to denote a very low order of intellect; but I must add, that the two children, a boy and girl, whose appearance bespoke the least mental power, were counted among the best scholars in their school, and acquitted themselves handsomely in my presence. They were the children of a poor woman who had been for many years cruelly abused by her master— so far as I could judge from her story and that of others, because she possessed an unruly tongue. She had suffered treatment so inhuman that I can not describe it here; I will only say, that not only her back but her breasts bore deep scars, the marks of unmerciful and brutal flogging. I could not help thinking that her children had suffered in looks and development from their mother's condition.

It is a fact that the whole population bears the marks of bondage. They do not look like the negroes of our Northern States, born and reared in freedom. Compared with these they struck me as decidedly a grade lower in the scale. But when we consider that a generation of freedom has worked this improvement in our Northern blacks, we need not despair of these Carolinians.

They dress, on week days, in a style which does not add to their appearance. The rags which surprised and amused me as worn by the school children were repeated on their parents. Their gowns do not often fit neatly; the clothes seem to hang upon a fieldhand, realizing the old sailor's figure of a "purser's shirt upon a handspike;" and to see a company of them together in the field made me think of an extraordinary collection of scarecrows. Of course, there are exceptions; those who were house-servants dress more neatly, and those now servants in houses do as well. But I speak of the greater number.

On Sundays the men and women put on their best, and present a bright and cheerful appearance. They are fond of brilliant colors, and might, I should think, be easily taught the art of fitting dress. I ought to say that all were clad with propriety; I saw nowhere indecent exposure of the person.

In their dress, and in the furnishing of their cabins, they have changed but little yet. Taste in these matters has to be acquired slowly; they have always been accustomed to a certain fashion of house and dress, and know nothing beyond or different. They have no models before them to imitate ; for in this region there were but two classes, the slaves and the masters — no middle class, enjoying cheap comforts, to allure the class below them to a more inviting mode of life.

The cabins are small, and contain two rooms — one called by the people the hall wherein is the great open fireplace; the other a dark hole, in which the older people sleep, and in which, too, I believe, their valuables are kept. Above is a loft, a general receptacle for those innumerable odds and ends which the slave cherished as "property." The younger people of the house sleep on rugs before the fire.

Every cabin is full of children, of all sizes. I stopped in one to speak to a sick woman, and was presently surrounded by half a dozen wide-eyed youngsters, the mother, with a babe in her arms, standing near me.

"You have a large family," said I to her.

"Yes, sah," said she, not quite taking in my question; "I've had twenty-three children." She did not look to be more than forty years old.

The cabins are, for the most part, whitewashed outside; inside they are smoke-stained, and on rainy days dark — for there are no glass windows — but not close, the fireplace acting as an excellent ventilator. In every cabin hung a hand-net, for fishing; near all the quarters. I saw piles of oyster- shells. On rainy days, when out-door work is impossible, the men sit at home and mend their nets, while the women sew. I was amused at the exclamation of an old woman:

" Why, dese Yankees, dey's the mos' wonderful people! when dey gives you needles, dey gives you tree to once!" She went on to explain that in the old times, her mistress gave each slave woman one needle to last a whole year!

Their cabins are not dirty, but they have a cheerless look to a Northern man. Doubtless those men who are now employed in the army and navy will bring back with them improved ideas and new wants, and will work a change both in dress and furniture. I noticed that on some walls were hung pictures from the illustrated journals; and I have no doubt cheap colored prints would find a ready sale.

You are to remember that not only have these people no standard, or model, according to which to make even slight improvements in their cottages, but they have never, until now, had the means, even if they knew how; and even now, if they have saved money, they can not buy — simply because they are not sold here — any one of the hundred trifles for which a Northern housekeeper goes to the "store" across the street, or a little way down the lane, or if she lives too far away, applies to the peddler when he comes along on his high-perched wagon. The day which sees the introduction on

these islands of the itinerant Yankee peddler will be an important
one. If he is only moderately honest, and quick-witted, he will be a
valuable helper in advancing civilization here.

To us, who have been long accustomed to a certain air of comfort
and tidiness, it seems extraordinary that these people should live
contentedly in the way they do, one moment longer than is abso-
lutely necessary. In our minds this squalor is linked with drunken-
ness and vicious improvidence and we unconsciously dislike those
who live in this condition. These were my emotions, I confess,
when I first entered the cabins of the people here. Those astounding
agglomerations of rags, this which seemed to me the most dreary
discomfort, the gloom through which, standing before the inner
room, you heard a voice — the voice of some old crone — without
seeing her figure; all this made my heart sink, at first, and I said to
myself: " Oh I dear! oh! dear! what can be done with all this?"

But I found that the rags were clean; that you can safely visit the
cabins — the only animal likely to assail you there being the flea,
which is at home also in the "mansion." I found that the whole affair
is not nearly so bad as it looks; and when I came to compare the
overseers' and the planters' houses with the " quarters," I saw in the
one as many traces of what Miss Ophelia called "shiftlessness," as
in the other. -The blacks could not learn from the whites, because
the whites themselves did not know what comfort or neatness was.
Beaufort was probably one of the wealthiest places in the South — it
was the home of wealthy families and their house-slaves. But it has
not a single one of the many conveniences which so quickly gather
about a New-England village or a Western town; and though there
are some hundreds of houses in the place, all large, roomy, and evi-
dently built by men who cared little for expense, there is, I am told,
but one in the place which contains what we include in the phrase
"modern conveniences."

Nor are you to forget that in a state of slavery these blacks were rigidly kept to a certain uniform, in dress and other surroundings, which was the mark of their servile condition, just as were the Jews in the middle ages. In fact, many things here reminded me of the oppressions practised upon the Jews in Europe almost down to our own days. Like the blacks they were regarded as of a peculiar race; the strongly marked physiognomy of the Hebrew set him and his apart quite as much, in Europe, as the negro's color separates him from us ; and any one who has travelled through Germany knows that the prejudice which existed there, till within" twenty years, was just as strong, as unreasoning, and apparently as unconquerable, as that which prevails in this country against the blacks. Americans know but little of the violence of this old-time prejudice against the Jews in Germany; but any German who reads this will bear me out in the assertion that the Jewish face was as bitterly despised and the Jew's rights as little regarded by the common people in that country thirty years ago as are the blackskin and the rights of its possessor in the South to-day.

I am making no excuse for the blacks in all this. They do not need it, for they display a disposition to make a better figure in the world, which proves that it is not they, but their masters, who are to blame if they make a poor show now.

"Stores" have been established on different parts of the island for the use of the blacks. Some of these were set up by superintendents, others by charitable societies in the North. Here goods are sold to the people at prices which cover the cost and expenses of transportation and management — that is to say, at the same rates at which the provident New-Englander buys in the wellknown "Union Store," whose sign would puzzle many a travelling English-man. The terms in these shops are "strictly cash;" nothing is sold on credit. I was assured that the wants of the people, judged by this excellent index, are increasing; every new supply laid in includes a greater variety of wares; and it happens even that negroes on St. Helena or Port Royal islands go to Beaufort to buy, because they can not obtain what they want nearer at hand. The people own more clothing than before — this was the universal reply to my questions upon this point. "For instance, men and women I know have a pair of fine shoes for Sunday and a pair of coarse shoes for working days," said one to me.

Mr. Philbrick, who has had great experience, amongst them, and who himself set up a "store" in the district of which he had charge last year, says that " their wants are increasing about as fast as their ability to pay." In his shop on Coffin's Point, the sales of one year, among a population or clientage of four hundred and fifty persons, amounted — at cost and expenses — to quite five thousand dollars; all, or very nearly all, paid for in money.

They have strong affection for their children. It is well known that few men run away to us alone; as a rule they come off bringing with them their wives and little ones — often from great distances, and at frightful risks. An intelligent observer remarked to me that he thought they were more careful of their little ones now that they — and not the masters — own them. Perhaps. The little things are fat enough, and are easily taught the virtue of obedience.

The people are universally polite. If you address a man, he touches his hat to you; as you ride past the quarter, on Sunday afternoons, when all are at home, the women gather in rows, outside, to see you, and the whole line courtesies, with a sudden bend of the knees, which has a somewhat comical effect at first.

While slaves, of course their days were claimed by the masters; and consequently they contracted a habit of transacting their own private business after nightfall. If you remember that a whole community was thus forced to provide for its interests after sunset, you will see what a singular state of affairs obtained in this way. Now this old habit still prevails; one superintendent remarked that the road in his district was more crowded, and more people passed, in one night than in three days. There results sometimes this, that a superintendent, going to his stable in the morning, finds to his surprise that his horse seems wearied and worn, as though he had been ridden all night — and no one knows any thing about it; or he finds, as one friend did, that his harness, taken off the horse the evening before, will not fit at all; it is too large, or too small; it has been let out, or taken in. In feudal Germany, some centuries ago, such incidents were common too ; and there superstition laid the blame to some evil-disposed spirit, some Rubezal or other mountain goblin, who thus amused himself at the expense of the master. But our more matter-of-fact Yankees know that the mysterious rider is a fellow with a black skin; and that the harness has been fitted, over-night, to the neighbor's pony, or to the lean Rosinante of the ploughman.

Another odd habit created by their enslaved condition, but lasting into freedom, is this, that men not unfrequently live on one place, and their wives in another, and at some distance away. It is curious to trace the steps by which a habit, once formed, covers up its tracks, so to speak, and hides its origin. Undoubtedly this separatism was brought about by the fact that men would more or less frequently take for wives women living at a distance, and whom their masters could not or would not buy. But it has come about, now, that young men prefer to live at home and cling to their mothers, while the young women in like manner cling to their fathers. Professor Zacchos, on Paris Island, related to me a story exemplifying this trait, which has a quaint antique flavor and manner about it.

It seems that a young fellow on Paris Island made love to, and took for wife, a young girl whose family lived on St. Helena's, separated from Paris by a narrow sound. The two really loved each other; they were married in regular form; but after living some weeks with her husband the girl returned one day to her father's house, and there remained. The husband tried, but ineffectually, to persuade her back; she was ready to receive him, anxious to see him, but she clung to her father and' mother, and these supported her in this course, and would not hear of her going away.

One day the husband, exasperated at this state of affairs, collected a number of young fellows, his friends, went in a boat to St. Helena's at a time when his wife's people were away in the fields, and forcibly carried her off.

There the affair rested for some days, till one day Dr. Zacchos, who knew nothing of this till afterward, was called to settle what threatened to be a severe and even a bloody quarrel. He hastened to the scene and beheld, drawn up on opposite sides, two bands of men, menacing each other with angry looks, and midway between them, appealing now to one and then to the other side, a young girl.

The parents had determined to recapture their daughter; the father had gathered a party of friends, and with them crossed, in his turn, to Paris Island, had seized the girl, and was conveying her to his boat, when the husband, collecting also a force, advanced to resist this novel rape. Neither party would hear reason, and a battle was imminent.

The presence of a white man produced a momentary calm. On a hearing of the case, in which I believe both parties agreed as to the material facts, he explained to the people that Mary had willingly married Sam; that she still loved him, according to her own declaration; and that whatever might have been the custom while slavery prevailed, it was now right that husband and wife should live together. The parents, he declared, had no more claim to their daughter.

At this there was evident dissatisfaction on one side; whereupon the faithful Sam, sure of his wife's affection, announced that it was best to leave it to her decision. Now mark what was her judgment, She said:

" I your wife, Sam; I love you; I love my fader and mudder too ; in de spring time and in harvest, when de hard work is in de field, I come live wid you; when no hard work to do in de field, den I go live at home and you come live wid me,"

And this judgment was thought so reasonable, that public opinion sustained the girl.

Port Royal, April 25, 1803.

The questions arising from the unsettled condition of family relations among these South-Carolina blacks have been among the most delicate which came up for decision before the constituted authorities. There was, I have been told, no such thing existing as polygamy; no man had, or pretended to have, two wives at the same time; but, in a number of cases, men desired to cast off the "old wives" whom their masters had 'given them, and take up with other women. One made the point in such a case that no marriage ceremony had ever been performed to bind him to this woman; that he exercised no choice in her selection even; and, no doubt, they did come together here much according to the will of the master or overseer, who parcelled out wives as he parcelled out blows or tasks in the field- In some cases the people were regularly married; in very many, not.

The rule made, in a General Order, to apply to these is, that where men and women were regularly married they must be faithful to each other, and the man must support his wife and children. Where no lawful marriage existed, this ceremony is performed by some minister; and if two women claim a man, he is ordered to cleave to the mother of his children. Concubinage and unfaithfulness to marriage vows are made punishable offences.

Now there come up such cases as this: A man who is somewhat notorious as a "rough" among his people, a strong, self willed, determined fellow — an exception to the rule, so far as character is concerned — comes to head-quarters, and says he has never willingly lived with the woman who, according to custom, was his wife; he does not love her, and she is not fond of him, for they never agree, (and he, I believe, sometimes beat her.) He now wishes to marry; but he has chosen a young woman for wife, with whom he has been living, secretly, for more than a year — and she is about to become a mother. It is made evident, by inquiry, that these two have a strong affection for each other; he is extremely anxious to marry her before her child is born. The former wife does not object, but consents.

No law was ever framed which did not bear hardly on some one. I have reason to believe that such cases as that I have just recited are decided in a manner to cause as little suffering and to do as little mischief as possible.

The marriage relation is, in general, held sacred. I have spoken in a previous letter of a negro now 'serving a term of ten years in the District of Columbia Penitentiary, who slew the seducer of his wife. He was held justified for the act by his fellows, and that is, perhaps, a fair index of the state of public sentiment among the people on this subject.

The young women are, so far as I could judge from careful inquiry, not eminently chaste. Public opinion did not compel them to virtuous courses under the old slave system. There is no reason to believe that indiscriminate intercourse obtained to any extent among the slaves, but it was held no shame to a girl to bear children under any circumstances; the planters, I suppose, encouraged that which put money in their purses; and a different and more rigid sentiment has not yet, I think, generally obtained. One of the ablest of the superintendents told me that he was in the habit, as the people were, at first, very destitute, of giving to each mother an outfit for her new-born child; of course, something very simple — a dress, and one or two other articles, perhaps. This was the custom of the planters; and he found it best to continue it, at least, for a time. "But," said he, "I made it a rule to refuse such gifts to the young unmarried girls who applied." If you think for a moment, you will understand what is implied in this remark.

To establish a different, higher standard of virtue among a people is slow work. These have many things to learn, and many to unlearn.

They have a habit or proneness to lying which is, I think, clearly one of the old effects of slavery. They can see no wrong in telling that story which shall seem in their judgment best calculated to produce any desired effect — to obtain a favor, to please a friend, or to harm an enemy. Those who are familiar with the character of the common Hindoo will appreciate this; for, in this, the negroes and they are precisely alike — and in both the spirit which has no faith in the efficacy or value of truth is bred of servility and is the fruit of tyranny. One of these blacks, fresh from slavery, will most adroitly tell you precisely what you want to hear. To cross-examine such a creature is a task of the most delicate nature; if you chance to put a leading question he will answer to its spirit as closely as the compass needle answers to the magnetic pole. Ask if the enemy had fifty thousand men, and he will be sure that they bad at least that many; express your belief that they had not five thousand, and he will laugh at the idea of their having more than forty -five hundred. "The intelligent and reliable contraband" is the dread of staff-officers, who pump him vainly for information on which they may depend.

In Irish trials you find the witness-box full of such witnesses as these, ready to swear to any thing which may serve the side for which their sympathies are enlisted. The traditional Irishman of the novel is precisely such an "intelligent and reliable" creature.

They have not, as a general thing, a craving for strong drink. Some have learned, while living among white men, as officers' servants, etc., to love whisky; but they cannot be called an intemperate people. It might be easy to make them so, however; I believe, with Captain Hooker, "that if ably-managed dram-shops should be established at suitable points on these islands the negroes would soon acquire the habit of intemperance — and thus, all distinctions of race in this respect would be swept away."

They display a desire to learn reading. It is not uncommon in Beaufort to see the workmen on the wharves, at the odd moments when they have nothing to do, busy with a primer or reader.

Their religious feelings are strong and easily excited. They all like to sing; are fond of devotional meetings, and have much of that curious excitability which is often developed in Western and Southern camp-meetings. What is called a "shout" is one way in which this excitement manifests itself; and this seems to be an effect of the same nature as what was called "the jerks" in the West and South-West — a kind of nervous affection, which, according to the best authorities, swept over nearly the whole South Western States some twenty years ago, affecting not a dozen or a hundred, but sometimes a thousand or two thousand people at once, when they were gathered together in open-air " meetings."

This excitability appears to many observers peculiar to the negroes; I think the people here show it, perhaps, more readily than any whites I have seen ; but any one who has been accustomed to camp-meeting scenes in Indiana and Ohio, a dozen or twenty years ago, will find here, on occasion of a " shout," I am sure, something he is quite familiar with.

If you remember that many hundreds of these people ran away from their rebel masters and came to our lines at the greatest risks, and well knowing that dreadful punishments awaited them if caught, I think you will find in that some evidence of courage. The higher officers here, who have used the black men as spies and scouts, will tell you that they are cool and bold enough. Men who return to the enemy's lines to steal off their wives and children do not lack enterprise ; and when the Government awards medals for good conduct and bravery in the face of the enemy, as well as for honorable and important services rendered, it ought not to forget Smalls, who brought the steamer Planter out of Charleston. He is not the only one who has come out past Fort Sumter. There is a sergeant in the First South-Carolina regiment who came out in a small boat, one dark night, to the blockading fleet. He is black, an intelligent and fin:-looking fellow.

I had occasion to see here, one day, how far the bitter and mean prejudices of a pro-slavery man will carry him. Smalls, of the Planter, was ordered to go to the Wabash to see the Admiral. He went alongside in a boat in which it happened that Brig.-General Seymour also was. The General called to the officer of the deck and said to him : " Officer, this hoy wants to see the Admiral; will you please let him know that the boy is waiting?" Then turning to Smalls, he cried out, in a sharp voice: " Here, Joy, you can go aboard, and the officer will tell you when the Admiral is ready to see you."

Now Smalls is not a boy; he is a man of, I should think, thirty years, and wears a beard sufficient to show it. I blushed for Gen. Seymour when I heard him use the old cant of the slave-master toward this man, who performed one of the bravest and most brilliant acts of the war. General Seymour is himself a brave man, and if a white man had done what Smalls did, he would no doubt have honored him for it. But because this gallant fellow happens to have a black skin, he speaks to him in away that seemed to me, unwillingly listening to him, contemptibly mean.

Smalls was engaged to be one of the pilots to take in the fleet to attack Charleston. He is thoroughly familiar, I am told, with the creeks and intricate channels along this coast; and his knowledge has been of great value to our army and navy. He seems a very quiet man, without the slightest swagger. How he looked or felt when he was called "boy" in this way, I can not tell you — for I dared not look in the poor fellow's face.

I have endeavored to give in these letters an exact account of what I saw in these Sea Islands, of the negroes, their qualities and character. I can sum up all, most briefly, in the words of General Hunter, who said; "In short, these people do work, they are not idle, they don't steal, they don't swear, they don't use obscene language, they are willing and faithful laborers and servants, polite to every body, always cheerful, docile, and easily ruled."

The Cotton States in the Spring and Summer of 1875

To the President of the United States:

Sir,

- I respectfully offer you a report on the political and industrial condition of several of the Southern States, the result of an exploration made by me during the spring and summer of the present year, at the request of Mr. James Gordon Bennett, for the *New York Herald*. The facts collected here seem to me likely to interest you, who, I sincerely believe, have failed to make the people of the Southern States contented, chiefly because, in your exalted position, it was unfortunately difficult for you to know the real condition of those States, which has rapidly and continually changed from year to year of your Administration. Had you been able to examine them for yourself in 1874–5, as you did in 1865, I can not doubt that your Southern policy would in very many particulars have been different from what it has been; for it is your duty, as it doubtless is your

wish, to secure the liberties and increase the prosperity, content-
ment, and happiness of all your fellow- citizens.

Very respectfully,

your obedient servant,

Charles Nordhoff

4

Preliminary

It was my fortune to spend the winter of 1874-75 in Washington, in almost daily attendance upon the debates of Congress, and in more or less intimate friendly relations with many of its leading members, of both parties. The Southern question was, during the whole of the three months' session, that which attracted most attention, and was in public and private most earnestly discussed. The Louisiana affair, the Vicksburg riot, the Alabama question, the Arkansas muddle, were all the topics of continual excited conversation in and out of Congress. I was extremely desirous to find a basis of fact on which to found a trustworthy opinion of the condition of the South; but was constantly confused by statements apparently partisan, and, at any rate, unsatisfactory. The leaders of both parties in Congress were, for the most part, no more accurately informed than I; and debate and legislation on Southern affairs during the whole winter were mainly based either upon a general notion that wo still live under a Constitution, or upon narrow views of party expediency or necessity. The Democrats for the most part dealt in incoherent and ineffective generalities about violated liberties. Of the Republicans, one faction steadily pressed coercive measures, which in the end failed of adoption; while -the other part opposed these measures but weakly, because they had no certain knowledge of the condition of affairs on which they spoke and were asked to legislate. Thus the Habeas Corpus and Force Bill and the Arkansas Message were defeated with great difficulty; the Civil Rights Bill was passed, only to become a dead letter in the South, and a source of annoyance to its supporters in the next Presidential canvass ; and the report of the first New Orleans committee, though based on evidence not afterwards controverted, was received with so much doubt that a second committee was thought necessary — to investigate the first.

Under these circumstances I accepted gladly an offer from Mr. Bennett to make for him an exploration of the principal Southern States, and see for myself what I had vainly tried to discover by questioning others. My journey began early in March, and ended in July. I visited successively Arkansas, Louisiana, Mississippi, Alabama, North Carolina, and Georgia; and the results of my observations were printed in letters to the *New York Herald.* These letters, with some additions and corrections, form the larger part of the present volume. They became, on their publication in the *Herald,* the subject of a contentious discussion in the journals of both parties. North and South, and, I must confess, had not the good fortune to please partisans anywhere. It was probably inevitable that they should offend those whose preconceived views or whose interests they did not advance, for I sought only for facts, and did not care what side they favored; but it has been a great satisfaction to me to receive many private letters from Southern men, both Republicans and Democrats, acknowledging the correctness of my statements, and the general justice of my views and conclusions.

Though my letters consisted almost entirely of statements of fact, I found, from first to last, opinions and conclusions imputed to me, by partisan writers, which I did not and do not entertain. It was but natural, perhaps, that each side should accept such facts as served its purposes, and draw inferences from them which were not my own. But I do not wish to be misunderstood, and propose, therefore, to prefix to the record of my observations my own deductions. And to make clear my point of view, it is proper to say that I am a Republican, and have never voted any other Federal ticket than the Republican; I have been opposed to slavery as long as I have had an opinion on any subject except sugar-candy and tops; and I am a thorough believer in the capacity of the people to rule themselves, even if they are very ignorant, better than any body else can rule them.

The following, then, are the conclusions I draw from my observations in the Cotton States:

1. There is not, in any of the States of which I speak, any desire for a now war; any hostility to the Union ; any even remote wish to re-enslave the blacks ; any hope or expectation of repealing any constitutional amendment, or in any way curtailing the rights of the blacks as citizens. The former slave-holders understand perfectly that the blacks can not be re-enslaved. "They have been free, and they would drive us out of the country if they thought we were about to re-enslave them. They are a quiet and peaceable people, except when they are exasperated; but then they are terrible. A black mob is a ruthless and savage thing," said a Southern man to me; and another remarked, "If ever you, in the North, want to re-enslave the negroes, you must give us three months' notice, so that we may

all move out, with our wives and children. They were a source of constant anxiety to us when we held them in slavery. To attempt to re-enslave them would be only to invite them to murder us, and lay the country waste."

In Mississippi alone did I find politicians silly enough to talk about the Caucasian race, and the natural incapacity of the negro for self-government; and even there the best Republicans told me that these noisy Democratic demagogues were but a small, though aggressive and not unpowerful, minority; and even in Mississippi, a strong Republican, a Federal law officer, an honest and faithful man, assured me that the northern half of the State, which, with the exception of the region lying about Vicksburg, is the most prone to occasional violence and disorder, was, when I was there, to his personal knowledge, as peaceful and orderly as any part of New York or Ohio.

Even the extreme excitement of a political canvass in Mississippi this fall, in which the Democrats are trying to rid themselves of the justly hateful rule of a corrupt faction, has led to but few disturbances; and we are not to forget that this State is a frontier country, in which every body goes armed ; and that it has for its governor a man who has neglected all the usual means of preserving the peace, or preventing disturbances. With a governor alive to his duty to the State, there would, I believe, have been none. Nor is it just to lay the whole blame of all that has happened on the whites. In the South the negro is not always a lamb. He is sometimes the aggressor.

2. That the Southern whites should rejoice over their defeat, now, is impossible. That their grandchildren will, I hope and believe. What we have a right to require is, that they shall accept the situation; and that they do. What they have a right to ask of us is, that we shall give them a fair chance under the new order of things ; and that we have so far too greatly failed to do. What the Southern Republican too often requires is that the Southern Democrat should

humiliate himself, and make penitent confession that slavery was a sin, that secession was wrong, and that the war was an inexcusable crime. Is it fair or just to demand this? Slavery is now seen, all over the South, to have been a huge economical blunder, and a proposition to re-establish it would not get fifty thousand votes in the whole South. That seems to me an extremely important point gained. As to the moral question, it belongs to the clergy, and has no place in our present politics.

3. The Southern Republicans seem to me unfair and unreasonable in another way. They complain constantly that the Southern whites still admire and are faithful to their own leaders; and that they like to talk about the bravery of the South during the war, and about the great qualities of their leading men. There seems to me something childish, and even cowardly, in this complaint. The Southern man who fought and believed in it, would be a despicable being if he should now turn around and blacken the characters of his generals and political leaders, or if he should not think with pride of the feats of arms and of endurance of his side; or if, having been plundered by Republicans since the war, he should fling up his hat for that party. I say this as a Republican, and believe the mass of Northern Republicans think just as I do.

4. Moreover, it is a fact that the men of brains, of influence, of intelligence, in the South, did, almost to a man, consent to secession, and take an active part in the war against the Union. It was, I believe, and most of them now believe, a great blunder on their part; but they have paid a heavy penalty for their mistake, for most of them were wealthy, and are now poor. It is not fair in us to demand that they shall be reviled and put down by their own people; nor, I believe, do Northern Republicans want that. A few days ago I received a letter from a Mississippi Republican, who related to me, with indignation, that at a Democratic meeting no cheers were so loud as those which followed a mention of Mr. Jefferson Davis's

name. Now, I do not admire Mr. Davis; I think him the weakest and the least respectable of the Southern leaders; and I happen to know that he is not highly thought of in many parts of the South, where his peculiar qualities are well understood, and were felt during the war. But I could not help but agree with a Southern Democrat who said to me, " I don't like Jeff Davis; but he was our leader, and we should be mean creatures, if, when he is spoken against, we did not stand up for him."

5. As to ostracism of Northern men, it stands thus : In all the States I have seen, the Republican reconstructors did shamefully rob the people. In several of them they continue to do so. Now, all the Republicans in the South are not dishonest; but who ever, in a State like Louisiana or Mississippi now, and Arkansas, Alabama, and others formerly, acts with the Republicans, actually lends his support and countenance to corrupt men. Is it strange that, if he is ever so honest himself, he is disliked for his political course? Did not Republicans in New York bitterly criticise and "ostracize" Mr. Tilden, Mr. O'Conor, Mr. Hewitt, and others, who chose to adhere to and act with the Democratic party, while that was controlled by the Tweed Ring? And do not the New York Republicans make it a reproach to this day, to such Democrats, that they thus did? But the cases are precisely parallel. It "costs something to be an honest Republican in the South," precisely as it cost something to be an honest Democrat in New York before the Tammany Ring was smashed.

6. As to "intimidation," it is a serious mistake to imagine this exclusively a Democratic proceeding in the South. It has been practiced in the last three years quite as much, and even more rigorously, by the Republicans. The Federal United States marshal in Louisiana has used cavalry to intimidate Democrats. Similarly, Federal officers confess they did in Alabama and elsewhere. The negroes are the most sav- I age intimidators of all. In many localities

' which I visited, it was as much as a negro's life was worth to vote the Democratic ticket; and even to refuse to obey the caucus of his party caused him to be denounced as "Bolter," and to be forsaken by his friends, and even by his wife or sweetheart. That there has also been Democratic intimidation is undeniable; but it does not belong to the Southern Republicans to complain of it. In North Carolina, a leading and intelligent negro told me that he and others of his race were opposed to the Civil-rights Bill, but they did not dare to let their opposition be known, because, as he said, they would at once have been denounced among their people, and would have lost all influence with them. In Wilmington, a young negro lawyer was mobbed by his people, because he ventured to oppose corrupt candidates for office. This was told me by a colored man.

7. There are no wrongs now in the South which the interference of the Federal Government under the Enforcement acts can reach. This interference is purely and only mischievous. It has disabled and demoralized the Republican State governments, whose members, sure that they would be maintained by the Federal arm everywhere, abandoned their duties, and took to stealing and maladministration. It has seriously injured the negro, by making him irresponsible to the opinion of his neighbors, and submitting him, in his ignorance, to the mischievous and corrupt rule of black and white demagogues. As a result, it has fostered ill-feeling between the races, from which in the end it is inevitable that the negro must be the greatest sufferer.

8. Those States which have been under Republican control have been shamelessly mismanaged, and are now deeply, and some of them hopelessly, in debt, and with very heavy State and county taxes. Such are Arkansas, Louisiana, Mississippi (this in county and local indebtedness), Alabama, and North Carolina.

9. On the other hand, Georgia, which has been since 1871 ruled by Democrats, has but a trifling State debt, scarcely any county debts, good credit, and low taxation.

10. It is a remarkable fact that, according to the best evidence I could collect on the subject, the negroes in Democratic Georgia own far more real estate, and pay taxes on more property, than in any one of the States which have been under Republican rule, like Arkansas or Louisiana.

11. Wherever one of these States has fallen under the control of Democrats, this has been followed by important financial reforms; economy of administration; and, as in Arkansas and Alabama, by the restoration of peace and good-will.

12. In Louisiana and Mississippi, which remain under Republican control, there is a continuance of barefaced corruption, and of efforts, made by a class of unscrupulous demagogues, to set the races in hostility against each other.

13. The misconduct of the Republican; rulers in all these States has driven out of their party the great mass of the white people, the property-owners, tax-payers, and persons of intelligence and honesty. At first a considerable proportion of these were ranged on the Republican side. Now, in all the States I have mentioned, except in North Carolina, the Republican party consists almost exclusively of the negroes and the Federal office-holders, with, in Louisiana and Mississippi, the Republican State and county officers also.

14. Thus has been perpetuated what is called the " color-line" in politics, the Democratic party being composed of the great mass of the whites, including almost the entire body of those who own property, pay taxes, or have intelligence; while the Republican party is composed almost altogether of the negroes, who are, as a body, illiterate, without property, and easily misled by appeals to their fears, and to their gratitude to "General Grant," who is to them the embodiment of the Federal power.

15. This division of political parties on the race or color-line has been a great calamity to the Southern States.

It had its origin in the refusal of the Southern whites, after the war, to recognize the equal political rights of the blacks; and their attempts, in State legislatures, to pass laws hostile to them. This folly has been bitterly regretted by the wiser men in the South. A Mississippian said to me, "It was a great blunder. We could have better afforded to educate and train the colored people, and fit them for the duties of citizenship, than to have had them alienated from us." He was right; it was a great, though probably an inevitable, blunder. It flung the negro into the hands of the so-called Republicans in the Southern States, and these, by adroitly appealing to his fears and to his gratitude to the Federal Government, and by encouraging his desire for official power and spoils, have maintained the color -line in politics, and by its means kept themselves in power.

It is an indisputable fact that there can be no permanent and beneficial settlement of political questions in any Southern State until the color-line is broken. While the white vote, or the greater part of it, is massed on one side, and the black vote, or the greater part of it, on the other, as is still the case in Louisiana, Mississippi, Alabama, and Georgia, it is impossible to get settled good government; for the political issues will, of necessity, be false, and will have no relation to any real question of administration, but only to questions of race.

The great mass of the Southern colored voters are illiterate; they are easily impressed by exhibitions of power; they are readily alarmed about their safety; and, like all ignorant masses, they are very apt to follow a leader. The Republican leader has always had the United States Government to back him. Packard, chairman of the Republican State Executive Committee of Louisiana, has, as United States marshal, the absolute command of Federal troops in Louisiana. Spencer, United States Senator from Alabama, and

Republican leader in that State, runs up to Louisville, and secures for the asking several companies of infantry and cavalry, to be stationed in Alabama, at a time when, as the United States marshal testifies, there was no need at all for troops; and Perrin, one of Spencer's underlings, at the same time deputy-marshal, supervisor of election, candidate for the Legislature, and distributor of Government bacon, shoots a hole through his own hat, and then orders Federal troops to hunt for imaginary Ku-klux. Governor Ames, as is publicly charged, refuses to stir to prevent a riot at Vicksburg; but after the riot, after forty or fifty blacks have been killed, and when the negroes are demoralized and feel utterly helpless, sends for Federal troops, which come at his command, and re-assure the blacks. Such manifestations of power strike the imagination of the negroes, as they would any ignorant population, and they follow very readily and blindly its possessor. Some colored witnesses in Alabama being asked why they all voted against Sheats, a Republican, for Congress, replied, "because Perrin told them to;" being asked if they would have voted the Democratic ticket if Perrin had told them to, they answered, unhesitatingly, "Yes." But Perrin, as United States deputy-marshal, commanded Federal troops, and gave away Federal bacon.

The leaders whom they thus follow do not instruct them in political duties. They do not discuss political questions before them. They appeal only and continually to the negro's fears and to his sense of obligation to the Federal power. In Alabama they were told that the bacon was sent by General Grant, and its receipt made it their duty to vote the " straight Republican ticket." In some parts of Southern Louisiana the negroes are still summoned from the field to political meetings, "by order of General Butler." I know of a case where a candidate for a county office circulated a printed "general order " commanding all colored men to vote for him, and signed "U. S. Grant, President;" and he received the solid colored vote.

One of the most intelligent and excellent men I met in Louisiana told me that in 1872 ho had made a thorough canvass of the part of the State in which he lives, addressing himself entirely to the colored people, by whom he is liked and trusted, and trying to explain to them the necessity for honest local government, and their interest in the matter. "But," said he, "I presently became aware that I was followed by a Republican, an illiterate and low-lived man, whom no colored man would have trusted with five dollars, but who overturned all my arguments by whispering, 'Don't believe what he tells you; they only want to put you back into slavery.'"

So pertinaciously has this base insinuation been used among the blacks, that when last fall the Democrats carried Alabama, I know of two instances in which colored men came into the nearest town to ask white Democrats, in whose honor and kindness they trusted, whether they would be allowed to choose their own masters, and whether they would be separated from their wives and children.

16. The Federal office-holders are largely to blame for the continuance of this evil. They are a very numerous class in every Southern State ; and have far greater influence than their fellows in Northern States, especially over the blacks, who have been taught to regard them as their guardians, and political guides and leaders. They are too often, and in the majority of cases indeed, *but by no means in all*, men of low character, Republicans by trade, and of no influence except among the negroes, to whom the lowest Federal officer, even a deputy marshal's deputy, is a very powerful being, armed with the whole strength of the Federal Government. Georgia has nearly, if not quite, three thousand men in the employ of the Federal Government in various capacities; and most of the States I have visited have an equal number. In such States as Louisiana these men "organize" the negro vote; and they do it as the only means to preserve their places. A Democratic Federal Administration -would

oust them; therefore they command and persuade the negroes, by all possible inducements, to vote the Republican ticket. The Federal Administration appears to me culpable in this matter, because it has not only permitted its officers in the South to take an active and partisan part in politics, but has apparently encouraged them in doing so. The United States Marshal of Louisiana, for instance, having the command at will of Federal troops, has been chairman of the Republican State Central Committee. The mere fact that he holds these two positions is a dangerous abuse, especially in a State where a great part of the voters are ignorant, and easily misled.

17. The color-line is maintained mostly by Republican politicians, but they are helped by a part of the Democratic politicians, who see their advantage in having the white vote massed upon their side.

18. Human nature being what it is, no one can be surprised that the Republican leaders who found it easy to mass the colored vote, who found also the Federal power flung into their hands, and themselves its ministers, who by these means alone have been able to maintain themselves in power, regardless entirely of the use they made of this power — that under these conditions they should become and remain both weak and corrupt.

The mass of ignorant men by whose votes they have been kept in power paid no taxes, and were not, therefore, directly affected by the public plundering ; and the plunder has been so great, and the number of white men engaged in it so small, that these were always able to divide with the more ambitious colored leaders, who, on their part, have been, as was inevitable, easily corrupted. Nor have the colored men been slow to learn the trickery and baser parts of political management. They were ignorant and poor, and saw power and wealth in their reach; and they did what poor and ignorant white men, having the same temptations set before them, have done the world over, and notably in the city of New York.

While the black vote is massed against the white, there is a continual irritation between the races; and this mainly because the white man, who is the property-owner, sees the black, who in most of these States seldom owns real estate, used by a few designing whites, to lay taxes, to make laws, to carry on the government, regardless of the wishes and rights of the great body of intelligent and substantial citizens.

I know many Southern counties in which the colored men pay in all less than one thousand dollars of the annual taxes, and yet are in so great a majority that their votes, massed by unscrupulous demagogues of both colors, constantly waste and misapply the taxes of the county.

Inevitably in such cases there must be a feeling of hostility by the whites toward the blacks, and it is an evidence of the good nature of the mass of whites that, in the main, they conduct themselves toward the blacks kindly and justly. They concentrate their dislike upon the men who have misled and now misuse the black vote, and this I can not call unjust. It is commonly said, "The negroes are not to blame; they do not know any better."

On the other hand, as the feeling is intense, it is often un-discriminating, and includes the just with the unjust among the Republicans. Hence what is called "ostracism" will last just as long as the color-line is maintained, and as long as Republicans maintain themselves in power by the help of the black vote, and by Federal influence. That this feeling of dislike and suspicion toward Northern men often goes to an unjust and unreasonable extent is very true, and it is not easy for a Northern man to hear with patience stories showing its manifestations.

There are scattered over the States I have visited a number of highly honorable and cultivated Northern families, who have lived there for years. Where, as is often the case, these are Republicans, they are, to a large extent, isolated socially, and this is not pleasant for them. But they seldom complain; and not a few have told me that they did not wonder that Republicans should be held in disfavor in their States, considering how badly corrupt Republican leaders have acted in the South.

19. The evil influence of the mass of Federal office-holders in most of these States is an important, but with us in the North unsuspected, element in protracting ill-feeling and preventing a political settlement. They have very great influence; they are the party leaders; if they do not show themselves zealous Republicans, they are removed; and they are interested in keeping men of brains and influence out of their party. Unfortunately, they have been allowed to control; and the Federal Administration has rejected the assistance in the management of these States of the only men whose help would have been important and effective; namely, the natural leaders of the Southern people.

20. Tradition lives longer among the Southern whites than with us. How else can one account for the fact that you hear everywhere of Whigs, and that the real division of political parties in those States which I have seen is between Whigs and Democrats ?

In Louisiana the Whig prejudice and dislike against Democrats is so strong that the party leaders found it necessary to adopt the name Conservative. In Arkansas the Whig leaders are quietly seeking out their followers. In Alabama, when you hear of an independent candidate, he is most likely to have been an old Whig. In Mississippi, even, there are Whigs, but they have as yet no ground to stand on.

Whenever Federal interference in the local affairs of these States ceases, the colorline will be broken, and the population will divide into Whigs and Democrats. The leaders of the present white party will, as a matter of course, strive to prevent this in such States as Louisiana, Arkansas, Georgia, and Alabama; but their efforts will be in vain. There are traditional animosities and differences, and these were not destroyed by the war.

The Southern Whig was usually a Conservative, and opposed to secession; less, I imagine, because he liked the Union, than because he disliked the Democratic leaders who urged secession, and whom ho believed to be incapable and often dishonest. The result of the war has not raised the Democratic secession leaders in the esteem of the old Whigs, but for the present they act with the Democrats, under the pressure of Federal interference and to defeat the Republican leaders.

But there are many signs to show that whenever politics in the States I have seen resume their natural condition, the Whigs will rally, and, with the help of such part of the colored vote as they can win over to their side, will try to secure the control of those States. The Whig feeling is especially strong in Louisiana, and there is little doubt that that State, and probably some others, could easily have been made permanently Republican, had the Republican leaders who came to the top there in 1868 been wise and honest men, and had they given the people good government and the means of industrial prosperity.

21. Thus there are in all the States I speak of naturally two parties among the whites. The leaders of one of these could have been induced by the Federal authorities in Washington, with proper efforts and at the proper time, to take a part in the reconstruction ; and they could have perfected this important work. Of course, it would have been necessary to take their advice as to the Southern policy; and to give them the selection of Federal officers in their States. To give them influence in their section they should have been called to prominent places under the Government; but they would, I believe, have insured a peaceable and harmonious settlement. They have, unfortunately, been proscribed in Washington for their share in the war, and thus forced into opposition; and are to-day, often

against their wishes united to the Democratic party. This has been the gravest error of the Republican Administration. Its true policy would have been to trust, and to put in places of authority and responsibility, the most eminent of the Southern public men; to take their advice as to the details of a Southern policy, insisting only that peace and equal justice should be rigidly established in those States. With such a policy there would have been to-day a respectable and powerful Republican party in every Southern State; and, what is of greater importance, a harmonious settlement of all questions.

22. The blunder of the Federal Republican rulers has been that they have not taken care to keep themselves informed of the rapidly changing condition of public sentiment, and the political and industrial condition of the Southern States. They were, in fact, physicians who were treating a patient who, in 1868, was in a highly feverish and dangerous state. They prescribed for him a remedy which, if severe, was yet effective; but it seems never to have occurred to them that under their treatment the patient's condition would change; that a convalescent needed different remedies; that what was necessary in 1868 might be extremely injurious in 1872-74. They have had no faith in their own remedies.

23. There was, in those Southern States which I have visited, for some years after the war and up to the year 1868, or in some cases 1870, much disorder, and a condition of lawlessness toward the blacks — a disposition, greatest in the more distant and obscure regions — to trample them underfoot, to deny their equal rights, and to injure or kill them on slight or no provocations. The tremendous change in the social arrangements of the Southern States required time as well as laws and force to be accepted. The Southern whites had suffered a defeat which was sore to bear, and on top of this they saw their slaves — their most valuable and cherished property — taken away and made free, and not only free, but their political

equals. One needs to go into the far South to know what this really meant, and what deep resentment and irritation it inevitably bred.

At the same time came the attempt of President Johnson to re-arrange the Southern States in a manner which the wisest and best Democrats I have met in the South have declared to me was unwise and productive of disorder.

I believe Mr. Johnson meant well and patriotically ; but my observations have convinced me that he was in error, at least in the time and manner of asserting his policy. He aroused the hopes and desires of the worst class in the Southern States, and disabled the large number of moderate and conservative citizens, who ought to have ruled during the reconstruction of society there, and who, unfortunately, were pushed aside. The result was violence and dis-order, not general, as has been charged so often, but still very serious, and not to be endured ; and this lasted until time and the punishment of criminals by Federal power under the Enforcement acts brought people to their senses.

I believe that there was, during some years, a necessity for the interference of the Federal power to repress disorders and crimes which would otherwise have spread, and inflicted, perhaps, irre-trievable blows on society itself. But, after all, I am persuaded time was the great and real healer of disorders, as well as differences. "We of the North do not always remember that even in the farthest South there were large property interests, important industries, many elements of civilization which can not bear long - continued disorders; and, moreover, that the men of the South are Americans, like ourselves, having, by nature or long training a love of order and permanence, and certain, therefore, to reconstitute society upon the new basis prescribed to them, and to do it by their own efforts, so soon as they were made to feel that the new order of things was inevitable.

That there were, during some years after the war, shocking crimes in the States I have visited, no man can deny; but a grave wrong is done when those days are now brought up and those deeds recited to describe the South of today.

24. There was, after 1868, in all the States I have seen, great mis-government, as I have said, mostly by men who called themselves Republicans, but who were for the greater part adventurers, camp-followers, soldiers of fortune, not a few who had been Democrats and " Copperheads " during the war, or Secessionists, and engaged in the rebellion — some Northern men, but also many native Southerners.

This misgovernment has been various. Its most marked or prominent features were the unscrupulous greed and pecuniary corruption of the rulers and their subordinates, who, in a multitude of cases, notably in Arkansas and Louisiana, were no better than common robbers.

25. But public robbery was, after all, not the worst crime of the men who arose in the name of the Republican party to govern these Southern States. The gravest offense of these "Republican" State governments was their total neglect of the first duty of rulers, to maintain the peace and execute justice. They did not enforce the laws; they corrupted the judiciary; they played unscrupulously upon the ignorant fears of the blacks and upon their new-born cupidity ; they used remorselessly the vilest tools for the vilest purposes ; they encouraged disorder, so that they might the more effectually appeal to the Federal power and to the Northern people for help to main-tain them in the places they so grossly and shamelessly abused.

I must, however, except here Arkansas. The reconstructors of that State were certainly, in the main, a set of ruthless robbers. But there were in Arkansas a few men — notably Governor Clayton, I think — who held society in an iron grip, and by main force produced peace. They put down with a stern and unflinching, and almost a cruel, hand the disorders which they found ; they made laws which are terrible to read, and they executed these laws with a rigor which saved society, and gave peace to the State by encouraging the orderly people of all parties to take public affairs into their own hands, and by discouraging and terrifying the lawless class. The result is that Arkansas is to-day a peaceful State; and as it has an excellent governor, who knows the extreme importance of maintaining law and order, the State is fairly on the way to prosperity.

26. The injury done to a community by the total failure of its rulers to maintain order, repress crime, and execute justice, is more seriously felt in Louisiana than in any other of the States of which I am speaking. It is a wonder to me that society has not entirely gone to pieces in that State: and I became persuaded that its white population possesses uncommonly high qualities when I saw that, in spite of an incredible misgovernment, which encouraged every vice and crime, which shamelessly corrupted the very fountains and sources of justice, and made the rulers a terror to the peaceably inclined in spite of this, order and peace have been gradually restored and are now maintained, and this by the efforts of the people chiefly.

No thoughtful man can see Louisiana as I saw it last spring without gaining a high respect for its white people. The State is to-day as fit for self-government as Ohio or New York. The attitude of the races there toward each other is essentially kindly, and only the continuous efforts of black and white demagogues of the basest kind keep them apart politically. The majority of the white people of the State are well disposed, anxious for an upright government, ready to help honest and wise rulers, if they could only get them, to maintain peace and order. I sincerely believe that whenever they are relieved from Federal oppression — and in their case it is the worst kind of oppression — they will set up a government essentially honest and just, and will deal fairly and justly with the colored citizens.

27. What those States which I have visited most need, for some years to come, is a vigorous and alert State government; a governor extremely vigilant in repressing and punishing crime, and possessing the energy and courage to use to the utmost his power "to maintain peace." Governor Garland, of Arkansas, set an excellent example in this respect, when, last spring, he caused a couple of miscreants who had shot at a man in pure wantonness, to be pursued not only through the State, but into the lower part of Louisiana, where they were finally captured and brought in irons to Little Rock to be tried. The governor openly declared that he would catch and punish these fellows, if it cost the whole contingent fund of the State. Unfortunately, Republican governors, like Ames in Mississippi and Kellogg in Louisiana, do not use the power in their hands, but tolerate crimes, or if these affect their partisans, make haste to call on the Federal Government for help.

28. The Southern white population differs from ours in one or two important respects. In the States I have seen there is a more marked distinction between the wealthy and the poor than is commonly found in the North. The numerous class of poor white farmers are a kind of people unknown among us. Settled upon a thin and infertile soil; long and constantly neglected before the war; living still in a backwoods country, and in true backwoods style, without schools, with few churches, and given to rude sports and a rude agriculture, they are a peculiar people. They have more good qualities than their wealthier neighbors, the planters, always allow them; but they are ignorant, easily prejudiced, and they have, since the war, lived in a dread of having social equality with the negro imposed upon them. This fear has bred hatred of the blacks, which has often, in former years, found expression in brutal acts to which, I believe, in the majority of cases, they were instigated by bad men of a class above them.

A mischievous class is found in a number of young men in the remoter parts of these States, who follow no regular occupation, but prey upon the community, white as well as black. They are gamblers and political bummers; they drink whisky and swagger in bar-rooms, armed with revolvers and knives; and it was, during some years after the war closed, their habit, when they needed excitement, to " shoot a nigger."

These are mainly the descendants of the overseer and negro-trader class in the South, and naturally despise honest labor, and take readily to brute force. They have sometimes sufficient education to make a political harangue; and they are a curse to the community. If the Republican leaders in such a State as Louisiana had done their duty, they would have exterminated this not numerous class, which is disliked and feared by the decent white people upon which it has often imposed itself. To have hanged them by the dozen would have been the first duty of a good ruler in Louisiana, and he would have won the gratitude and support of the decent people who form the mass of the community.

In Arkansas this scum was crushed out. In Louisiana it was tolerated by the Republican rulers, and has been kept down mainly by the respectable people themselves. In some parts of Mississippi it forms still the most vociferous part of the Democratic party, though by far the least numerous.

As this is really a criminal class, it will continue to commit crimes; but they will not be political crimes, nor will they be beyond the power of a reasonably energetic State government, encouraging and demanding the help of the decent people, to punish and repress. As these young bloods have sometimes influential connections, and as they are known to be ready with the pistol, they may, here and there, overawe a local jury ; and if their crime is given a political aspect by the action of Federal officers, they may even temporarily win the sympathies of unthinking people. But a vigilant and energetic governor will have no difficulty in mastering the situation, even in the most lawless parts of Mississippi. He need not call on the United States. There is nowhere such a combination as a determined governor can not put down, nor anywhere crime which he can not punish. In the last resort a governor may declare martial law in a county, and if he is wise he will take that occasion to hang up a few disorderly wretches. He will make votes for the next election by doing so, for lawlessness is not general; the mass of the people wish for peace and order.

The country has seen recently two conspicuous proofs of this; the first in the conduct of the governor and the people of Georgia, a Democratic State, in the "negro insurrection" affair, where order was maintained absolutely under great excitement; and where the governor, a candidate for reelection, and naturally anxious to fall in with the popular impulse, conspicuously asserted the law, and saw justice done to the blacks. The other case is that of Mississippi, where, when some election troubles recently arose, prominent citizens in different counties at once and publicly offered their services to the governor, to assist him in maintaining order; and Ex-Senator Pease, a radical Republican politician, Postmaster of Vicksburg, telegraphed the Attorney-general of the United States that a posse of citizens of both parties could be got by the governor, to maintain order, in every county in the State, if necessary.

29. No thoughtful man can examine the history of the last ten years in the South, as he may hear it on the spot and from both parties, without being convinced that it was absolutely necessary to the security of the blacks, and the permanent peace of the Southern communities, to give the negro, ignorant, poor, and helpless as he was, every political right and privilege which any other citizen enjoys. That he should vote and that he should he capable of holding office was necessary, I am persuaded, to make him personally

secure, and, what is of more importance, to convert him from a *freedman* into a *free man.*

That he has not always conducted himself well in the exercise of his political rights is perfectly and lamentably true ; but this is less his fault than that of the bad white men who introduced him to political life. But, on the other hand, the vote has given him what nothing else could give — a substantive existence ; it has made him a part of the State. Wherever, as in Arkansas, the political settlement nears completion, and the color-line is broken, his political equality will help — slowly, but certainly — to make him a respectable person. I will add that in this view many Southern Democrats concur. "If the North had not given the negroes suffrage, it would have had to hold our States under an exclusively military government for ten years," said such a man to me.

30. General manhood suffrage is undoubtedly a danger to a community where, as in these States, the entire body of ignorance and poverty has been massed by adroit politicians upon one side. The attempt to continue for even four years longer such a state of things as has been by Federal force maintained in Louisiana would either cause a necessary and entirely justifiable revolt there, or totally destroy society.

There are scores of parishes and counties where the colored voters are to the white as four, six, eight, and even ten to one; where, therefore, ignorant men, without property, and with no self-restraint or sense of honor in pecuniary trusts, would continue to rule absolutely; to levy taxes which others must pay; to elect judges and fiduciary officers out of their own number ; to be the tools of the least scrupulous and the most greedy wretches in the community. There are scores of parishes and counties in Louisiana, Alabama, and Mississippi, where the voice of the people is not the voice of God, but the voice of the worst thief in the community.

But the moment the color-line is broken, the conditions of the problem are essentially changed. Brains and honesty have once more a chance to come to the top. The negro, whose vote will be important to both parties, will find security in that fact. No politician will be so silly as to encroach upon his rights, or allow his opponents to do so; and the black man appears to me to have a sense of respectability which will prevent him, unencouraged by demagogues, from trying to force himself into positions for which he is unfit. He will have his fair chance, and he has no right to more.

31. Whenever the Federal interference in all its shapes ceases, it will be found, I believe, that the negroes will not at first cast a full vote; and, as this with, perhaps, be charged to intimidation, it is useful to explain the real reason.

It was everywhere asserted to me by the Republicans that without white men to "organize" the colored vote — which means to mass it, to excite it, to gather the voters at barbecues, to carry them up with a hurrah to the polls, to make " bolting " terrible, to appeal to the fears of the ignorant and the cupidity of the shrewd: without all this the negro will not vote. This was the universal testimony of all Republicans I met in the South, good and bad.

Now the " organizers " of the colored vote are almost altogether the petty Federal office-holders. These have little else to do, and they give themselves to the work. In Alabama, for instance, in 1874, the Republican State Executive Committee was allowed to nominate the United States deputy-marshals for the whole State. Many of these persons were candidates for the Legislature or for local offices ; many candidates were also Federal supervisors of election. They appealed to the negro clothed in the majesty of Federal office; they spoke in the name of General Grant; a deputy-marshal could summon troops, and could summarily arrest white men. He was a very great man to a negro. Indeed, a United States deputy-marshal is a very great man to a Southern white man, for he has really extraordinary powers; and in the South nobody nowadays thinks for a moment of resisting "the Government." "We may fight among ourselves," said a Mississippian to me; "but if the whole of my town were engaged in a riot, to produce peace you need not even bring in a squad of Federal troops. You need only stuff the clothes of a Federal sergeant with straw, and bring that effigy into the market-place, and in five minutes you would have absolute quiet." And he did not exaggerate.

Well, take away these petty Federal "organizers," and the negro, left face to face with the white man, no longer marched up in column to the central poll of the county, but voting in his proper precinct, argued with, hearing both sides for the first time ; knowing by experience, as he will presently, that the Democrat is not a monster, and that a Democratic victory does not mean his reenslavement, will lose much of his interest in elections. "They won't vote unless they have white organizers," is the universal testimony of the Republican leaders wherever I have been.

Of course, as soon as parties are re -arranged on a sound and natural basis, the negro vote will re-appear; for the leaders of each party, the Whig or Republican and the Democrat, will do their utmost to get his vote, and therein will be the absolute security of the black man. I believe, however, that for many years to come, until a new generation arrives at manhood perhaps, and, at any rate, until the black man becomes generally an independent farmer, he will be largely influenced in his political affiliations by the white. He will vote as his employer, or the planter from whom he rents laud, or the white man whom he most trusts, and with whom, perhaps, he deposits his savings, tells him is best for his own interest. He will, perhaps, in the cities, sell his registration certificate, as in Montgomery in May last. But, at any rate, he will vote or not, as he pleases.. And it is far better for him that he should act under such influences than that his vote should be massed against the property and intelligence of the white people to achieve the purposes of unscrupulous demagogues.

32. It struck me as probable and natural that some constitutional modification of the suffrage should come about in such States as Louisiana and Mississippi. An education qualification, applied equally to white and to-day is due to the Southern planters, who have been wise enough to adapt themselves to the tremendous change in their labor system, and honest enough not to discourage the ignorant free laborer by wronging him of his earnings or by driving unjust bargains with him.

The system of planting on shares, which prevails in most of the cotton region I have seen, appears to me admirable in every respect. It tends to make the laborer independent and self-helpful, by throwing him on his own resources. He gets the reward of his own skill and industry, and has the greatest motive to impel him to steadfast labor and to self-denial.

I have satisfied myself, too, that the black man gets, wherever I have been, a fair share of the crop he makes. If anywhere he suffers wrong, it is at the hands of poor farmers, who cultivate a thin soil, and are themselves poor and generally ignorant. It is a curious evidence of the real security of the negro, even in the rudest parts of the South, that some thousands of them have emigrated from Alabama and Georgia into the Yazoo Bottom in Mississippi, and into the cotton regions of Arkansas and Louisiana— parts of the South where, if we might believe the general reports which have been spread through the North, no negro's rights and life are safe.

34. The black laborer earns enough, but he does not save his money. In the heart of the cotton country, a negro depending on his own labor alone, with the help of his wife in the picking season, may live and have from seventy-five to one hundred and twenty-five dollars clear money in hand at the close of the season. If he has several half-grown boys able to help him in the field, he may

support his family during the year, and have from one hundred and seventy-five to two hundred dollars clear money at the year's end. Few laborers as ignorant as the average plantation negro can do as well anywhere in the world.

Of course he lives poorly; but he thrives on corn-meal and bacon, and has few doctor's bills to pay. Unfortunately, as yet, he commonly spends his money like a sailor or a miner, or any other improvident white man. Very few lay by their earnings; yet the deposits in the Freedmen's Bank showed how very considerable were the savings of the few; and I am sorry to say that the criminal mismanagement of this trust has struck a serious blow in the South, for it has given a fresh impetus to the spendthrift habits of the blacks. Moreover, in Democratic Georgia, where alone I was able to get official statistics, the negroes pay tax this year on over seven millions of property, of which nearly four hundred thousand acres are real estate.

They have as yet far less desire to own farms than I hoped to find. They are, like almost all rude people, fond of owning an acre or a house lot; and in Southern towns and cities it is common to find them such owners. But, except in Georgia, a comparatively small number, as yet, are freeholders in the best sense of the word. This, however, will come with time. They have been free but ten years, and in that time have been unsettled by the stress of politics, and have scarcely known, until within the last two years, whether their freedom was a substantial fact, or only a pleasant dream. Moreover, they have, very naturally, enjoyed the spending of their own money, and have had to acquire mules, farm implements, household goods, not to speak of very ancient and shabby buggies, sham jewelry, and gewgaws of all kinds.

In the cities and villages it is a pleasant, and indeed a touching, sight to see the little colored children going to Sunday-school, bright, clean, neatly dressed, frank and fearless, with no trace of the slavery which was the lot of their parents. I think no humane man could see this sight unmoved, remembering, as he must, how short is the time since slavery came to an end.

35. The character of the Southern negro is essentially kindly and good. He is not naturally quarrelsome, and his vices are mostly those which he retains from slavery. For instance, it is the almost universal complaint of the planters that they can not keep stock, either cattle or hogs. It is the bad custom in the South to turn such animals into the woods to shift more or less for themselves, and here they fall a prey to the colored men, who kill and eat them. They have not yet learned to respect property rights so loosely asserted. But this will come with time. Nor are the planters' chickens safe. In fact, petty theft is a common vice of the plantation negro. He learned it as a slave, and has not yet unlearned it.

He spends some of his money for whisky, too ; but he is not an habitual drunkard, and is usually good-natured in his cups. Men and women, and even children, smoke, and in some regions they " dip " snuff.

It is an easily contented and happy population, and I do not doubt the judgment of those planters who assured me that they possessed the best laboring force in the world. Nor let any one persuade you that it is dying out. Wherever one travels he sees multitudes of fat, chubby, comical-looking pickaninnies— the country is full of them, and their shining black faces and wondering, staring eyes are the commonest sight in the South.

36. They are anxious to send their children to school, and the colored schools are more abundant in those States which I have seen than I expected to find them. I think it may be said that the colored people, so far, have got their fair share of schools and school money. In such places as New Orleans, Mobile, Selma, and Montgomery, the colored schools are excellently managed and liberally provided

for. By general consent of both colors, there are no mixed schools; nor would it be wise to force this anywhere.

It must be remembered that few of the Southern States had public schools before the war. The whites are unaccustomed to them; and enlightened and influential Democrats, as in Georgia, have difficulty in obtaining appropriations for schools sufficient to place these on a sound basis. The poorer whites are still in doubt about the usefulness of a thorough public-school system. But wherever I have been the blacks have a fair share of school privileges. Democratic Georgia gives as much every year for the support of a colored university as for the old State University; and in places like Mobile, where the schools are under Democratic control, I was surprised at the excellence of the colored schools, and the liberal manner in which they were maintained by the Democratic trustees.

37. The negroes have developed quite a genius for the lower political arts. They have among them not a few shrewd and calculating demagogues, who know as well how to "run the machine," to form a ring, and to excite the voters to their duty, as any New York City politician. Office is of course a great temptation to men used to fieldwork at small wages; and the moderate pay even of a juryman, with its accompanying idleness, seems very delightful to them. They have long ago discovered their numerical strength in many parts of the South, and do not hesitate to say in some places that, as they cast the votes, they ought to have the offices. At least a dozen times I came upon this saying in different places; and there are signs which show that if the present political divisions could continue, the black leaders would, in counties where the blacks predominate, in two or three years crowd all the white men out of the Republican party; or, at least, all who aspired to office. But they would not attempt this unless they felt assured of the protection of the Federal power; when they lose that reliance, every body, of both parties, says they will lose the power of cohesive action.

It is not strange that, on the whole, the blacks, under such white leadership as they have had, should have badly misused their political power. They were both poor and ignorant; they had no characters to lose by misconduct, for it is the misfortune of slavery that a slave is a being without reputation; and it will require a generation or two to establish in them, as in the ignorant part of our foreign -born population, that quality which we call character. In their political relations among each other, they are as intolerant and as unscrupulous as ignorant men suddenly possessed of political rights are sure to be. The caucus rules with a singular tyranny among them. The slightest assertion of political independence is resented. The restive negro's name is sent through the county or district, with "Bolter" affixed to it; and this fixes upon him the stigma of treason. The church, his friends, the young women if he is unmarried, all avoid him ; and he is effectually under, a ban of excommunication.

38. Unfortunately, the North and South do not know each other. Few Northern Congressmen have visited the South; and those who did too often fell into the hands of partisans, and obtained, whether Republicans or Democrats, only partisan impressions. Party feeling runs high in the South, and nothing is easier than to get a thoroughly onesided view, for each side has a share of truth on which to build up its statements. An advocate, on either side, could easily make up a very effective case. In Washington the Southern Republican's statement was received, partly because he was a Republican, and generally a Northern man or a negro; partly because he appealed, not to reason or statesman ship, but to the sympathies of his listeners; and often because he was a very adroit demagogue, who knew how to make his points. In the South I was often horrified by tales of brutal murder or intolerance; but if, when my indignation was at its height, I thought to ask, "When did this take place?" the answer was almost always, "In 1865," or "1868," or "1869." It is a common

trick of the outrage-monger in the South thus to recite to his Northern visitor tales of some years ago as representing correctly the present condition of Southern society; and this has constantly been done by Southern Republicans in Washington.

39. I come last to speak of the future of the Southern States: I was deeply impressed with the natural wealth, mostly undeveloped, of the States I saw. The South contains the greatest body of rich but unreclaimed soil on this continent. Louisiana seems to me to have elements of wealth as great as California. Georgia has a great future as a manufacturing State, and will, I believe, within a few years tempt millions of Northern and European capital into her borders to engage in manufactures. Alabama now exports iron to Europe — in small quantities, to be sure — and her coal-fields and iron ores will make her the rival of Pennsylvania at no distant date. Mississippi and Arkansas have immense undeveloped tracts of rich cotton lands. North Carolina has mineral as well as agricultural wealth, which ought to secure her a remarkable future.

40. Almost everywhere, except in Louisiana, Mississippi, and perhaps Arkansas, I noticed an increase of the towns. I saw many new buildings, and others going up; and observant Southern men remarked upon this to me also. Wherever the people have been even moderately prosperous, these improvements begin to make a show. The reason for this growth of towns was pointed out to me by Mr. Goodloe, a North Carolinian, and an Abolitionist before the war, whose essay touching this question seemed to me both curious and valuable. Under the slave-system, whenever a man had saved a thousand dollars he bought a slave; and the accumulated wealth of the South was almost entirely invested in this species of property. Hence there was no money to build dwellings in the towns, to carry on retail shops, to make all those improvements which mark our Northern civilization. "But," as Mr. Goodloe remarks, "the money paid for slaves was substantially wasted, because the negro will work

in freedom." A horse, a cow, or a sheep must be owned, in order to be of service to man. Not so a man, a negro man. It was not necessary to enslave him in order to make him industrious and useful to the community of which he forms a part. Experience since the war shows that he will work without being owned. It is true, therefore, that the money invested in slaves was wasted, so far as the general community was concerned; it was a misapplication of capital. With the extinction of slavery, this waste of the savings of the Southern people stopped. As wealth once more begins to accumulate, some other and sound forms of investment are, and will be, sought for it. It will be turned into houses, town improvements, and, above all, I believe, into factories of various kinds. Of course, the accumulations of the community will no longer be in so few hands as before; but this also is already found to be a great advantage in the South, where employments are becoming more varied, and there is more work for mechanics of different kinds.

41. I noticed, also, at many points a tendency to a more varied agriculture; to smaller farms; to the cultivation of fruits and vegetables for distant markets; and in these ways much remains to be done, which, when done, will very greatly increase the wealth of the Southern States. Already in all the Cotton States planters begin to raise corn sufficient for their home supply — an extremely important matter in a region where in winter the roads are bad, and where it is literally true, as an Alabamian said, that "it would pay a planter better to raise corn at home, at a dollar a bushel, than to have it given to him eight or ten miles away."

No one who has seen the States of which I speak can doubt that they have before them a remarkable future. Nothing but long continued political disturbances can prevent them from making very rapid strides in wealth. Their climate fits them for a greater variety of products than any of our Northern States. The orange and lemon crop of Louisiana, for instance, will some day, I believe, bring more money to the State than the sugar crop now does. The vegetable gardens about Mobile are already an important source of wealth to the place; and this industry is as yet in its infancy. In ten years these market gardens which are growing up will bring as much money to that city as the cotton used to; and, when the Louisiana question is finally "denationalized," as a zealous Packard man put it in New Orleans, the revival of industry in Southern Louisiana will in a few years make that wonderfully rich country as productive as it ought to be, and re-establish the fortunes of New Orleans.

Meantime it is a fact that, if the planters are poor, they owe but little money. Planting has come to a cash basis; and a good crop is good for the land-owner and the laborer, and not mainly for the factor. There is no doubt that there has been much suffering in the South since the war among a class of people who formerly scarcely knew what even prudent economy meant. The emancipation of the slaves destroyed at a blow, for the slave-owners, the greater part of the accumulated capital of these States. The labor is still there. The community will presently be wealthier than ever. But in the redistribution of this wealth the former wealthy class is reduced to moderate means. It is by no means a public calamity; but it makes many individuals gloomy and hopeless, and is one cause of the general depression.

42. Finally, these States have made a new experience in taxation. Aside from the plundering of the Republican rulers, there is a natural and inevitable increase in taxation, growing out of the fact that the former slaves are now citizens, who are taught in schools, tried in courts of justice, confined in State and other prisons, supported in asylums, and in many other ways are, as all citizens are, a source of public expense. This is too often forgotten by Southern men when they complain of high taxes. Formerly a negro thief received thirty-nine lashes from the overseer, and there an end; now a constable catches him and a prison holds him for trial, a grand jury

indicts him, a petit jury hears evidence for and against him, a judge sentences him if he is guilty, and thereupon a penitentiary receives him just as it does his white brother-in-law; or, if this happened in Alabama under the Republican rule, his father hired him of the State at twenty cents a day, and let him loaf about the cabin until his term expired, or he became a candidate for another term. The misfortune is, that the Federal interference has held these States under Republican rule against the will of the intelligent part of their citizens, and has prevented these from learning by experience what are the real difficulties and necessities of government under the new order of things. In Alabama, last spring, for instance, the Democrats, who are in power, began to discover that "the price of government has gone up," and that they could not very greatly lower the State taxes, against which, among other things, they had long grumbled. In a State like Louisiana or Arkansas, of course merely to stop the stealing will at once and enormously relieve the community, and a good deal can be effected by economy in government in Alabama as well. But the people will discover that they can not get back to the old extremely low taxes.

These are my conclusions concerning those Southern States which I have seen. If they are unfavorable to the Republican rule there, I am sorry for it. No men ever had a greater opportunity to serve their fellow -men and their nation than the Republicans who undertook the work of reconstruction in the South; and they could not have desired greater power than was given them. Had they used their power as statesmen, or even only as honest and unselfish citizens, not only would the States I speak of to-day have been prosperous, and their people of both races contented and happy, but there would now have been, in every one of them, a substantial and powerful Republican party. Nor are the Northern Republican leaders without blame in this matter. They chose for their allies in the South men like Spencer in Alabama, Ames in Mississippi, Kellogg and Packard in Louisiana, Dorsey and Brooks in Arkansas, not to speak of hundreds of subordinate instruments, corrupt, weak, or self seeking. They suffered the most shameless public plundering to go on in those States without inquiry. They confided the Federal power and patronage to men, many of whom would to-day be in State-prisons if they had their dues. And they have, as the result of their carelessness, seen State after State fall into the hands of the Democrats, and, in a large part of the Union, the name of Republican made odious to all honest and intelligent men; while they have crushed to the earth a considerable number of honest Republicans in the South, who, naturally, found no favor in the eyes of such men as Spencer and Ames.

5

Arkansas in March, 1875

The State of Arkansas celebrated on the 25th of March, 1875, a great deliverance. By proclamation of Governor Garland that day was kept as one of thanksgiving for the action of Congress, which, it is hoped and believed, restored the State to permanent and peaceful self-government. I arrived in Little Rock a few days before the holiday, and that day was singularly quiet. Banks and shops were mostly closed; many people went to church; there was turkey for dinner; and there were, among-the older and substantial citizens, not a few heart-felt words of gratitude for quiet and peace, and the hope of prosperity.

And that, so far as one could see, was all.

The streets were not crowded, though the day was as long as a June day with us. I heard absolutely no political discussion either in streets or hotels. Poker Jack's arrival in the morning did not create even a ripple; and though there were probably a good number of disappointed men among the adherents of Brooks, it looked very much as though both parties were glad to see the battle ended.

Indeed, there is no doubt about the matter, for everywhere throughout the State reports show that the general settlement is accepted as final, and industry is reviving. More cotton and grain are being planted than in previous years; houses and fences are being repaired; fewer men are idle; there is a notable and sudden decrease of street-loungers, black and white, in Little Rock.

People are going to work again. It is creditable to both parties that, so far as I hear and have been able to observe, there is no bitterness of feeling, no resentment. The victors are too well pleased to be any thing but good-humored, and the vanquished take their defeat in good part. One of the most zealous, and, during the winter, which he spent in Washington, ferocious Brooks men, a colored man, said to me, "What we need now is men and capital; we have peace secured; we are done with politics for a while, and will all go to work in earnest to recover our losses and make the State rich. Give us only a good crop this year, and we'll be out of the woods."

The truth is, it was time for strife to end. Nobody of either party who had any thing, even his labor, to lose, could any longer afford it. Here are a few figures which prove it:

Arkansas has less than 650,000 people. It has about 120,000 voters. These owed in 1868, when reconstruction began in this State, about $3,500,000, and had $319,000 in cash in their treasury. The debt was State debt. The counties owed little or nothing.

To-day, after seven years, the State owes at least $15,700,000, and most of the counties have debts of their own sufficient to make them bankrupt. And for this huge indebtedness, which amounts for State, counties, town, and school districts to probably $20000,000, the people have nothing to show, except some miles of railroad, on which they must pay for their passage whenever they travel. There are no new public buildings; neither science nor the arts have been advanced; the old State-house looks as dilapidated as when the reconstruction began, and has been changed in nothing except having its door- lintels mutilated that a Brooks cannon might be squeezed into the hall; the schools are almost all closed because the school fund was stolen; and Little Rock is unpaved, though the conquerors of 1868 issued nearly shinplasters enough to pave all the streets handsomely with the paper itself, and bonds enough besides to make dry crossings at the corners.

The State debt alone amounts to-day to more than $115 for every voter. State, county, township, and school debts, including scrip of all kinds, would probably bring the voters in debt $175 per head. And the whole of this prodigious burden has been laid upon an impoverished, and never very prosperous, people in seven years.

Arkansas was, in 1868, a tempting prize to speculators. It had a trivial debt, a handsome little sum in cash in the Treasury, hardly any railroads, and a people singularly innocent of political wiles. The young and enterprising men who then flocked in and seized on power, and who held it so many years, had had some experience in what we call "politics." "We showed them some new tricks," said one of them to me; "the damned fools didn't know a thing about organization. They just went around the State making stump-speeches, and thought that was politics. But that thing's played out."

The new regime framed a constitution admirably suited to their ends, of which I shall speak further on. And then they began the work of plunder with an act granting State aid bonds to railroads to the extent of 800 miles, at $15,000 per mile, or $10,000 for such roads as had also land-grants. Under this law 271 miles of road were built, of which the Fort Smith road is well built and well planned for 100 miles, and is to be completed. It has received $1,000,000 of bonds. The Memphis and Little Rock Company built 45 miles, and received $1,200,000, or $750,000 more than it should have got. The Ouachita Company built 28 miles, and got $600,000, or $180,000 more than it should have got. The Arkansas Central built 38 miles, and got $1,350,000 ; under the law it was entitled to but $570,000. This was called Senator Doreey's road. The Pine Bluff Company built "70 miles, and got $1,200,000, or $150,000 more than its share.

The whole issue of railroad aid bonds made by the State in less than four years amounts to $5,350,000. Many of the roads were not needed ; all but the Fort Smith and the Memphis are unfinished, and will for some time remain so; $1,110,000 more bonds were issued than even these fragments of roads were entitled to; the roads were to pay the interest, but of course did not; and the State now owes the whole sum, and, when it can, must pay the interest as well as the principal. Citizens of Little Rock point out to a visitor a number of pleasant residences at the new or court end of the straggling town, which, they say, were built by the men who handled these bonds.

Next, in 1871, were issued $3,005,846 in levee bonds. The law authorizing this issue provided that no levees should be built except on the application of a majority of the property -holders to be benefited, and then only in a specified way, and the land benefited was held for the payment of interest and principal of the bonds. Regular surveys were to be made, and competent engineers were to decide, after all, whether the levee should be built. In practice, one or two engineers and half a dozen contractors made a ring and built levees wherever they pleased; no formal petitions were required, no proper surveys made; logs and timber, and even empty flour and beef barrels were crammed into the bank, and meantime the levee commissioner issued bonds whenever any body whom he knew asked for them, and actually kept no books to show to whom, for what work, or when they were issued. The first freshet washed most of these levees away, and of those that stood, many were so misplaced that planters were ruined, because the levees, intended to keep the water out, only kept it in.

Fortunately, the contractors and swindlers took their pay and plunder in bonds. The swindle was too gross, and the bonds fell in value till they sold in the market for six or eight cents on the dollar. The planters resisted in the courts the payment of interest demanded of them, and so carelessly had the whole work been done, that the courts have held them exempt, because the most simple forms of law had not been complied with, and it is now believed that the Levee Ring failed to get rich by its plunder. But the State owes on these bonds still.

Next came the issue of scrip. The taxes and bonds were not enough for the reconstructers. They began to issue State, county, township, and even school scrip — notes of hand of these corporations, some interest-bearing. They issued State scrip at such a rate that by May, 1874, $3,240,000 of this stuff had been taken up and destroyed, and there is supposed to be $1,500,000 of it afloat still.

But these big thefts are not nearly as amusing as the smaller ones. One man. Speaker of the Assembly, for instance, got the people of Clark County to issue $100,000 in bonds to the Ouachita Valley Railroad, of which he was president. He found a broker in New York who offered him eighty per cent, for these bonds, on condition that he would get a responsible bank to guarantee the payment of the interest for five years. He deposited with a bank $30,000, which was the interest for five years at six per cent.; received at once $80,000 for his bonds, and of course pocketed $50,000 by this pretty transaction. He did not even take the trouble to return to Arkansas, and is now said to be living in Colorado.

In 1873, Faulkner County was formed out of fragments of surrounding counties. This making new counties was a custom of the reconstructers. They thus created new offices. The new Faulkner County had no debt. It had no public buildings, and has none yet, except an eight-by-ten court-house given it by a Methodist church. It contains 7000 people, and has a property valuation of about $900,000, Two young New Yorkers were appointed sheriff and county clerk by the governor. They collected the first year about $40,000 in taxes; and this being insufficient for their uses, they issued county scrip for $50,000 more. They collected the taxes in greenbacks, and turned them in in depreciated State scrip, some of which they bought at thirty-five cents on the dollar. They sold offices, released prisoners, engaged in fraudulent registration, and, finally, they departed with their plunder, and the State knows them no more.

In Little Rock, the collector of taxes openly engaged in broker-age, took out a Federal license as a broker, and then drove a thriving trade with the citizens when they came to pay their taxes. You must understand that all State and county scrip was receivable at par for taxes. If a citizen had to pay $50 for taxes, he might buy scrip at thirty cents, and pay it in at par. But the collector bought scrip beforehand, when the market was low, and made his own bargain with the citizen. It is said he made his office worth $100,000 a year. His way was to demand a moiety of the tax, but in greenbacks. For this he gave a receipt in full. Then he kept the greenbacks, and turned into the treasury in their place the scrip he had bought up cheaply. This atrocious form of swindling became so universal that I have been told only one county tax collector in the whole State has uniformly turned into the treasury the same money which he received; and this when the allowances of the assessors and collectors were so great that in some years it cost twenty per cent, to collect the State revenue.

The reconstructers were wise in their generation. They not only robbed at wholesale and retail, but they took care to preserve their own supremacy. The constitution of 1868 gave the governor the appointment of almost all the local officers, even to the justices of the peace and registrars of elections. The governor, of course, selected his own adherents, and did not scruple to send them from Little Rock, sometimes a hundred miles away, into a strange county. So loosely was business conducted that when the new county of

Howard was created, in 1873, an illiterate carpenter of Little Rock, being appointed county clerk, began his career by having county scrip printed before he even went down to take up his office, and issued the first of this scrip in Little Rock in payment for an ambulance to take his family to Howard County. Scrip of this county is now worth from ten to fifteen cents — and no wonder.

Again, in Little Rock the merchants got alarmed at the overissue of scrip in 1869, and took the plates from which these shinplasters were printed from the mayor's office and destroyed them. But presently it was discovered that no account had been kept by the mayor of the quantity printed and issued, and to this day, though ten thousand dollars' worth of the stuff has been redeemed more comes in, and no man can tell how much remains behind.

There is a small bridge in Eagle township, near Little Rock, which cost to build it five hundred dollars. Jack Agery, a colored man, was engaged to make some repairs on it. He brought in a bill for nine hundred dollars; scrip was then worth ten cents, and he received his pay in it, amounting to nine thousand dollars, which the county must some day redeem at par.

Sam Mallory, formerly engine-driver on the Erie Railroad, became here a general of militia, and State senator in 1871; was later made commissioner to audit old militia bills, and among the accounts allowed by him and paid was one for coffee-mills at seventeen dollars apiece.

Meantime taxes rose, until in Pulaski County, of which Little Rock is a part, they were at five per cent., and in some counties seven and three -tenths. Pulaski County scrip went down to ten cents, school-warrants were bought at six, and some were worth no more when I was there. Other counties were but little better off, and the book-keeping has been such that it is impossible to tell how much is really owed. In Pulaski County even the register of bonds has been, as an official advertisement in the papers says, "lost or stolen," and the bondholders are now requested to come forward and register their bonds before the coupons shall be paid.

To return to the railroads. Where their embankments would serve as levees they were allowed levee bonds in addition to the aid bonds; and, not content with this, in one case twenty miles of track having been laid on a road, accepted, and the bonds received, the iron was taken up and removed to another road, where it sufficed to obtain from the treasury another three hundred thousand dollars in bonds.

The reconstruction constitution in 1868, under which Arkansas was supposed to enjoy a Republican government, is an able and ingenious instrument, said to have been framed at Washington. It established an extremely centralized and despotic administration.

The governor appointed nearly all the local officers in counties and townships, and he had the power to fill vacancies even in the few offices he did not originally name. He appointed judges, collectors, and assessors of taxes, justices of the peace, prosecuting attorneys, registrars of elections, who in turn appointed the judges of elections. Where new counties were created, which was a favorite device of the rulers, the governor appointed all the officers. Moreover, where any subordinate proved refractory — which means honest and public-spirited — he was removed on a writ of *quo warranto* brought by a convenient attorney-general before the Supreme Court, at the head of which sat Poker Jack. Then the governor filled his place.

Under this monstrous system of centralization, as extreme as that of the later French empire, the ring had their adherents scattered all over the State. They absolutely controlled the elections; they ruled the people despotically. The governor was even careful to appoint, in many instances, local officers who did not live in the counties they were to rule, and who, of course, had no interest whatever in good government or in the decent administration of justice.

One instance, out of many, will show how audaciously they carried out their schemes. A new county was formed in the north-western part of the State. A sheriff was sent to it who lived in Little Rock. This person chanced to own a farm in the county. The people chose for county seat a village near the centre of the county; but the sheriff determined to establish it on his own farm, five miles away. He and his fellow office-holders manipulated the registry-lists, but failed to eliminate a sufficient number of voters' names, and when an election was held for a choice of three commissioners to determine on the county seat, his candidates were beaten. He went at once to Little Rock, where the election was, at his instance, set aside ; new commissioners were appointed, and the court-house, which cost over thirty thousand dollars, was actually placed on his farm, in spite of the demand of nine-tenths of the people to put it in the village, where it would be convenient for the public.

All these local appointees of the central government had unlimited power to steal, and knew it. Indeed, they were expected to divide their plunder with the ring at headquarters. They issued county and town bonds for railroads; they erected, or pretended to erect, new and unneeded public buildings, for which bonds and scrip were issued; they put out scrip on every possible excuse, and kept no books or records to show the amounts issued; or stole the records, or in several notorious instances burned down the court-houses and thus destroyed the records; they pocketed the greenbacks paid in by tax-payers, and turned into the treasury depreciated scrip; they protected thieves and swindlers for pay, and sold justice at a convenient price.

When the county scrip became too much depreciated for their use, the Supreme Court — Poker Jack chief-justice — rendered a decision making that only receivable for county taxes; and when this Speculation had served their turn, the Supreme Court — Poker Jack still chief-justice — reversed this decision, and made only State scrip receivable for taxes.

So monstrous was the robbery that even now, when the plunderers are beaten off and confidence is restored, the average value of county scrip over the whole State is less than thirty-four cents, and it is doubtful if one-quarter of the counties know certainly the amount of their debt.

Meantime champagne was the commonest beverage of several hundred people at Little Rock, and it was at one time said that nowhere in the United States was so much of this wine consumed as in the dilapidated little capital of Arkansas. Champagne and poker were the chief enjoyments of the thieves in office, and they indulged themselves without stint and openly, without shame.

The governor appointed the registrars of election, and they were naturally tools of the ring. Registration was an imperative prerequisite to voting. The law was so framed that the decision of the registrar as to the right of a citizen to vote was final, the only appeal lying to the Supreme Court, which refused to hear such cases. On election-day, even if a citizen showed a certificate proving that he had been registered, this did not entitle him to vote if his name was not actually found on the register. Moreover, the registrars appointed the judges of elections at the polling places, and, of course, chose partisans.

What happened was this: As registration went on, the partisan registrars kept a sharp eye on the lists. When these were completed they had some days to revise them. During this time they counted votes, and judiciously marked out Democratic names enough to secure the required majority. "If red ink don't hint them out, take red paint and a paint-brush," was the blunt order said to have been sent to one registrar.

Meantime the colored vote was manipulated to such an extent
that the colored people were enticed away from their vocations for
weeks before election-day, and gathered in crowds at barbecues and
other camps. At first the ring had a largo majority, for they con-
trolled the negroes, and about twenty thousand of the old citizens
were disfranchised for participation in the rebellion. In November,
1872, a constitutional amendment was adopted by the people which
enfranchised these voters, and enabled them to begin to help them-
selves. As the people became more and more dissatisfied, the ring
began to quarrel among themselves, and thus disorganization crept
into this band. Meantime it is confessed that occasionally some
public thief, who had outraged the people of a county beyond en-
durance, was shot, and public sentiment quietly justified the deed.
But at every such murder a howl was raised that Union men were
persecuted, and in danger of their lives; and the North, anxious
to protect the oppressed, ordered the Federal power to protect the
oppressors.

These did not shrink from measures for their own protection.
The Legislature adopted in March, 1869, a Ku - klux bill of the most
stringent character, which was so well executed that all outrage of
this kind disappeared in a very short time. In 1873 it adopted a Civil
Rights bill, which is as peremptory as that which was advocated
by General Butler. In the same year they brought forward a bill
to establish a "metropolitan police." Six thousand men were to be
appointed by the governor, to act as a police over the whole State.
It was in effect to be a standing army, with power to interfere in
all civil affairs, everywhere, at all times; to make summary arrests,
and to bring those they arrested from the most distant parts of the
State to Little Rock for trial. After prolonged efforts, this atrocious
scheme was defeated in the Legislature.

At the same session was brought forward a scheme to release all
the railroads from liability for their old bonds, by a law compelling

the State to assume these, and redeem them by a new issue. It was the avowed intention of the plotters to cause the issue, first of all, of the remaining railroad bonds, between six and seven million dollars, and to declare the levee bonds unconstitutional and worthless, which, it was believed, would appreciate the value of the railroad bonds.

This proposal also was beaten. It was advocated in the Republican newspaper; and it was commonly said Governor Baxter had been offered a Federal judgeship, or sixty thousand dollars in money, to cease his opposition. This, however, was never proved.

About this time came a change. The new constitution was adopted, Garland became governor, and the men who had so long robbed and misgoverned the State were at last threatened with loss of power.

Then they appealed to the Federal Government. Unluckily, the President fell into the trap of these Arkansas jobbers. He had forced Brooke out of the State-house in 1874, and in 1875 he demanded of Congress that Brooks should be forced in again. Now, to install Brooks as governor was to continue the robbers in power; and these, rendered desperate, and knowing that, even if Garland were overthrown and Brooks put in, their lease of power would be brief, because a Democratic Congress was at hand, meant, it is said, first of all, to issue all the remaining railroad bonds, and divide this huge piece of plunder, amounting to at least five, or probably seven, millions of dollars. Their swag secured, they were ready to retire, if they must.

The first effect of the President's Arkansas policy would have been to saddle the State with all these millions of additional debt.

I find, by the State auditor's account for the year 1859 and 1860, that at that time the cost of administering the State government was $307,596 for two years, or, roughly, $150,000 per annum. Making every fair allowance, it should not have cost, from 1868 to 1874, more than twice this sum, or $300,000 per annum, or $1,800,000 in all for the six years. But in that period there was collected from the people in taxes the prodigious sum of $6,674,000; the bonded debt was increased $8,753,000, aside from railroad subsidies; a floating debt of scrip, demoralizing to the community, was added, of $1,865,000; and thus the reconstructors cost the State alone, in six years, over $17,000,000, instead of $1,804,000, which would have been a fair charge. And for this vast expenditure there was no return, except in despotic government, broken credit, ruined industry, and a deplorable corruption of public morals, growing out of a depraved currency, and unbridled and open theft in high places. But this still leaves out the county and other local taxes, of which I have no exact record, and the county, city, and township debts, an unascertainable total, thought by the best experts to amount to no less than $2,500,000 more.

Of one thing I can speak with positiveness, and that is, that Arkansas is, in March, 1875, as peaceable a State as New York, Massachusetts, or Ohio. I assert this on the authority of leading men of both parties. No one whom I was able to see pretended a doubt on the subject. In Little Rock itself, where most of the political sore-heads are found, there is not even political discussion. The editor of the Brooks, or Republican, organ assured me that there is no violence, and that a close perusal of the county journals and his own correspondence in different parts of the State convinced him that industry had revived all over the State; that the people were at work; and that Arkansas promised this year, if the season were favorable, to produce more corn, wheat, and cotton than ever before. All this was corroborated by leaders of the Garland party; and as the well-informed men of both sides thus concur, it may be accepted as fact.

Moreover, of Governor Garland, leading men of the Brooks side have told me that he is a man of good character, firm, determined to execute the laws, and able to do so. Ho himself assured me that he meant to put down with a strong hand any attempts at lawlessness, should such occur, and he struck me as answering very well the description his political opponents gave me of him, as a man of decided character, no blusterer, but firm, solid, and likely to be calm, and to carry out a definite policy in a straightforward manner. Of course, it is a great piece of good fortune for the State to have a man of such make at the head of affairs at this time.

It is admitted by every body that the State has among its people men of a ruffianly character, idle, vicious, and prone to murder; these it is the business of the governor to hold to accountability for their misdeeds. They are not numerous, and there is no good evidence that they now shoot with political purposes. A couple of months ago, two young men, drunk and reckless, shot at the engine-driver of a railroad and another person. The latter was a Northern man, but a supporter of Garland; and this last fact showed that there was no political purpose or animosity in this attempt at murder.

What followed, however, shows the spirit of Arkansas just now. The sheriff of the county, a negro, pursued the two men; and the whole county, white as well as black, turned out to help him in the hunt. The criminals escaped into Louisiana, but, under the energetic pursuit of Governor Garland's law officers, were captured, brought back, and are now in prison awaiting trial.

There is just now a difficulty in Scott County. This lies in the northern part of the State, where there are but few negroes, and the cause of quarrel is exclusively among white men, and has no relation to politics or the negro.

The negro sheriff, Furbush, in Lee County, was reported in February to have been murdered; but I saw a letter from him of recent date, in which no allusion was made to political or other disturbances in his county.

To the one vital question which Northern men ask, "Are Union men, white and black, secure of life, property, and political rights in Arkansas?" I am, therefore, persuaded the answer is, "Yes, they are so."

And this answer rests on the very best testimony, that of Republicans and Brooks men themselves.

I may add that the phrase " Union men " is not used in Arkansas. "We are all Union men," said a Confederate general to me; "and you Northern people do us a serious injustice when you rank only the Republicans at the South as Union men. We have here life-long Northern Republicans acting with the Democratic party; and, on the other hand, some of the very leaders of the Republican party in this State were not merely Democrats in the North, but Copperheads during the war," and he cited ex-chief justice M'Clure (Poker Jack) as such a man.

In casting about for proofs of the actual condition of the State as to peace and liberty, it occurred to me that if there had been unrepressed violence, lawlessness, political assassination, and terrorism, such as we heard of during the winter of 1874-75, and such as the Brooks men during the Arkansas struggle in Washington described, there must have been frequent appeals to the Federal commissioners for protection under the Enforcement acts. I therefore made inquiry of the clerk of the United States Court at Little Rock, under whose eye every such matter must come, and he assured me there had not been a single case for a year. He thought that complaints had sometimes been made to the district attorney, but they had never been brought before the grand jury, and were, therefore, presumably groundless.

The United States district attorney was absent, but the Federal judge corroborated the testimony of the clerk.

The sum of my information on this point is, that not a single case for redress of grievances, either political or civil, under the Federal

Enforcement acts has been made in the eastern district of Arkansas for a year past; and in the western district, so far as I could learn, the only cases were appeals on the part of Democrats, complaining of Republican registrars of election in 1872.

There are fifty-three Federal commissioners in the State, who receive, I believe, no salary. The Federal supervisors of election for the whole State cost twenty-five hundred dollars for an election, when the full list is appointed. Now, it is hard to prove a negative; to show, namely, that the State is not disorderly. But it seems to me clear that if white and black Union men had been seriously or continuously harassed and in peril, they would have appealed to the Federal authorities established for that purpose, to protect them and punish their oppressors.

The fact is, that the Dorsey-Clayton Republicans between 1868 and 1873 ruled Arkansas with an iron rule, and did put down, peremptorily and effectually, all political disorders. For this they deserve credit; for there is no doubt that when they took possession of the State in 1868, and for some time afterward, there was a grave and perilous condition of society. In March, 1869, they adopted a Ku-klux law of uncommon and even dangerous severity; it prohibited all secret political organizations, and declared their members infamous and public enemies; it made even the possession of a uniform of such an order a criminal offense, or the knowing of its existence without giving immediate information to the public authorities; it authorized the arrest of a member of this organization anywhere, at any time, by any citizen, without a warrant; it prescribed a penalty of five hundred dollars fine, and from one to ten years in the Penitentiary, and forbade the member of such society to be a juror before or a witness after conviction; it allowed the grand jury to summon witnesses and enforce their presence, and gave the informer from half to three-fourths of the fine. This

law was sternly enforced, and the "Knights of the White Camellia"
disappeared almost at once.

This law remains on the statute-book at the instance of the
Democratic governor, Garland, who gave notice that if it were not
strong enough he would ask the Legislature to make it still more
severe. This was his reply to a charge made in Washington that
Republicans had been intimidated from voting.

Nor is this all. In February, 1873, the Republican reconstructors
adopted a civil-rights act so much stronger than that recently passed
by Congress, that, when I asked whether the Federal act made any
trouble, people laughed at me. Under this State law hotel -keepers,
bar-keepers, and owners of places of public amusement are required
to give accommodation to colored people, and these are to have
equal school facilities, but separate schools. Violators of the law are
subject to a fine of from two hundred to one thousand dollars, or
to imprisonment from three to twelve months. Even accessories or
agents are punishable, and an action for civil damages lies, besides
the criminal prosecution. Officers of the law may be prosecuted for
failure to enforce it, and prosecuting attorneys, sheriffs, coroners,
justices of the peace, and even constables, are to institute proceed-
ings, and are obliged to do so. Many of these officers throughout
the State are colored men. I was told there had been but a single
case under this act, in which a saloon-keeper was fined twenty-five
dollars. I noticed that some drinking-saloons had two bars, one for
each color; but I also saw in several cases black and white men
drinking together. The negroes have shown no disposition to make
the law offensive.

As to elections, while the justly odious features of the old
registration law have been repealed, under the new constitution a
candidate may appeal to the court with proof that voters intending
to vote for him have been prevented; and if he proves his case, the
votes so claimed are counted as actually cast for him; and if they

give him a majority, he secures thereby the office without a new election. This makes it to the interest of candidates and of each party to look after and support the rights of voters, and gives them power to remedy wrongs.

Finally, it is acknowledged by the best men of both sides, that the present State and local judiciary is composed of an excellent and capable class of men, of high character. So far as the colored people are concerned, and considering their lack of education and training for public business, it seems to me that a fair proportion were chosen to office by the Garland men, or Democrats, for there are now one hundred and sixty colored justices of the peace in the State, ninety-five constables, twenty-nine sheriffs and county clerks, assessors, and county surveyors, one militia field-officer, and eleven militia company-officers. The militia officers were appointed by Governor Garland, and all the civil officers were commissioned by him. The enrolling clerk of the last (Democratic) Assembly was a negro, and he was chosen by a Democratic house. The door-keeper of the same body was a one-legged negro, who had been a Federal soldier. The counties of Lee, Phillips, and Jefferson, where the negro vote is very strong, sent colored Representatives and Senators to that Legislature. The Democrats even nominated a colored man to represent Little Rock in the Constitutional Convention; but his Republican friends persuaded him not to accept the nomination.

Moreover, the condition of the two political parties in the State is such as in itself to secure good government if the present opposition — the Republicans, that is to say — wish it. Arkansas has, I am told, about one hundred and twenty thousand voters, of whom, roughly, sixty-five thousand are Democrats and fifty-five thousand Republicans. Of the latter about forty thousand are colored men. The ruling party has not, therefore, a large majority. It can hold the State only by good and economical government, and of this fact I found the Garland men very conscious. They do not, by any means, think themselves in a secure position ; and they see the necessity, politically, of a moderate and just policy, and of general conciliation.

It is quite true that many of the prominent leaders of the Republican party have no political future in the State. Dorsey will, it is said, leave the State. M'Clure also talks of taking his little carpet-bag into New Mexico. Brooks has fallen into general contempt among his own adherents by accepting the Little Rock postmastership, to secure which he caused to be ousted a man universally respected and trusted by both parties. Snyder, late member of Congress, compounded any future preferment in the State for the little fifteen -hundred dollar post-office at Pine Bluff, and flung out one of his own adherents to get it. But with all this, the Republicans are not without leaders; and, now that the Federal government has taken its support away from them, these begin to assume the natural attitude of an opposition party, talk of the prosperity of the State, of the necessity for economy, of the benefits of peace, and so on.

Both parties will try to secure the colored vote, and it may be confidently said that the color-line in politics is broken in the State. The Republican leaders are already coquetting with white Democrats, whose votes they must secure to regain the ascendency; and the Democrats have for a year past been busy in establishing friendly relations with influential blacks.

It is plain, from what is above stated, that not only is Arkansas at present peaceable, but, what is of greater importance, the conditions necessary to secure permanent peace and security are all present in the State. A strong governor, determined to punish lawlessness and crime; an excellent judiciary ready to help him; and an absence, for the present, of all political excitement and animosity, are the means; but the cessation of Federal interference, and the necessity which lies upon both parties to court the negro vote, and to maintain, and promise to maintain, peace and order, are the main elements.

It is just now (in March, 1875) probable that the Democrats will carry the State in 1876; but it is by no means certain. A thorough reorganization of parties is certain: when it will happen is only a question of time. The Democratic side has a dissatisfied element, which may bolt, and endeavor to form a coalition with a part of the Republican party. The leaders on both sides are distrustful, and one hears here, curiously enough, the old word "Whig" as a potent political watchword. If one could imagine such a resurrection, he would think that these Arkansans would by-and-by split off into Whigs and Democrats.

But, whatever happens, the negro is safe, for his vote — which can only be got by kind treatment — will be sought by the leaders of both parties, and he who wrongs a black man will lose votes. That, in the long run, the old planters will secure a large share of the negro vote is highly probable. They would be impracticable fools if they did not, for they know the negro's weak and strong points better than any one else. What pleased me was to hear constantly from old Arkansans — former slave-holders — when I inquired about negro peculiarities, the answer, "They're just like white men; take them under any circumstances, and they'll act just as white men would."

The reconstructors of Arkansas have been too busy issuing bonds and scrip and manipulating laws since 1868 to pay attention to industrial statistics. Hence I could get but scant and uncertain answers to many questions affecting the real interests of the State. A leading politician could tell me readily enough how many black voters there are, and why these are more numerous in proportion to population than white voters, which is because, formerly, mainly adult negroes were brought in as slaves, and since the war the small colored immigration has consisted largely of colored men, seeking political and other adventures. But when I asked the same man the more important question, how many colored real-estate owners the State has, he had not the least idea. I believe Governor Garland means to draw information of this kind from the sheriffs of the counties, who are also often tax-collectors.

Arkansas, as viewed from a railroad car, is not a charming country to a Northern eye. It seems to contain a good deal of thin and worthless land, and where you meet with cultivation the farms have a ragged and uncombed look, the farm buildings are usually of a poor character, and very high fences show that stock is allowed to run wild. Fields are oftenest full of stumps; and in the cotton region " deadenings," or fields with girdled and decaying trees standing upon them, give the landscape a melancholy aspect.

But, after all, it is useful for a Northern man to remember that dead trees and stumps are more economical than a cleaner culture where labor is scarce, and that the Arkansas farmer does not need as solid a house as his countryman in New York or Massachusetts. Though the farms and plantations of the State have too often an unprosperous look, the census-tables of 1870 disclose the singular fact that the value of the agricultural product of that year in the State equaled the assessed value of all the farms and plantations, which, if it is a correct statement, would make Arkansas one of the richest of our agricultural States.

The State is divided, by natural configuration, into two sections, the south and east producing mainly corn and cotton; the north and north-west, which is mountainous, yielding wheat and other grains. In the latter part there are but few colored people, and here, during the war, were found Union men, who fought vigorously for the old flag, either as volunteers or guerrillas.

The richest and most productive lands of the State are, of course, the river-bottoms, and here are found the most colored people. The Arkansas negro prefers, it seems, to raise corn and cotton. He suffers less from malaria than the white, and he likes the bottomlands.

Of the forty thousand negro voters in the State, it is believed that at least one in twenty owns either a farm, or a house and lot in a town. This would give but two thousand such independent land-holders — a small number, but yet a beginning, showing that, even amidst the intense and incessant political turmoil of the last seven years, a part of the colored men have been persistently industrious and economical. In that part of the cotton country which I saw, I heard of a number of negroes who had bought farms, and not uncommonly a manager or planter would say, "There's Jim; he's going to buy land next year if this crop turns out well." In one negro cabin the woman told me her husband had lost six hundred dollars in the Freedman's Bank, and seemed delighted when the planter told her she would probably get back a part of it.

I was shown a black man who bought a farm of eighty acres last year — all cleared cotton land — for four thousand dollars, paying seven hundred dollars down. On the remainder he was to pay ten per cent, interest, and the planter who sold it to him told me he would make it all safely out of the farm. This man had genuine energy, for he employed other negroes to cultivate his own farm, and himself worked fifty acres of rented laud. " He gets more out of his people than I could," said the planter to me; "he'll hire some women, and get a man's work out of every one of them."

The usual manner of working the cotton lands is to let them, either on shares or for a fixed price per acre. Some planters hire their laborers by the mouth or year, but it is not thought a profit-able plan, and I believe it is not so well liked by the negroes. The rich bottom-lands are worth from thirty to fifty dollars per acre, according to location nond condition. Where land is let for a share of the crop the renter usually pays the owner from eighty to ninety pounds of clean cotton per acre. If he has good luck he can raise four hundred pounds to the acre, and he aims to get also corn enough for himself and his stock. In such case the owner gins all the cotton, and he supplies, besides the land, fencing, fire-wood, a house which even if very good will not cost more than two hundred and fifty dollars, and often is a mere log-cabin, and range for stock. The renter must have his own teams and tools, and must pay for extra labor for picking his cotton if he needs it. For twelve acres he ought to have a mule, plow, hoes, and seed; and he may get eight bales of cotton, of which two would go for rent, and the net remainder would be worth three hundred dollars, besides the value of his corn. The planter or land-owner usually expects to make his people advances of food and clothing; and it is evident, from what I have seen and heard, that the greater number of the people are careless and do not lay up money. That they can, however, is shown by many instances.

Where a planter hires laborers, colored men receive from fifteen to eighteen dollars a month and board, or one dollar a day if they feed themselves. Women, employed in hoeing cotton, receive as much as men if they do a full day's work. I could not learn that any difference in wages is made by reason of color; but negro laborers are thought to be more peaceable and more easily provided for than whites. General Churchill, now State treasurer, told me that some of his former slaves were still on his plantation as renters. Several managed forty or fifty acres each. He found no difficulty in collecting his dues from them, and liked them as renters; but -he remarked to me that the young colored people do not farm so well as their fathers, and more of them seek some other employment.

The favorite method, I think, is to rent cotton land for a fixed price per acre, usually from six to ten dollars, the owner ginning the cotton in the latter case. The negroes usually use the labor of their women and children in the fields, and a man takes more or less land according to the number of his family. If a renter takes fifty acres at eight dollars, his account in an average year would stand somewhat thus: Thirty acres in cotton would yield twenty

-five bales, worth thirteen hundred dollars. Of this he would pay out four hundred dollars rent, and, probably, one hundred and fifty dollars for extra labor in picking, etc., and would have left seven hundred and fifty dollars cash, and twenty acres of corn as food for his family and stock.

Such results not only satisfy the negro, but they even tempt white men to come in from the less fertile uplands, and on some plantations there are Swiss and Germans, who, as a rule, become prosperous, I am told.

The planter keeps on the place a store at which renters may buy their supplies, and where they get a moderate credit. He also keeps a cotton-gin and a grist-mill, for the use of which he makes a charge ; and he takes care to get his year's rent out of the first of the crop. In practice, furthermore, the planter finds it necessary to ride daily through his fields to see that the renters are at work, and to aid them with his advice. During the winter, he hires them to chop wood for his own use, and to split rails and keep up the fences.

All the plantations have a quantity of unused woodland, in which stock roams at large, and this is free to the renters. It is a wasteful and wretched way to keep stock, and one result of it you see in the steers which are used to draw wood into Little Rock, some of which are not much bigger than a good -sized Newfoundland dog. It makes trouble, too, about hogs. The hog is in Arkansas what the umbrella is elsewhere — the prey of the first man who needs it. Pork is called "meat;" and when your planter friend explains to you that he has to buy all his meat, he will add that "the negroes will steal hogs; you can't keep a hog about the place."

The cabins of the renters, white as well as black, are usually pretty cheerless affairs, and there are few signs of a desire for tasteful or even orderly surroundings. But in this respect the planter's own home surroundings are often but little in advance of his tenants'. Here and there you find a man who keeps a kitchen -

garden; and most of the people have chickens; a forehanded negro will own some cows; and they all buy coffee, sugar, molasses, and wheaten flour, which last they prefer to corn-meal. A plantation store which I examined was pretty thoroughly supplied, not only with dry-goods and groceries, but with furniture, saddles, cooking-stoves, and all kinds of kitchen and tableware of the plainer sorts, of course. A placard announced "Scotch snuff;" and to my inquiry the store-keeper told me that many of the women, white as well as black, use it in the way called " dipping." I was sorry to discover that at some of the plantation stores whisky is sold to the renters.

On one of the plantations I was told that negro renters are preferred, because they are easier to get on with, and less apt to grumble and find fault than native whites; and I judge, from all I heard, that the negroes are quite as economical, and as apt to buy land out of their savings, as the poorer class of whites who become masters.

Cotton-picking, which, it used to be said, could never be satis-factorily done with free labor, because it requires the concentration of so much labor at a certain time, is, it seems, better done now than ever under the slave system. In the picking season women and children gather upon the plantations from towns and villages, and from all the surrounding uplands; and as they are well paid, and by the hundred-weight, the work is quickly and well done. "During slave times we never got through picking so early, or saved the whole crop in such good order as now," said a planter to me; "some-times the cotton was not all gathered before March, and now the fields are usually stripped clean before frost comes."

Every neighborhood has a church and school for the colored people, and usually also a school for the white children; but the school fund having been mostly wasted and stolen, many of the schools are closed. On Sunday the women go to church in bright dresses, and this is a great occasion. The colored preachers are usually cotton farmers, renting land, and I imagine they also have some political influence among their people. Political meetings are held in the churches.

To conclude. Wherever I met colored people, they seemed comfortable and at ease; and I neither saw nor heard the least evidence that they are regarded by the whites otherwise than as an integral and important part of the population. They appear to me to have withstood, very creditably, the demoralizing influences of political junketing, barbecues, and excitement incident to the earlier years of reconstruction. On the plantations white and colored renters seem to hold like relations to the owners of the land. Cotton-land is still so abundant that there is no difficulty in buying it in such quantities as laboring men, white or black, want. In Little Rock I saw negro policemen as frequently as white, and in the State-house and elsewhere in government offices I saw them employed.

Arkansas is at peace. The condition of parties seems to make proscription for opinion's sake impossible, for neither party can afford to sacrifice adherents. There is the best evidence that industry has revived all over the State, that the people of both parties strongly desire peace and order, and that the cessation of Federal interference has removed the only cause of disorder by throwing the politicians on their own responsibility, and leaving the people to control their own local affairs, and to remedy abuses at the polls, which before they were unable to cure or remove by lawful means, and were therefore tempted to resort to the shot-gun and the revolver.

"In my county," said an Arkansan to me, "the county clerk and collector of taxes were appointed by the governor. They were not citizens of the county, but strangers. They wasted the taxes; issued scrip to a heavy amount, and stole that; gave us neither improvements nor good management; and we had no appeal, no way, at elections or by any other method, of ridding ourselves of them.

Taxes went up to seven per cent, on a high valuation. What should we do? One of these scoundrels was shot, and the other ran away. And then came a howl of political ostracism and persecution of Union men. But now we can protect ourselves at the polls, and we will keep the peace."

The public debt of Arkansas is very great, and its management is full of difficulties for the present. But the natural wealth of the State is great, too. It is now under the rule of honest men; and the people, individually, owe less, in proportion to their property, than ever before in the history of the State. Their prospects, therefore, are favorable, and a good crop this year will, every body thinks, make them prosperous.

6

Louisiana in April, 1875

The long-talked- of "compromise," or Adjustment, determined on by the Congressional Committee, -was completed on Saturday, April 10th, by the installment of a Conservative in place of a Republican State senator. Its terms did not entirely please the leaders of either party. The Conservative leaders conceived themselves to be getting less political strength than the election of 1874 actually gave them, and the Radical leaders, or at least some of them, declare that it is for them a surrender of political power in the State.

Meantime, however, a wing of the Conservatives very strongly favored the compromise, and was able to bring most of its side into it; while a wing of the Radicals, among whose leaders were Governor Kellogg and Ex-Congressman Sheldon, accepted the compromise, and General Sheridan's advice silenced Pinchback, Senator West, and other Radical opponents, who were at first determined to defeat the measures of peace.

Thus matters stood when the House formally accepted the Adjustment, and unseated the Radical members whom the committee of Congress declared to have been wrongly seated by the returning board. But when the resolution of acceptance was proposed, a number of Conservative members voted "No;" among them Mr. Wiltz, whom some of the Conservatives desired to make Speaker. This attitude of Wiltz encouraged those in his own party who did not want him to be Speaker, and these succeeded, with the help of a considerable Radical vote, in defeating Wiltz and electing Estillete as Speaker.

This was the really important and decisive result of the Adjustment, for it declared which of the two branches of the Conservative party should control its organization.

The State of Louisiana had, according to the census of 1870, 87,076 white and 86,913 black males over twenty-one years of age. It has since been proved by undeniable evidence that the census understated considerably the number of whites. It was taken in the summer, when many white people always leave the State, and the census-takers did not, it is asserted, thoroughly record that part of the white population which is scattered over the pine hills back of the bottom-lands, on which a large number of white farmers are settled. I suppose the truth to be that Louisiana has to-day at least ten thousand more white than black voters. The Conservatives claim at least fifteen thousand more.

Now, in the election of 1874 parties were divided, unhappily, almost entirely on the color-line. Mr. Packard, who unites in his person the two important, and I should think incongruous offices of United States marshal and chairman of the Republican State Central Committee, told me, in New Orleans, that only live thousand whites voted the Republican ticket in 1874, and that the same number of blacks voted with the Conservatives. It is, I think, a fair statement that, with the exception of the office-holders. State and Federal, and their relations, there were no white Republicans in the State in 1874, or, at the furthest, but an inappreciable number. The reason for this condition of things I shall try to explain. It must suffice now to say generally that the inefficiency and corruption of the State government in all its parts — leaving lawlessness unpunished, countenancing the most monstrous and shameful frauds, and continued thus for six disgraceful years, at last united all the whites in one party, whose aim was simply and only to oust the thieves. Opposed to them in 1874 stood those rulers with almost, but not quite, the whole negro population at their backs.

The situation was one not different in kind from that in New York City in 1871, when all honest men. united against Tweed and Tammany Hall. The rank and file of the party which calls itself Conservative consists in part of Democrats who are naturally opposed to Republican rule, but in part, also, of old Whigs, Know-nothings, and the mass of citizens not interested in politics. These entered the Conservative party only to save the State from further misgovernment and spoliation. It was and is, therefore, an "honest men's" party, and was called " Conservative," and the name Democrat dropped, because there are in Louisiana a large number of good citizens who are so strongly opposed to the Democratic name that they will not actively, if at all, work with a party bearing that title. Many of its most substantial citizens were opposed to secession, and to-day think that act was "blundering Democratic statesmanship," as one said to me the other day. A Northern man may very commonly hear men who have been active and foremost in the Conservative movement declare that, "as soon as we have driven off the Radical thieves and robbers who have so long spoiled us, we shall quickly show these Democrats that they can not hold the State."

There is little doubt that whenever Federal interference in the State definitely ceases, and honest men have been put into power, the " Conservative " party — the white man's party — will incontinently split into two nearly equal halves, and each will try, with the help of the negroes, to beat the other. But it is tolerably certain that, until the present so-called Republicans are driven from power, the white men will stick together, for they can not afford to do otherwise.

The Republican politicians stigmatize one wing of the Conservatives as "last ditchers," and it was these who desired Wiltz to be Speaker, and thus the head of the party. Now, they are not "last ditchers," or impracticable men at all; but they are Democrats, and wish, as is but natural for them, to make the State Democratic. To this end they would like to keep the present Conservative party together permanently, and use its strength for the Democratic party. I can not see any thing wrong about this. It is their natural course to attempt it.

But the other wing of the Conservatives, which, in the struggle over the speakership, was, curiously enough, led by Leonard — that editor of the *Shreveport Times* whose extreme and blood-thirsty utterances last year were so widely quoted as proving the dangerous condition of Louisiana — this other wing determined to beat Wiltz, and in doing so had the sympathy, I think I may safely say, of the greater part of the business community of New Orleans.

Leonard, who is a bold politician, did not hesitate to accept the help of the Kellogg wing of the Republicans ; and the Wiltz men, on their part, tried to secure the help of Pinchback. On Friday morning it was understood that Kellogg, Sheldon, Judge Steele, and the better class of the Republicans had given assurances to the Estillete men that they would co-operate for thorough reforms with that wing of the Conservatives, while Pinchback, it was said, was ready to throw a considerable colored Republican vote (twenty-three was the precise number given) for Wiltz; and with this help it was then believed Wiltz would be chosen. At the last moment, however, Pinchback abandoned Wiltz, and thus he received but thirty-seven votes, in a house of one hundred and eight members, in which his own party had fifty-eight men.

P.B.S. Pinchback

As it is very common to charge corruption where party-lines are thus broken, I will add my belief, founded upon pretty intimate knowledge of the negotiations on both sides, that there was nothing of the kind here. Mr. Wiltz is a person of a high sense of honor, and his adherents made no promise for him or themselves to Pinchback, except that Wiltz, if elected Speaker, would, in appointing officers of the house, give a fair share of the places to colored men. Pinchback probably deserted Wiltz at the instance of General Sheridan, who is known to have conversed with him on Friday morning in pretty energetic language. On the other side, Estillete's adherents insisted only on a solemn engagement from Kellogg that he would aid them in all reform measures.

The disappointment of the Wiltz men was very great, and that of the corrupt Republicans was even greater, and with reason ; for, unless Governor Kellogg should be weak and wicked enough to falsify his pledges, and fling himself once more into the hands of the corrupt part of his party — which means, I do not hesitate to say, the very great majority of its white and black leaders— these are left out in the cold. Those Republican leaders, meantime, who sincerely desire honest government — and they are not very numerous — hope that they have split the white man's party in the State, and that the result of the Speaker's election will be a final breaking-down of the color-line.

Meantime, so sore are the white people of the State over the too-long-continued misgovernment, that they view every movement and every man with suspicion ; an^ only the most unswerving, bold, and determined course, the most rigorous punishment of corrupt men, could satisfy the State sufficiently to gain the new combination prolonged life. You can not travel far in Louisiana without discovering that the politicians who, in the name of the Republican party, rule it, and have done so for the last seven years, in all the departments of its government, State and local, are vehemently and unanimously detested by the white people. I have been amazed to sec how all white men, and many blacks to my own knowledge — whether rich or poor; whether merchants, mechanics, or professional men; whether Americans, French, Germans, Irish, or Italian by birth: absolutely all except the office-holders and their relatives — unite in this feeling of detestation of their rulers. It expresses itself so vividly at the polls that, as I noticed before, only five thousand whites out of over ninety thousand supported the Republican ticket at the last election; and it is a fact that most of these five thousand are officeholders, the greater part are strangers in the State, and very many of them may justly be called adventurers. It is so universal a sentiment that I have found scarcely a colored man out of office, who did not complain to me that the Republican whites are as faithless to their duty as they believe the other side would be. Now, this small band of white men have for more than six years monopolized all political power and preferment in the State. They have laid, collected, and spent (and largely misspent) all the taxes, local taxes as well as State; they have not only made all the laws, but they have arbitrarily changed them, and have miserably failed to enforce any which were for the people's good; they have openly and scandalously corrupted the colored men whom they have brought into political life; they have used unjust laws to perpetuate and extend their own power; and they have practiced all the basest arts of ballot-stuffing, false registration, and repeating, at election after election. In the last election, it was proved before a committee of Congress that the Republican leaders had, in the city of New Orleans alone, made no less than five thousand two hundred false registrations. A few days ago I went down the river to attend court, in order to see the working of a negro jury. The court had to adjourn for lack of a jury; and no panel had been drawn, because, the names being taken from the registration lists of the parish, thirty-six out of forty-eight were found to be fictitious — and this in a country parish. The Republican returning board was condemned as a transparent fraud by two Congressional committees, and has, so far as I know, no defender in Louisiana or in the country. I know of one case in the last election where, the Conservative ticket being elected, the records of the election were carried by the supervisor from the parish to New Orleans, and concealed in a house of prostitution, one of whose inmates was sent to drive a bargain with the Conservatives for their return. So common is corruption, and so unblushing still, that the grand jury of New Orleans, only the other day, began an investigation to discover who had altered, after its passage, an important appropriation bill, passed by the Hahn (Republican) Legislature; and the discovery of so gross and daring a fraud scarcely excited attention in New Orleans, where I have myself seen colored members of the Legislature — men who were slaves but ten years ago, and began life with nothing at that time — now driving magnificent horses, seated in stylish equipages, and wearing diamond breast-pins. Whatever we in the North may think of the white people of the South, we can not forget the fact that Louisiana has a long established and wealthy community, with large and complicated business and social interests, and a great accumulated capital, invested not merely in lands, but also in machinery and important public works. New Orleans is one of the largest commercial ports in the United States. It has a numerous body of intelligent and wealthy merchants, the equals of any of their class in New York, Philadelphia, or Boston. The sugar-planters of Louisiana are, in fact, manufacturers; they have large sums invested in machinery, and their business requires much technical skill; and they are, as a class, the equals in intelligence and character of Northern manufacturers.

Now, then, all these men, the cream of the population, with scarcely a single exception are united in opposition to the present rulers of Louisiana, whom they not only detest, but dread. It is not the cotton-planter only of the remote districts, therefore, or the country trader, who opposes the Republican rule. How, in spite of so united au opposition, a handful of politicians, most of them strangers in the State, have maintained themselves in power I will now try to explain. The constitution of 1868, under which Louisiana was reconstructed, and which is still in force, is in some respects a sufficiently harmless-looking instrument. For instance, it pretends to give the people the election of almost, but not quite, all their local or county officers; it pretends to limit the powers of the Legislature and of the executive; it even, like many other State constitutions, forces the people to elect the judges and the subordinate State officers. But while thus apparently popular, it gives to the governor the exclusive power to appoint and remove all the officers concerned with the registration of. voters, the conduct of elections, and the counting of votes in every parish of the State; and also the appointment and removal of all tax-collectors— officers who have also an important part in the assessments. And, having thus given into the governor's control the purse and the voice of the people, by one or two inconspicuous clauses this instrument enables an adroit and unscrupulous governor and Legislature to deprive the people of even those powers and remedies which are apparently secured to them, and without which free government becomes a farce. In fact, this constitution, as it has been applied by legislatures and governors, and construed by State judges since 1868, provides all the machinery needed for the party in power to perpetuate its rule forever, in spite of the will of the people. 1st. The governor appoints and removes the registrars of election and their assistants all over the State, and the decision of these officers is final and conclusive as to the right of a person to vote. The registrars appoint the local supervisors, or commissioners, who conduct the elections. But, as New Orleans is largely Democratic, the mayor and sheriff of that city are prohibited, under severe penalties, from holding or interfering in " any election whatever," that work being given to the metropolitan police, whose officers are appointed by the Governor. 2d. The governor appoints and removes the tax-collectors all over the State; and in New Orleans he appoints also the assessors. 3d. He appoints the officers of the metropolitan police, paid for by the city of New Orleans; and this body, so controlled by him, is constituted a metropolitan brigade, which he may send into any part of the State to make arrests; and a steamer is provided for this purpose. 4th. He appoints the Board of Public Works of the State. 5th. He may, whenever he deems it necessary, appoint and commission, as an extraordinary force, a chief constable, and as many deputies as he thinks necessary in any parish of the State, and these have, ex officio, power to make summary arrests. The chief constable is paid four dollars a day. 6th. He is, of course, commander-in-chief of the State militia, and appoints and commissions its officers. 7th. The constitution empowers him to fill all vacancies in office throughout the State. Under this apparently harmless clause, he, in effect, controls even the lowest local offices in the remotest parts of the State, such as constables, justices of the peace, and parish surveyors. In a single number of the Louisianan, the official gazette of the State, I find the following examples of the exercise of this power:

"Appointments by the Governor"

"The following appointments were made by Governor Kellogg yesterday:

"Parish of Orleans.—K. W. Connog, assistant supervisor of registration of the First Ward.

"Parish of Natchitoches—Henry Percy, parish surveyor, vice W. H. Boult; R. E. Hammett, justice of the peace of the Third Ward; P. L. Grappe, constable; F. Jennings, justice of the peace of the Fifth Ward; S.M. Cramps, constable; L. Van Schonbruck, justice of the peace of the Sixth Ward; M. L. Bates, constable; James E. Turner, justice of the peace of the Seventh Ward; Will Cobb, constable; A. R. Dowden, justice of the peace of the Eighth Ward; J. C. Bush, constable; J. B. Vienne, justice of the peace of the Ninth Ward.

"Parish of East Baton Rouge—Charles Q. Pages and Robert Morris, clerks to the supervisor of registration.

"Parish of Claiborne —Charles S. Blackburn, supervisor of registration; L. M. M'Cormick and L. B. Blackburn, clerks.

"Parish of St. Mary. —Richard Brooks, constable of the Third Ward.

"Parish of Sabine —'R. A. Forhis, justice of the peace of the Fourth Ward ; S. Whattey, justice of the peace of the Ninth Ward;

James Hardy, constable of the Fourth Ward; O. Seuter, constable of
the Ninth Ward.

"Parish of Lafayette—Hugh Wagner, justice of the peace of the
Second Ward; Joseph Ledoux, constable of the Second Ward, vice
C. Doncet, who failed to qualify; Vincent Bertraud, justice of the
peace of the First Ward, vice Alfred Peck, who failed to qualify : Gal-
bert Bienvenu, constable of the Third Ward ; Jules D. Boudreaux,
constable of the Fourth Ward, vice H. Theall, who failed to qualify;
Alexander Billond, inspector of weights and measures.

"Parish of Winn.— Sam Peace, justice of the peace; John Patton,
constable.

"Dr. J. J. Finney was commissioned as a member of the Board
of Health."

A more thoroughly centralized government France did not have
under either empire. Nor have these great powers been hesitat-
ingly used.

Officers have been nullified to an extraordinary degree, and at
every new creation the governor had the appointment of a favor-
ite. New parishes (counties) were formed by the division of old
ones, and in every case the governor appointed all the officers.
Judicial districts have been re-arranged and new ones formed, and
the governor thereupon made his friends or allies judges. A trick
became common by which officers elected refused to qualify, and
thereupon the governor filled the artificial vacancies with men who
could not have been elected. Finally, so careful have the leaders in
this conspiracy been to maintain their influence and their creatures
in the pettiest offices, that the members of the Legislature are
usually members of the local school boards, and degrade the schools
by making the teachers their political tools; and I have been in
some petty villages of fifteen hundred or two thousand inhabitants,
which have not for four or five years been allowed to put in office
the town officers they elected; but after each election the result

was disallowed, and the vacancies thus created were filled by the governor.

As an example of the way such matters were managed, Shreveport will answer, the better because it lies in a region where the whites have been accused of discontent with the Republican rule. Shreveport before reconstruction had a simple and economical city government. The mayor received a moderate salary, the Common Council were unsalaried. In 1871 the Republican Legislature imposed upon the place a new charter, which put it in charge of a mayor and four administrators, all salaried, all provided with clerks, and with office contingents. The governor was authorized to appoint these officers, and to fill all vacancies, until 1873, and they were authorized to issue bonds, and dispose of them " for the best interests of the city."

They seem to have issued not only bonds but scrip, and this fell to forty cents on the dollar at last. In the spring of 1874 the administrators proposed to issue bonds to the amount of one hundred thousand dollars, to improve the streets. A tax-payers' association had been formed, and, having defeated this project, they offered the mayor to undertake the same work which had been proposed, and do it to his satisfaction, if they were allowed to raise money on tax receipts from citizens. Permission being given, they did the whole work for thirty-six thousand dollars. The police were demoralized by being paid in depreciated scrip; the tax-payers asked the mayor to discharge the police, and authorize an unsalaried citizens' patrol; and this, too, was done, and the city became at once orderly. In the fall of 1874 the Republicans were beaten, a Conservative city government was chosen, and the scrip stands to-day at ninety. But this is not all. The new charter was passed in 1871. In 1873 the Legislature incorporated the Shreveport Savings-bank and Trust Company, and gave it for fifty years the "sole and exclusive right" to erect works to supply the city with water and gas, and to run a ferry across the river. Now, at that very time Shreveport had already a well-established gas company; a satisfactory ferry had long been in existence, and was a source of revenue to the city; and for waterworks there was no need. The company was to pay for all its privileges the petty sum of five hundred dollars a year. Now, then, among the incorporators named in the statute which gives these "exclusive rights," I find C. C. Antoine, then and still lieutenant governor; William Harper, State senator; S. A. Hamilton, tax-collector; Frank T. Hatch, supervisor of registration; M. A. Walsh, the appointed mayor, and George L. Smith, member of Congress. The story is completed when I add that the incorporators were not merely endowed with "exclusive rights," but also allowed to transfer these to other persons unimpaired.

No ruler of a civilized community ever possessed greater powers than the governor of Louisiana under this constitution. It gives him actual and direct control of the whole of the election machinery, and of all the officers who handle the taxes, and, indirectly, be has had the appointment of almost all the local or parish officers of the State, as well as of the judiciary; for when a judge or other officer elected by the people did not serve the purposes of the corruptionists who controlled the State, if no other way to remove him offered, the Legislature was ready to create a new parish, or a new judicial district, or a new court, and thus enable its governor to put in a serviceable person. Here is au example: The constitution provides that all district judges shall be elected by the people. New Orleans has a strong Conservative majority, and elected Conservative judges; and, this being inconvenient to the rulers of the State, the Legislature of 1871 created a new tribunal, called the Eighth District Court, and authorized the governor to appoint a judge to hold until the next election. But, in 1872, Mr. Elmore, Conservative, was elected to preside over this court. Thereupon the Legislature, as soon as it met, abolished both this and the Seventh District

Court, to both which Conservative judges had been chosen, created the "Superior District Court," authorized the governor to appoint its judge, to hold until 1876, and vested in this court, so organized, exclusive jurisdiction of all prerogative writs and the trial of all actions in which the title to any office— State, parish, or municipal — was involved. Another act of the same Legislature authorized the removal of cases where the office of judge was contested in any part of the State to this Superior District Court of New Orleans.

Again, the criminal jurisdiction in the parish of Orleans was formerly vested in the First District Court of that parish. In 1872, a Conservative, E. Abell, was elected judge of this court. Thereupon, in 1874, the Legislature deprived this court of almost all its important powers, and gave them to a new tribunal, called the " Superior Criminal Court;" and this was specially vested with exclusive jurisdiction in all cases of violations of registration or election laws — and the governor was directed to appoint a judge to hold office until 1876. Now, remember that the Radicals, or Republicans, who thus created this court, were proved before the Congressional committee to have made live thousand two hundred false registrations in New Orleans alone in 1874. Of course, having their own court, no one was punished for this.

Again, by the charter of New Orleans, the police magistracy of the city was vested in certain "recorder's courts," whose officers were to be chosen by the "Administrators," or Common Council of the city. But the people elected in 1872 a Conservative board of administrators, and these chose Conservative recorders. Thereupon, Act No. 95 of 1873 was passed by the Legislature, which abolished the recorder's courts, created in their place metropolitan police-courts, and gave the governor authority to appoint the magistrates to preside in these courts.

In other parts of the State the same trick has been repeatedly played, of legislating au obnoxious — that is to say, an honest —

judge out of office by creating a new district, thus giving the governor the appointment of one judge, or even several new judges. Take one instance as an example: In the parish of Natchitoches, in 1872, the grand jury indicted a parish officer for embezzlement. The parish judge, his personal friend, protected him by neglecting to draw a jury.

This was so common a trick that a law was finally passed which compelled the drawing of juries; but this law is evaded, for no jury was drawn in the parish in which I write this at this term of the court — people tell me because the parish judge was afraid that if a grand jury met it would indict him for a gross misapplication of trust funds.

However, in Natchitoches the case went before the district judge and a negro jury, who gave a verdict for forty thousand dollars. Thereupon, at the next session, the Legislature broke up th« judicial district, and the governor appointed to be judge of the new district, which included Natchitoches parish, that parish judge who had corruptly protected the embezzler of public funds. The judge has since been driven out of the county — so he tells me; reputable citizens of the parish accuse him of being concerned in embezzling the school fund. The tax-collector, Boult, also driven from the parish, stands published as a defaulter in the last official State auditor's report, and acknowledged to me that he had, while tax collector, been engaged in partnership with the Democratic member elect of Congress in buying up depreciated county warrants, which the county must redeem at par.

Both Myers and Boult continued, when I was in Louisiana, to hold office, and the condition of affairs in the parish may be gathered from the following details, which were confirmed to me by several citizens as existing in 1874: District Judge Myers was also treasurer of the school fund, and continues to be, though he has not been in the county since last July. Dr. Boult was tax-collector and member of the school board. His son, William Boult, was deputy-tax-collector and also deputy parish treasurer — two offices one of which ought to be a check on the other. A negro "police jury " — a body which is the equivalent of our county supervisors — appointed an illiterate parish treasurer, who made this Boult his deputy. Another son, David Boult, was parish judge.

Nor is such a state of things uncommon. Before the Congressional committee appeared one Green, of Lincoln parish, and in answer to questions admitted that he was State senator, one of his sons tax-collector, another parish judge, and a third supervisor of registration. Of the members of the present Legislature some are parish judges, some tax collectors, one is assistant secretary of state, and a considerable number are charged by their constituents with sharing the emoluments of office-holders whose appointments they have caused.

The complaint is universal that the officers charged with the execution of the laws are not only inefficient, but corrupt; that justice is not only denied, but openly sold; and in many cases the people have, after vain remonstrances, taken the law into their own hands.

"I have seen a district attorney, appointed by the governor, sell out a case for as little as ten dollars," declared a laboring man with whom I conversed, and the story was confirmed to me by several citizens of the parish whom I asked. One of the prominent citizens of the parish of Rapides said to me, "We have had neither protection nor justice for years. Matters became so bad that even the negroes got tired of bad government, and began to vote with us. We bad no intimidation at the last election, because it was not necessary. But we would have intimidated if it had been required, for we could stand it no longer."

"When we drove out the parish judge and other rascals, our taxes had got up to seven and nine- tenths per cent, on a high valuation;

and we concluded that we might as we stop there, and refuse to pay
any more taxes," said the citizen of another parish." Nor are even
the highest judicial officers of the State untainted. In the North
Louisiana Railroad case, the Supreme Court of the United States, in
its decision delivered last winter, said:

"A property upon which had been expended nearly two million
dollars, together with a large stock-subscription, a large grant of
lands, and considerable movable property, was bought for fifty
thousand dollars by the very persons who defeated a sale for a much
larger price, and the purchase money was retained by themselves.
It is impossible to characterize this agreement as anything else than
a gross fraud. Its obvious purpose was to remove competition at
the sale. It was a flagrant breach of trust on the part of Home, and
it was a fraud in Ludeling, with knowledge of the trust Home had
undertaken, to persuade him to violate his instructions and sacrifice
the interests of his constituents, himself becoming a party to the
violation. * * * And it is farther ordered, adjusted, and decreed
that the sale made by John T. Ludeling and his associates, and the
adjudication of the sheriff to them, together with the sheriff's deed
to them, be declared to be fraudulent and void, and be set aside and
canceled; and that a perpetual injunction issue commanding them
and all the defendants to refrain from setting up or claiming any
right, title, or interest under said sale or under said deed, etc."

Now, the .John T. Ludeling here declared guilty of fraud and
breach of trust is the present chief-justice of the Supreme Court
of Louisiana, appointed by a Republican governor, and has been
allowed by the Republican Legislature to retain his seat on the
Supreme Bench of the State in the face of these terrible words of the
United States Supreme Court. Public and political demoralization
could hardly go farther than this.

Considering the character of the men with whom he acts, he was
the right man in the right place ; and it was but part of a general

system when " Ludeling, Ch. J." decided, in 1870, in a case brought before his court, where it was attempted to upset an act of the Legislature on the ground that it had been procured by bribing the members, that "courts are not permitted to go behind an enrolled, duly authenticated and promulgated public statute, to inquire into the motives which may have influenced the members of the General Assembly in enacting it. Therefore, evidence tending to establish bribery and corruption against the members of the General Assembly, which, it is alleged, procured its passage, is not admissible."

Federal, State, and parish officers have banded together to maintain themselves in power, and have used the ignorant fears of the negroes to help them. They called to their aid every man unscrupulous enough to take part with them. By alarming the blacks, by false registration, by arbitrary arrests and threats of arrests just before the elections, by cheating in the returning board, by tampering with the courts, by debauching the Legislature, by monopolizing offices, they have persistently prevented the honest people of the State from securing honest government. See here an example:

A young fellow, a white man, in the present Legislature, came to New Orleans from New York six years ago, so far an adventurer that his first occupation was to teach boys to travel on the velocipede. He was presently engaged as a subordinate clerk in the Legislature, and when that body adjourned he went to Mississippi, where, the Legislature of that State being still in session, he was also employed as a clerk. In the fall he returned to New Orleans, where Warmoth, then governor, made him supervisor of registration and election in an up-country parish where he had never been or lived. After the election he brought down the returns, which, by a coincidence not at all remarkable in this State, showed him to have received the unanimous Republican vote, and to be elected to the Legislature from the parish where he had managed the registration and election. Two years later (in 1872) he did not receive the Republican nomination; but, noways discouraged, he announced himself as an independent candidate. On his way to the parish, however, he was intrusted by the State committee with the Republican tickets for the parish voters, and it was discovered that his name and that of a Democrat had been mysteriously placed on these tickets. Thereupon the negroes threatened to lynch him, and he returned to New Orleans until just before the election. The returns showed his defeat; but the returning board seated him, regarding him as too useful a man to leave out. I am told that he found it necessary to call in the help of the last returning board also to seat him in the present Legislature.

Such cases were so far from rare that the Legislature of 1869 was made up almost entirely of supervisors of registration and colored men. Warmoth, the governor, selected as registrars a large number of men left in New Orleans after the war, and remaining there without regular employment These were sent into the country parishes to register the voters; and they so impressed the negroes with their official power and dignity, that a majority of them were returned to the Legislature from parishes which they had never seen until they went there to superintend the election. Many negroes were dragged in as a matter of bargain; they had wit enough to demand a share of the honors. The Legislature so elected sat sixty days, at a cost to the State, for per diem, mileage, and contingents, of nine hundred thousand dollars. Each member is said to have received seven thousand dollars for the session; and it is related that a single committee of the House had eighty-seven clerks, who were paid ten dollars a day each.

Henry Clay Warmoth

A government so highly centralized as that of Louisiana can scarcely fail to be costly and corrupt. But it ought at least to secure peace and order.

I asked Governor Kellogg what was the real condition of the State in this respect, and he gave me a long and deplorable catalogue of disorders: parishes which refuse to pay taxes; others where the judges have been driven away; others where murders have been committed, and so on. Other Radical politicians spoke rather boastfully of these things, as a New York newsboy took pride in his sore toe. They related to me by the half- hour melancholy instances of crime and outrage — most of them dating back to 1866.

What they did not tell me was some such story as this, which, nevertheless, is true: In the parish of Plaquemiue, which lies under the governor's nose, along the Lower Mississippi, below New Orleans, and which has had Republican rulers ever since 1868, thirty-three murders have been committed since 1868. Of these, thirty -one were of blacks by blacks, one of a white by a white ; and one of a white man, a Northern man, a Republican and an office-holder, the tax-collector of the parish. This man was shot by a colored man for seducing his sister and turning the young girl adrift with her baby. Of these thirty-three murderers, not one has been hanged. Those who were apprehended mostly broke out of jail, and only last fall the Republican deputy-sheriff, who acted as jailer, was indicted for permitting three murderers and a defaulting tax-collector to escape out of his custody.

In other cases which I have on my notebooks, men sentenced to imprisonment for life for murder have been pardoned. No one, not even the governor, pretends that murder and lawlessness have been punished, though in many instances white citizens have helped the authorities to arrest white murderers. I am satisfied that since the year 1870, except in the Coushatta and Colfax affairs, most of the murders in Louisiana have been nonpolitical in their origin, and a great proportion of them hare been of negroes by negroes, mainly on account of jealousy in their relations with their women.

This does not lessen the degree of criminality. Nor does it take away from the duty of the rulers, possessing, as these did, greater and more unlimited powers than the rulers of any civilized State in the world, to punish these crimes. The governor of Louisiana appoints, in effect, almost the whole judiciary and constabulary of the State; he has express authority to use the metropolitan police as a standing army in any part of the State, and to appoint an extraordinary constabulary force in any parish ; his own judges superintend the selection of the juries, both grand and petit, and these are usually largely composed of colored men; he has also the militia; and, finally, he has the army of the United States ready to help him at his call. Is there any excuse for him if he permits lawlessness, murder, violence? When he and those who rule with him speak of murder and violence unrepressed, do they not fatally condemn themselves as incapable and unfit to rule the State? A United States army officer, an extreme Republican, after giving me an account of some murders of which ho had heard, and which he believed to have happened, added, "But I must say that if the governor had been a man fit for his place, such things could not have happened. Let me be governor, and I would quickly, with the great power he has, put a stop to such things."

It can not be truthfully said that the State of Louisiana has been peaceful ever since the war. In the early days, between 1865 and 1868, there is no doubt that many barbarous and heart-rending murders and outrages were committed on the blacks. The white people, sore at their defeat in the war, refused to tolerate free negroes, fearful, to a degree that seems to a Northern man absurd, of combinations and conspiracies among the blacks to murder the whites and outrage their women, and rendered frantically furious by the sight of negroes assembled in political meetings, often at night, did, without doubt, commit atrocities of which I should be sorry to see any formal record made. Such crimes decreased from year to year, but I doubt if they entirely ceased until 1870. They happened oftenest in counties — of which Louisiana has a good many — where the negro population is as three, four, and in some cases even as nine, to one white; where a few white families, isolated from each other, are surrounded by a dense negro population; and where the dread of a rising to exterminate the whites is to this day the secret terror of every white man, the dread which makes him frantic and desperate when even a rumor of conspiracy reaches his ears. I speak here that which I know.

Now, into such regions came white men, strangers, often fanatics, often knaves, who gathered the freedmen together at barbecues and in camps, and told them of their "rights." I was shown yesterday a colored man who still keeps in his house the mulehalters he got in 1868, when a white man traveled through St. Mary's Parish telling the blacks that "they had made the land what it was; had cleared it and cultivated it; and they ought to own it; and the Government, which had set them free, was going to give them each forty acres of land and a mule." The blacks believed it. Many of them believe it still — just as there are planters down here foolish enough to believe that the United States Government will pay them for their losses in the war.

All this irritated the whites, and aroused the fear of negro insurrection; and it led, in the remoter parts of the State, to many inexcusable acts of barbarity. Then came the reconstruction, in 1868, and the negro was made, not only a voter, but an office-holder.

It was, I believe, absolutely necessary to confer these rights upon him; he would never have been a free man without them. But it was a misfortune that demagogues and adventurers were his introducers to political life, and led him to regard not fitness, but color and numbers, as the reasonable claim to office. I have been opposed to slavery ever since I sat on my father's knee, and was taught by him that slavery was the greatest possible wrong; but when, in New

Orleans last Wednesday, I for the first time saw negro legislators, I was unpleasantly startled — not because they were black, but because they were transparently ignorant and unfit. What, then, must have been the feelings of men who saw blacks, but lately their own slaves, and as ignorant as the mules they drove, preferred before them for office, set over them in authority, making laws for them — and making them very badly at that — openly plundering the State, bribed by rascally whites, and not merely enjoying, but, under the lead of white adventurers, shamefully abusing, place and power?

Even in 1874, in one of the northern parishes, the Republican candidates for sheriff and parish judge could not write. The negroes on many police-juries (supervisors of counties) are totally illiterate; yet they have complete power over the parish taxes, roads, bridges, and all county matters. Negro juries are called to sit upon intricate cases of commercial law and other matters which even intelligent men find it difficult to understand; and the black man himself has, it would seem, an instinctive appreciation of the absurdity of this, for it is notorious that a negro criminal always asks his counsel to get a white jury, if possible, to try him. Things which are commonplace here are unheard of with us. It was a matter of complaint to me the other day that in a certain county not a single colored man had been drawn on the grand jury this year. My instant and thoughtless reply was that I had never known a negro to be drawn on the grand jury in the county in which I live. But the cases are widely different; and it is absolutely necessary that the negro in the South shall take some share of the responsibilities of citizenship.

But you can not quiet unreasonable fears or change wrong habits by act of Congress. I asked a citizen of a northern parish, a frank and intelligent man, whether they had schools for the colored children. He replied, " Of course, as many as for the whites;" and added, "At first all our people were bitterly opposed to negro schools; when, after some time, we had come in to that, then we would not for a while allow white men to teach in them. But now we are all agreed that it is just as well not to interfere; and one of my own neighbors, a weakly man, is teacher in a colored school, and nobody thinks the less of him for it."

A prominent citizen of New Orleans said to me, " When, in 1868, the blacks were for the first time to vote, I was a candidate for office; and I heard, just before the election, that John, a man I had raised, who was my personal servant, and who, since his freedom, had lived with his family in a house of my own rent free, was going to vote against me. Now, I love the boy like a brother, but I called him to me and asked the question, and I was deeply irritated. He replied that if I was on the Republican ticket he would gladly vote for me; but if not, he would certainly vote against me. I told him that if he did, he must leave the house in which he lived, and must never show me his face again.

The next day was election-day. I watched the poll, which was near my house. I saw John come to vote; he did not see me, but he pulled out his ticket, unfolded it, held it up over his head, and said in a loud voice, ' I'm votin de Republican ticket.' I drove him out of his house, took away all his employment, and ordered that he should not be admitted to my house. I was very sore and angry toward him. My pride was hurt. It lasted several months, and I missed John. One day, on the anniversary of the death of one of my children, he sent me a bouquet of flowers; and I did not refuse the peace-offering. He lives with me now, and will till he dies; but since then I have never tried to control a black man's vote. I have learned better. Nowadays they come to me to ask how I would like them to vote; and as those I employ necessarily lose a day if they go to the polls, I noticed that in 1874 many did not vote at all."

How clearly such instances show that the freedman would never have been a free man without political rights; but, also, that the adjustment of his new relations needed time as well as law to complete it!

One thing more was very much needed, and that was a rigorous enforcement of the laws. Unfortunately the reconstructors of Louisiana have utterly failed in this. It was not only murder and personal outrage they should have punished and repressed, but malversation in office, public robbery, bribery, fraud. When the United States Supreme Court, in a solemn and public decision, denounces as an inexcusable fraud and breach of trust the act of a man who is now Chief-justice of the Supreme Court of Louisiana, and when neither the Legislature nor the governor takes measures, after that decree, to purify the highest judicial court in the State, that is only a straw which shows the general drift of political demoralization. All sense of honor, of honesty, of propriety and self-restraint, seems to me to have been lost by these men who have so long misruled the State.

That I am not speaking extravagantly or in mere idle denunciation, let this recent instance show you. The Republican (or Hahn) Legislature, that which, after the dispersion of the Wiltz Assembly in January, 1875, was recognized by the Federal Government, among other acts passed a new charter for the city of New Orleans — an instrument calculated, I am told, to facilitate still greater robbery and misgovernment of the city. Governor Kellogg did not sign the bill ; but neither did he veto it. The Assembly adjourned while it was still properly in his hands, and under the constitution he must return it signed or vetoed on the first day of the next meeting. The merchants and property-owners were alarmed at the mischief which would be wrought if this bill became a law. They petitioned against it, and the governor quietly gave them to understand that if they would unite to prevent the election of Wiltz as Speaker, he would veto the bill. Now, I do not believe Wiltz to have been the best man for Speaker, but that does not excuse a governor for trading upon the fears of citizens.

More than this, an honorable Republican, a man respected by the other side, told me, with indignation, that a number of Radical members of the Legislature had made it a condition of their supporting the Adjustment, that an injunction issued by a State court stopping the proceedings of a corrupt board of audit should be dissolved; and it was so dissolved the day before the Legislature met.

As for minor robberies, take this as an example: The parish of Plaquemine lies on the Mississippi, below New Orleans. It contains a large number of sugar- plantations; and, besides these, its people (mostly French Creoles and colored men) cultivate rice and the orange. It is a charming, quaint country, and the small farmers, who mostly speak French better than English, are a quiet and simple-hearted people. In the year 1868, when reconstruction began, this parish had no debt, and six thousand dollars in cash in its treasury, which sum was turned over to the reconstructors. Among these was one who owned a small sugar-plantation in the parish, into which ho had come as an officer during the war; he was elected to the State Senate, and, by a curious coincidence, the Legislature, of which he was a member, passed a law removing the parish seat from Point à la Hache, where it had been time out of mind, to a spot at Jesuits' Bend, farther up the river, and on this man's plantation. Of course, to get the county town removed to one's farm is not a bad speculation. Lawyers and many other people must live near the Court-house, and they make a market for town lots. The records of the county were, in fact, removed; but the people made such a clamor that, after a struggle of a year, the project was given up. Presently this man became a bankrupt; but he is all right, for the governor has appointed him tax-collector of the parish, a place said to be worth ten thousand dollars a year.

A colored man from the island of Nassau also came in 1868. A white man, formerly in General Neal Dow's corps, which campaigned in this region, was another politician. He was made supervisor (member of the police-jury they call it here), and, soon after the reorganization, the parish authorities began to issue scrip in such abundance that in two or three years it fell to fifteen cents on the dollar. But it was always receivable at par for parish taxes. In 1872 the colored man above mentioned was State senator; another colored man was member of the Assembly, and another was sheriff. The Legislature passed a law authorizing these three, and two white citizens, to ascertain and report the outstanding debt of the parish, and to fund it. The three colored men are accused of issuing: bonds illegally, and without consent of the whites, to the amount of $30,000 in exchange for scrip, much of which had been bought up by them and their friends at a great discount. On an investigation by citizens it was found that the seal of the court, which had to be affixed to these bonds by the parish clerk to make them valid, had not been affixed by him; but had been surreptitiously obtained and used by the three bond-issuers. The parish debt is now $93,000, and Judge Pardee, a Republican, but praised by every body here as an honest and incorruptible man, has granted an injunction prohibiting the conversion of the remaining $57,000 of scrip into bonds. Finally, the last grand jury of the parish, composed of twelve colored men and four whites, indicted Butler for bribery and embezzling the school fund; Mahoney, for stealing the school fund; and Prescott, the parish judge, a white man, stranger in the parish, for subornation of perjury.

Now, then, the financial statement it Plaquemine parish stands thus: In 1868, no debt, and $6000 in the treasury; in 1875, a debt of $93,000. Meantime, in every year since 1868, taxes to the amount of from $20,000 to $25,000 have been levied and collected. And for all this large sum, amounting, taxes and debt, to over $200,000 in six years, the parish has received neither roads, nor schools, nor levee repairs, nor public buildings. Before the war the taxes never exceeded $7000 a year.

In the report of the State Superintendent of Public Instruction, the management of school affairs in Plaquemine parish is thus mentioned:

"A controlling portion of the school board could not resist the temptation to use their position as a means of political advancement, and a large portion of the school funds was expended for private and partisan purposes. Furnished with ample funds from the State treasury, which were liberally increased by local taxation, the money has been squandered or expended without even ordinary judgment. * * * Access to the books and papers pertaining to the office of the treasurer was denied me from time to time upon frivolous pretexts, and, finally, peremptorily and insultingly refused. Obstacles of every possible character were thrown in my way to prevent me from obtaining reliable information, the treasurer even attempting my imprisonment on the charge of larceny. * * * The result of a somewhat protracted investigation can be summed up in a few words. The accounts, as they appear in the remarkable document before alluded to, are, in many cases, falsified by being 'raised;' fictitious claims are allowed and paid to fictitious personages; unworthy, incompetent, and dissipated teachers have, in some instances, been employed to perform political services of questionable honesty, and the public money expended to the last cent, leaving a heavy load of debt. * * * Knowing as I do the details of this most disgraceful matter, I charge the then treasurer of the board with embezzlement, aided and abetted by the then president and the parish judge, who also was a member of the board, and am prepared to establish this before any competent tribunal."

The treasurer of the school hoard here denounced was also at the same time State Senator and member of the police-jury (supervisor). Mahoney, who was president of the school board, was at the same time member of the Assembly and police-juror.

I find that in a great many parishes the members of the Legislature are members and officers of the school board. As the latter office is not salaried, I was dull enough not to see the object of the Senators and Representatives in holding it, until an intelligent colored man, a Republican and an office-holder, explained to me that in this way the public schools are made political engines throughout the State. The Senators or Representatives, being also officers of the school boards, appoint the school-teachers, and select men who are their own political adherents, and who, living among the colored people, help to keep their patrons in office.

"In this parish," said the man to me, "we have many more colored schools than white; but it is a fact that most of the teachers are ignorant men or lazy, or, sometimes, drunkards. They are appointed by our Senator and Representatives, and their work is not to teach school, but to talk up the man who appoints them. If a teacher were the smartest man in the township, and he went against the man who appointed him, he would be turned out; but this is not all. Over here there is a colored school, and another one close to it. There is no need for two so near together; but neither of them is worth any thing; for they were both set up for politics, and the teachers are only politicians, and the schools are hardly ever open."

The colored man who told me this is a Republican and an office-holder. I shall not mention the name of the parish in which he lives, because I do not wish to get him into trouble; but his testimony was confirmed to me by many other men of both colors.

The school report to which I have referred gives a melancholy picture of the Louisiana school system. Of 272,334 children between six and twenty- one, only 57,433 were enrolled in the public schools; and as my eye runs over the pages I find that in one parish the treasurer of the school board has used the funds for his private purposes, and paid the teachers in scrip to the amount of three thousand dollars. In another thirty thousand dollars were spent, and the schools were open less than a year — this in a country parish. In two parishes the school treasurers "had absconded with quite a large amount of money belonging to the school fund." In another "the money appropriated to establish schools was invested in private business and speculation." In yet another "all the forms of law which should govern school affairs have been totally ignored and disregarded." In the parish of St. Martin, the treasurer of the school fund was discovered to be a defaulter to the amount of three thousand seven hundred dollars. In St. James the school board had prudently burned their records when they left the office, and J. W. Hunsaker, president of the board, after giving bail of five thousand dollars to answer to the charge of fraud, left the State.

Do you wonder, in the face of such things as these, that, according to the admission of Marshal Packard himself, only five thousand white men voted the Republican ticket in 1874? That is to say, the office-holders and their relatives. Is it matter for surprise, that but for the fear of the Federal power, the people would sweep away this State government in an hour — that, in fact, these rulers would disappear of themselves if they did not know that they have the Federal government behind them? Do you wonder that enterprise languishes, and property is valueless, when men see a fair election defeated by a fraudulent returning board, and the chief officer of that board, the engineer of the fraud, which was denounced as such by two committees of Congress, receiving directly afterward a Federal office?

It is not contempt which the people of Louisiana feel for their rulers, but fear. The man who takes part in the State government, even if he should be honest himself, gives his influence to public plunderers, and he must expect property-owners to be shy of him. Did honest men associate with the Tammany thieves in New York?

Or, if they did, were they not, in the public opinion, stained by the contact?

"Do you see that man?" said a citizen in an interior parish to me: "he is our parish judge; he is as ignorant of law as a horse. During the last election I heard him openly, and to his face, charged with theft. Not only that, but at a public political meeting where he was speaking, in his presence he was accused of taking a bribe of ten dollars while be was prosecuting attorney, and the man who accused him was the man who paid him the money. In spite of this, the colored people were persuaded to elect him judge. Every decent colored man in the parish will tell you that it was an unfit nomination; but he got on the ticket and they elected him. The whole bar of the parish firmly believes that he sells justice. He says he is ostracized; but can you expect me to invite him to my house? He could not to-day get invited to the house of any respectable colored man in the parish."

"Can you expect us to like people under whose rule such frauds go on for years, and are unpunished?" asked another;" who allow the fountains of justice to be corrupted, who never punish crime, and are too corrupt to check corruption in their subordinates; who degrade the very schools to serve their partisan purposes; appoint rogues to collect the taxes; and frame a returning board to cheat us by a clumsy and glaring fraud, when we try at the elections to procure better government?"

A friend writes me from the North this question, "Are white and black Union men safe in life, liberty, and property in Louisiana? That is the question which we of the North want to have honestly and seriously answered."

I answer: first, the population of Louisiana is divided politically into Republicans, called here Radicals; and Democrats, called here Conservatives. They are all Union men. It is absurd and wicked to keep up the old war animosity by giving to the Southern Republicans the special title," Union men."

The Republican party in Louisiana contains a great many men who were bitter Secessionists, not only during, but after, the war. One of the most conspicuous Republicans who came before the Congressional committee with complaints, and who was proved there and then by documentary evidence to be a rogue, was a Breckenridge Democrat before the war. Another, Green, who admitted that he and his sons held pretty much all the offices in Lincoln parish, made a speech in the Legislature after the war advocating payment for slaves. I could mention dozens of such cases.

On the other hand, in my limited acquaintance in the- State, I know at least fifteen Northern men who were strenuous Republicans in the North, most of whom still openly act with the National Republican party in Federal elections, but who vote and use all their influence for the Democratic or Conservative party in State and parish affairs. There are hundreds of such men in the State. Even the Republicans themselves are not so absurd as to arrogate to themselves the title of " Union men." They would be laughed at.

What my correspondent, and no doubt many other Northern men, want to know is, whether Northern men and negroes are safe, and can get security and justice in Louisiana; and to this I reply, unhesitatingly " Yes."

William Pitt Kellogg

It is perfectly true, as I have said elsewhere, that between 1865 and 1868 there was a good deal of savage and brutal wrong inflicted on blacks; and in the same period, and probably for a year or two later, Northern men who came here to take possession of the State politically, and who at once began a prodigious system of public plunder, were not always safe from the anger and resentment of the native whites. But several of the most prominent Republican politicians of New Orleans have told me positively that the State was peaceable and quiet from 1868 to 1872, and that since then the whites had been dissatisfied mainly because they believed sincerely that Kellogg was not fairly elected governor, and that his rule was that of a usurper. If General Sheridan ever turns in his famous list of 2500 murders, and if he puts dates to them, it will be found that the political murders happened before 1868, with the exception of the Coushatta and Colfax affairs. The corrupt judge -who claims to have been driven out of Natchitoches Parish assured me that that parish was one of the most quiet in the State until 1874, -when he and a swindling tax-collector were driven out.

That parish has become so notorious as the most unruly in the State, that I have taken some pains to ascertain the facts; because there, if anywhere, persecution of Northern men and negroes would be found. Now, then, first, an official report, properly authenticated, of the murders committed in this parish from 1868 to 1875 lies before me. They number 41, and of these there were whites murdered by whites, 13; colored murdered by colored, 13; whites by colored, 4; colored by whites, 3; whites by an unknown person, 3; colored by unknown, 1, colored by officers of justice in serving process, 3; Indian by a white man, 1. Somebody may object that this record is not correct, but to that the reply is that the parish has been almost continually since 1868 under Republican officers, and that the coroner is reputed here, as elsewhere, to be an officer very zealous in the collection of fees. It is not creditable to the Republican rulers that for these 41 homicides not one man has been hanged, and only one has been punished in any way. I should add that there is no evidence that any of these murders arose out of political causes.

Consider that the parish had for years a corrupt judge and a thieving tax-collector — who managed to get all his sons into offices — and a police -jury (county supervisors) made up mainly of illiterate negroes. Governor Kellogg, for instance, in 1874 appointed as police-jurors three colored men, who could neither read nor write, one white man of an infamous character, whom even his fellow Republicans publicly protested against, and one decent white man. Under such rulers, the parish tax, which amounted to $13,475, with a valuation of $8,000,000 in 1860, rose to $46,894 on a valuation of but $2,000,000 in 1869; it rose to $54,902 in 1870; and in 1873 to $82,207. This was the parish tax alone, exclusive of the State tax.

The supervisors allowed themselves one year fifty cents a mile mileage for every time they met. They paid out $1500 for a bridge which should have been built for $300, and gave the contractor a privilege to levy toll upon it for his own use when it was built. The parish judge acknowledged before the Congressional committee that he had for two years retained $7500 of parish money in his possession, in violation of an order of a district court to return it to the treasury; he refused repeatedly to draw juries, in order to shield his confederates ; and yet this person was appointed by Governor Kellogg district judge, a higher office.

The people formed a tax-payers' association, and warned the judge and one of his confederates, the tax-collector, to leave the parish. The sons of the latter to-day hold offices in the parish, and none of them have been killed. The two men walk about freely in New Orleans, and are not molested ; but they tell fearful stories of intimidation and danger to their lives, and call themselves "Union men."

The Tax-payers' Association was composed of Republicans as well as Democrats, and had among its members 200 negroes. Myers calls it a white league, of course, and talks about intimidation of Republican voters; but the official returns of the registration and election show these figures : The parish had, by the census of 1870, 7312 whites and 10,929 blacks. Of these, one in five and a half blacks registered as a voter, and only one in seven and a half of the whites, in 1874, the year of the disturbance. Of the 3665 who registered,

3131 actually voted, and the Republicans carried the parish by 315 majority. It was shown that many negroes voted with the Conservatives, and many others staid at home because they were disgusted with the theft of the school fund.

I have taken Natchitoches as an example, because it has an especially evil reputation. Contrast with this a parish in which the Republicans have given the people an honest and economical government, and where there has been no disturbance. There are but four or five honestly governed parishes in the State. I happen to be well informed about one of these, Tensas, like Natchitoches, a cotton-planting county, and with a large preponderance of negroes. There has never, since 1868, been any disturbance in Tensas, nor any pretense of intimidation. Here is its story since 1868: The Republicans who came into it from the North happened to be honest and sensible men. Their leader was Judge Steele, later assistant attorney-general of the State, an able man. They persuaded some of the most substantial of the old residents to take parish offices. They took care to put always three prominent whites and two colored men on the police-jury. The parish judge had been a Confederate officer, and is a capable man, and a property-holder in the parish. They have always persuaded the negroes to elect such men to the local offices. Tensas had, in 1870, 1400 whites and 11,018 blacks. With economical management, they have extinguished since 1866 a debt of $190,000, contracted for levees before the war, paying off $130,000 of it. The rest was proved fraudulent in the courts. The parish has good roads, bridges, thirty schools, four graded schools — two for each color; it has money in the treasury; its assessment is very low; the courts are respected, the laws are enforced, peace obtains; even stock-stealing has been put down. Meantime, the Northern men have not ceased to be Republicans, nor have they given up their share of the offices. The State Senator and Representative and some of the local officers are Northern men and Republicans. The negroes are satisfied; and when once some drunken ruffians from a neighboring county threatened to come in and attack a Northern man, the largest meeting of whites ever assembled in the county promptly gathered, and sent word to the rowdies that they would be shot down if they showed their faces in the parish.

Surely the story of these two parishes tells the reason why discontent and sometimes disorder are found in parts of Louisiana. "It is not the Radicals, but the thieves, that we hate and oppose," said more than one Conservative to me. And I believe this to be the truth. I have not time to wander all over the State; but I have examined every case where I have heard of complaints of especial hostility to Republicans, and in every case I have found that there had been gross and long-continued misgovernment, extravagance, denial of justice, and tolerance of disorder by the courts.

I was told, for instance, that Madison Parish was "not a pleasant place for a Republican." Very well. I find that in four years — from 1868 to 1872 — the Republican reconstructors ran up a debt in this parish of over $142,000. It had, in 1870, by the census, only 936 white persons. It registered in 1874 only 255 white voters and 2135 blacks. The few whites were, of course, the owners of almost all the property. Such monstrous mismanagement, borne by so few tax-payers, might very well create ill-feeling and strife; but the parish gave, in 1874, 1614 Republican majority, and the vote ran but 55 short of the registration. Intimidation is, of course, out of the question.

In the North we have heard so much about murders that I was very glad to get hold here of some parish statistics on this subject. The State government, which has almost entirely neglected to punish murderers— being too busily engaged in stealing — has, of course, no such official returns of crime as it ought to possess. I have been able to obtain returns, chiefly made by county clerks and coroners, from only 13 parishes, not counting Plaquemine, which I have before given. From 1868 to 1875 there have been in these 13 parishes 313 murders. Of these, 93 were of whites by whites, 143 were of colored by colored, 28 were of whites by colored, 32 colored by whites, 3 colored by officers of justice, 5 colored by persons unknown, 7 whites by persons unknown, 5 whites by mobs, and 5 colored by mobs.

The State has 57 parishes. Most of the 13 of which I have given returns have a population nearly equally divided between white and black, and I suspect the figures give more than an average number of murders of whites by whites, and less than the average of murders of blacks by blacks. Plaquemine, for instance, not counted in the above list, registered, in 1874, 510 white and 2160 black voters, and there I found that there had been, since 1868, 33 murders, of which 31 were of blacks by blacks. There is good evidence for the statement that the large majority of murders in the State in the last six years were of blacks by blacks, instigated by whisky and jealousy. The negroes drink less whisky this year than two or three years ago, when they were getting much higher wages; but their demand for it is so strong that I find the planters generally sell it to them in the little plantation-stores, having discovered that if they did not, their hands would be running off elsewhere to get it, or some negro would peddle it in the cabins. The plantation negroes commonly carry a razor as a concealed weapon, and, absurd as this seems as a weapon of attack, they inflict serious and often; fatal wounds with it. The razor seems to be their favorite weapon elsewhere also, for I found it so in Delaware. They take to it probably because it is the cheapest tool with a keen edge.

It is not only a fact that crime has not been punished in the State under the Republican rule — neither crime against the person nor against property; but there is a great complaint that the pardoning power has been abused. I have found but one return on the subject, which shows certainly a liberal use of this prerogative. From

January 1, 1873, to March 5, 1874, Governor Kellogg pardoned thirteen murderers (almost one a month) besides six men convicted of manslaughter. The whole number of pardons during this period was eighty-four, and among the offenses thus condoned are poisoning, rape, shooting into a dwelling, burglary, assault with intent to kill, perjury, and bribing witnesses. Now, when society is said by Governor Kellogg to be in a disordered state, and when he himself acknowledges, as ho did to me, that crime is not generally punished, surely it is a serious error to pardon with so free a hand persons convicted of such grave and dangerous crimes as I have mentioned. It can not fail to increase disorder. Unhappily, it can not bring the courts into greater contempt, than their general corruption and inefficiency all over the State, and from the lowest to the highest, have already brought upon them.

To return to the question of my Northern friend: Louisiana is at peace. The people universally accept the Union — nothing is more certain than this. Also, there is no disposition to re -enslave the negro. The planters have discovered that free labor is far more economical than slave. Everywhere planters have been ready to demonstrate to me the profitableness of free labor, and to acknowledge that all their fears of disorganization had proved groundless.

The bitterest Democrat I have met in the State said to me, "We are fortunate in one thing which I little expected at the close of the war: we have the best laboring force in the world." Ho went on to tell me that before the war he had often to pay, for extra bauds which he hired, from one hundred and sixty to two hundred dollars a year, two suits of clothing, rations, and medicine. Now he pays thirteen to fifteen dollars per month and a ration. "And they work just about as well, except when some accursed politician comes up) from New Orleans with a brass band, and sends word, as was done last fall, that General Butler has ordered them all to turn out to a political meeting."

One of the hopeful signs is that I have not heard a single man in the State speculate about "the future of the negro." That sort of nonsense has disappeared. Nor have I anywhere found the negro shy of speaking his mind on political subjects. I laughed at a planter only last evening, who told me how well his hands worked on a system of shares in the crop, of which I shall speak in another place, and how faithful and serviceable they were. He said, " But the scamps all voted against me at the last election." " I'm glad of it," he added, " for I could not have refused them any thing they asked if they had voted for me, and it saved me probably live hundred dollars, for they know how to get a favor for a favor."

I do not exaggerate when I say that the only cause of disorder in the State lies in the corruption and inefficiency of the State and parish governments. Even Marshal Packard tells me the State is now at peace. It has, as every Southern, and, for that matter, every Northern State has, a proportion of lawless and ruffianly persons. This class is not numerous, but is composed of idlers, drunkards, and bravos, who go armed; and when a community is excited, they are ready to commit outrages, not only on blacks, but on whites, even on each other. I was touched by the remark of an elderly man from a remote parish, who said, "The State government, and the courts and officers it gives us, are so inefficient that we have to deal with these ruffianly young men ourselves. I have more than once taken my life in my hand to preserve the peace, when the sheriff was too cowardly or inefficient to do his duty. We have not had a murderer punished in our parish in five years, except one, and he was pardoned out of the penitentiary before his sentence expired. We live near the Texas line, and desperate men come and go easily. Instead of being abused as disorderly, we people deserve praise that we have kept as good order as we have, when the governor has time and again appointed corrupt and inefficient officers, and when, in fact, society has had to be maintained against the abuses and inefficiency of the government by the private effort of the good citizens."

This man spoke the truth. It is a solemn and undeniable fact that the Republican rulers of Louisiana have disorganized society, instead of protecting the good citizens. The only danger to the peace of Louisiana to-day lies in the corruption and inefficiency of her rulers, who call themselves Republicans, and have thus gained the countenance of the Northern Republican party and the support of the Federal Administration. These men have committed a great crime against the State and against the country, the greatest crime which civilized men can commit; for their misrule has struck a blow at the very foundations of society in Louisiana; they have corrupted the public morals, they have degraded and debauched the negroes, whom they were sent to lead into the exercise of citizenship; and, surveying the story of their misrule, I am constrained to say that their plunder of the State, monstrous as it has been, is the least of their offenses, because it is a graver crime to debauch and demoralize a State than to steal its treasure.

Here are a few figures which give some idea of how the affairs of Louisiana have been managed under the Radical rule since 1968:

For mileage, per diem, and contingent expenses the General Assembly of the State cost, in 1860, before the war, $99,435; in 1861, $131,481; in 1866, the year after the war, $164,906; in 1868, the year of reconstruction and of the beginning of Republican rule, $363,156; in 1869, $370,214; in 1870, $722,231; in 1871, $958,956; in 1872, $350,000; in 1873, $461,450; last year, a much smaller sum, over $200,000; but still, the Comptroller of the State says, $60,000 above his estimates of the proper cost.

In 1860 the State printing cost $40,900. In 1867, the year before reconstruction, it cost $75,000. The Republican Legislature of 1868 adopted a system under which each parish has an official organ, which prints at the public cost, not only the laws, but the entire journals of the Legislature and the proceedings of police-juries. This abuse has been checked, but not yet entirely stopped. During its height, these petty journals were, with a very few exceptions, owned by members of the Legislature. Hence these persons every year voted themselves handsome subsidies ; and the State-printing bill, which amounted to $75,000 in 1867, jumped to $431,345 in 1869, $313,920 in 1870, $397,600 in 1871, $154,752 in 1872, and $100, 866 in 1873. That is to say, the reconstructors managed to spend out of the treasury in five years for printing alone very nearly $1,500,000, and a great part of this they voted into their own pockets.

In 1861 the State tax amounted to 29 cents on $100; in 1867, the year before reconstruction, to 37 1/2 cents; in 1868, to 52 1/2 cents; in 1869, to 90 cents; in 1871, to $1.45; in 1872, to $2.15; in 1873, to $2 15; and in 1874, to $1.45, at which it is fixed, now, I believe, by the constitution.

In spite of this enormous increase in the tax rate, the debt of the State has trebled since 1866. In that year the absolute and contingent debt (by which the State accountants here mean the debt owing, and for which the State has engaged itself for the future) amounted to $11,182,377. In 1868, the year of reconstruction, it amounted to $16,885,682. In 1870 it had been run up to $40,456,734.

The report of the Joint Legislative Committee to investigate the State auditor's office — the committee is composed entirely of Republicans — gives the following summary of the State debt at the beginning of the present year. I copy it literally, as it is official:

Floating debt.................................$2,165,171 71
Bonds loaned property banks............. 4,830,683 33
Bonded debt proper.......................22,134,800 00
Contingent debt reported by auditor......10,895,000 00
Contingent debt not reported by auditor.. 9,605,500 00
                                          ——————————
                                          $49,604,155 04
Add trust bonds and bonds missing......   993,194 91
                                          ——————————
      Total...............................$50,597,394 95

The committee add to this statement these remarks :

"In conclusion the commission find that a large portion of the public debt has arisen from extravagance, profligacy, and misuse of the revenues of the State; that as to all that portion created since 1865, the State did not realize over fifty cents on the dollar, nor was the amount realized expended for the benefit of the State to the extent of more than one-half; in other words, the State has not been actually benefited in an amount exceeding one-fourth of the debt created, nor to an amount exceeding one-half of the taxes collected since 1865. The entire balance, say one half of all the taxes and three-fourths of all the present debt, has been squandered, or done worse with, by the administration of the government since that date."

The State revenues, as given in the auditor's reports for the different years, were:

1868	$3,452,069
1869	4,937,759
1870	6,537,939
1871	6,616,843
1872	4,312,033
1873	4,016,690
1874	3,514,332
Total	$33,387,665

— collected in taxes from the people for the support of the State government alone in seven years, besides city and parish taxes.

The various petty monopolies and swindles to which State aid was so profusely given account for a small part of this huge debt and expenditure. Such extravagance as is mentioned by the auditor in his last report (1875), in the following words, accounts for more:

"Thus the number of pages (in the Legislature), which by Act No. 11 of 1872 is limited to ten, at a compensation for each of $180, was increased more than sixty, and vouchers issued to them at from $150 to $180 each; nor was this practice confined to this particular class of employees, but was carried to other classes, such as enrolling and committee clerks, porters, etc."

He also, in the same report, complains that he has vainly tried to get the Legislature to adopt a new plan of assessing property for taxation which "would save the State $156,000 a year." In the auditor's report for the year 1871, complaint was made to the Legislature of the great cost of collecting the taxes. "In 1870," says this report, "the actual commissions paid on account of assessors was $181,975, and the amount paid to taxcollectors $215,411. In 1871 the commissions of tax-collectors amounted to $320,252, and that of assessors to $250,838."

Of course there were some heavy jobs, which helped to run up the debt. For instance, in the auditor's report for 1871, I find a statement that during the two previous years the State, under an arrangement with the firm of Jones & Hugee, lessees of the penitentiary, had issued $500,000 in State bonds for machinery for that institution. The lessees were to pay one-half their clear profits to the State. They paid nothing, and in 1870 transferred their contract to another set of men, the State agreeing thereafter to accept $5000 a year in lieu of all profits, with an increase of $1000 a year. Between 1869 and 1871, in two years, "the penitentiary had cost the State $796,000." "In 1868 the New Orleans, Mobile, and Chattanooga Railroad was chartered in Louisiana, and it was determined to connect Mobile and New Orleans with Houston, Texas. In 1869 the Legislature agreed to Indorse the second-mortgage bonds of the road to the extent of $12,500 per mile, and to make the indorsement for every section of ten miles built. The company built seventy miles, and the State indorsed $875,000 of their second-mortgage bonds. The next Legislature agreed in addition to give the road a State subsidy of $3,000,000 of bonds, and of this they drew $750,000. The company now proposed to build a railroad from Vermillionville to Shreveport, and in 1871 the State agreed to take stock in this enterprise ($2,500,000), paying for it in bonds, and the whole of these bonds were delivered to the company when they had done one day's work on the road. They have never done any more.

That is to say, the company have built in all seventy miles of an uncompleted, and, therefore, worthless road, and received from the State $4,250,000, or over $58,000 a mile, besides a grant of the use of a part of the New Orleans levee, valued at $1,000,000; and they have kept it all. Finally, it remains to be said that two different companies of Northern capitalists offered to build the Houston and New Orleans road without subsidy or State aid of any kind, but the Legislature would not give them a charter.

A great deal of money has been spent and squandered since the war on the reconstruction of the levees and their repair, and Democrats as well as Republicans have taken part in this jobbing, the greatest waste, however, being since 1868. Between 1868 and 1871, $4,750,000 of State bonds were issued for levee purposes, and still there are no levees worthy of the name. Most of the money was spent by a "State Board of Public Works," whose members were appointed by Governor Warmoth. In 1871 a deficient system was adopted, which is still in force, and under which a large part of the revenues of the State has been handed over for a long term of years to a private corporation, with privileges which enable it to misuse and squanders them in a most shocking way.

By the act, this corporation, which was to furnish a million of dollars in capital stock, agreed to build and repair the levees of the State, and to be responsible in damages to the planters and farmers who should suffer loss by overflow or crevasse. In return for this, the Legislature gave it a million dollars down, before it began work, and the proceeds, annually, for a term of years, of a tax of four mills on the whole taxable property of Louisiana ; and authorized it to charge, against this great fund, sixty cents per cubic yard for the work. But a great part of the levee work, when done by plant-ers for themselves, has cost only from fifteen to eighteen cents per cubic yard, and thirty cents for the average of all kinds of work all over the State would be, experts tell me, a high rate. In fact, the first charge was so exorbitant that it has been reduced to fifty cents; and in 1874 the levee tax, which the company continues to receive, was reduced to three mills. But the company never had any money; the levees have not been kept in proper repair, and the losses from overflow have never been so great as since it went into operation ; and, having no capital of its own, if it is sued for damages it must pay these out of the State fund; and thus, in fact, the tax -payers pay their own insurance. The company receives about $720,000 a year.

This was one of the most notorious jobs perpetrated by the Legislature, and attracted attention at the time because a great many members not only received bribes for its support— which was too common an occurrence to be noticed — but actually gave their receipts for the money paid them. The following letter, of which the original is before me, shows how openly legislative bribery was carried on under Warmoth's administration. The writer of it was then member of Assembly, is now State Senator, and member of the State School Board, and, I am sorry to say, is a negro:

House of Representatives, State of Louisiana, New Orleans, February 25th, 1871.

Gentlemen of the Finance Committee of Louisiana Levee Company

"Sirs, —

Please pay to Hon. A. W. Faulkner the amount you may deem proper to pay on account of Levee Bill, I being absent at the time under orders of the House. But would have voted for the bill had I been here. Mr. Faulkner is authorized to receive and receipt for me. Very respectfully, gentlemen,

"Your obedient servant,
"T. B. Stamps"

Surely the brazenness of corruption could go no further than this — when a legislator claims a bribe on the score that he would have performed the corrupt service had he been in his place, and sends his friend not merely to receive, but to receipt for it.

The city of New Orleans is made to pay a very great part of the State tax, and has been, besides, burdened in various ways by the Legislature, which has set apart a large part of its revenues for State or special purposes. It has now a debt of its own of about $22,000,000, and its tax-rate has been run up to three per cent. About $17,000,000 of its bonds are worth but thirty-five cents on the dollar in the market. Here is an example which tells the tale of wasteful misgovernment: An estate, which could have been sold in 1867 forever $1,000,000, showed on its books, in 1872, this remarkable condition : After paying for insurance and usual repairs, the taxes levied that year on the property exceeded the entire rental by $540. In the next year, 1873, the receipts exceeded the taxes, repairs, and insurance by $900. Yet, in 1867, this property netted seven per cent, on over $1,000,000 — that is to say, more than $70,000, after paying insurance, taxes, and repairs.

It is not the wealthy alone who complain. I have spoken with at least a dozen small property-owners in the city, and they all tell the same tale. In the country the small farmers complain that they are forced to pay the heavy taxes, while in many cases their rich neighbors resist, and are allowed to refuse payment or to delay.

I was struck with the story of exasperation told me by a man who said, "One piece of property after another belonging to members of my family had been sold out for taxes. Two years ago we came nearly to the end. We could not sell, and we could not pay the terrible taxes. I went to the sheriff", I and said to him, 'This property which you are advertising is the last possession of my mother and sisters, and their only support. I warn you that on the day you put it up at auction I am going to attend the sale with my double-barreled shot-gun.' And it was not sold. Next year we were fortunately able to pay."

Now, I know the man very well who thus did, and I know him to be a peaceable, law respecting citizen, one of the most important and most useful members of the community in which he lives. He saw that I was shocked and pained at his story, and said, "What could I do? We were wealthy people before the war; we have been contented in our poverty since, and I have worked hard, and lived very economically. My sisters now teach in a public school. But the times are so hard and the taxes so high that it is all we can do to live, and when I saw the last little dependence of my mother and sisters about to be sold to satisfy these cormorants and thieves, I could not stand it."

In the parish of St. Landry alone, as I think I have before stated, there were between November, 1871, and November, 1873, eight hundred and twenty-one sales of plantations and lands for taxes. Yet Louisiana is by nature one of the richest States in the Union, and New Orleans is one of the greatest commercial ports. Is it surprising that the whole white population of the State, except the office-holders and their relatives and intimates, united, in 1874, in the endeavor to overthrow a party which has so abused its powers?

I spent some days looking through the acts of the Legislature of Louisiana since the first reconstruction Legislature, in 1868, and a more amusing and preposterous exhibition of wholesale legislative plundering it would be difficult to imagine. The bare titles of the acts whose sole and transparent purpose was plunder would fill half a dozen of these pages. I must content myself with a brief mention of but a few sample laws granting exclusive privileges, giving away the State's money, creating new offices, or adding to the taxes.

One of the earliest acts of the reconstructors — who are believed to have come into the State as the missionaries of great moral ideas — was the passage of a law giving the exclusive monopoly of selling lottery, policy, and "combination" tickets in the State to a company which calls itself the "Louisiana State Lottery Company."

Lest the profane should imagine that this monopoly was intended to promote the merely selfish advantage of the incorporators, it is distinctly stated in the charter, which forms part of the act, that the lottery company is a purely charitable and beneficent body, created for the unmixed benefit of the people of Louisiana. "The objects and purposes of this corporation are, first, the protection of the State against the great losses heretofore incurred by sending large amounts of money to other States and foreign counties for the purchase of lottery-tickets and other devices, thereby impoverishing our own people; second, to establish a solvent and reliable home institution for the sale of lottery, policy, and other tickets; third, to provide means to raise a fund for educational and charitable purposes for the citizens of Louisiana."

The monopoly is to last twenty-five years; it is made a criminal offense in any one unauthorized by the company to sell any kind of lottery-ticket anywhere in the State; the company is exempted from all taxes and license fees whatever — State, city, or parish; and for these monstrous privileges and exemptions it pays into the State treasury — for the educational fund — the petty sum of forty thousand dollars per annum!

The company is now composed almost entirely of a few men living in New York and New Jersey; on a million of capital they are believed to make not less than seven hundred and fifty thousand dollars clear profit every year; they have established policy-shops and petty gambling dens around the markets and other public places in New Orleans, which perpetually demoralize the laboring class, and particularly negro men and women, and over which the city government has no control; and they have agents and solicitors all over the State, tempting the poor and ignorant to gamble, providing for this end what they call a "combination game," which can be played even by the owner of a ten-cent piece.

In 1868 the Legislature chartered the Mississippi Valley Navigation Company of the South and West, and in 1870 an amendment to the charter gave the company $100,000 of State money, for which the State was to receive stock. The company got the money, but I can not hear that they are in business to-day, though they were authorized to "construct steamboats, warehouses, docks," etc. Another scheme was the Red River Navigation Company, which was authorized to receive $135,000 in State bonds.

The bayous or river estuaries of the State early became a fine field for swindling. For instance, the Legislature of 1870 passed an act incorporating a company to improve Bayou Bartholomew, in the northern part of the State, and granting State bonds to aid the enterprise. Within sixteen days after the passage of the act. State warrants to the amount of $118,000 had been issued to the company. The auditor at that time happened to be an honest man ; he refused to recognize these warrants; suit was brought by the company, and the Supreme Court twice declared the proceedings fraudulent, Ludeling, chief-justice (whom the United States Supreme Court last year denounced for fraud in another matter), alone dissenting; and on a motion to remand the case for a rehearing, which Ludeling granted, Judge Wyly, dissenting, said, "Act 59, to improve the navigation of Bayou Bartholomew, never authorized a contract to exceed $40,000. I regard the contract for $118,000 for that work as a deliberate fraud upon the State. Not a single requirement for letting out and making the contract according to Act 59 seems to have been complied with."

Now, then, mark what follows. The claim was twice denied by the Supreme Court. The Legislature of 1874 created a board of audit, with power to settle outstanding liabilities; and this board, -while I was in New Orleans, quietly allowed a large part of this claim.

A company whose main purpose appears to have been cattle-stealing was organized and chartered in 1874, under the title of "Society for the Prevention of Cruelty to Animals." The Legislature gave it sole and exclusive charge of all the pounds in New Orleans, with authority to seize and arrest animals of all kinds in the streets, and impound them, and charge the owners five dollars a day for their detention, and to sell them outright at the end of eight days. The summary arrest of goats in the outskirts of the city came near creating a mob of Irish women; and, to prevent cruelty to animals, the company at one time, I am told, began to arrest horses left standing in the streets while their riders were transacting business in the shops.

An act of the Legislature to improve Bayous Glaises and Rouge gave the incorporators sole and exclusive power to navigate these bayous with vessels of all kinds, exempted their capital stock from taxation of every kind, and allowed them to levy a toll on all vessels except their own, or which they allow to be used on these bayous. The improvements to be made were very slight.

In 1871 the Mississippi River Packet Company was incorporated by act of the Legislature. . Among the incorporators were Antoine, now lieutenant-governor, then senator; Kelso, Monette, Pinchback, Ingraham, and Barber, all State senators, and Pollard, member of Assembly. The object of the company was to run steamboats on the Mississippi River. The State was pledged to subscribe $250,000 on the organization of the company; and, so far as I can see in the act, it was to enjoy no benefits or privileges whatever.

The same Legislature established the Louisiana Warehouse Company "to promote the interests of commerce." Among the incorporators I find mentioned in the act Senator West, then administrator of improvements in New Orleans, and Collector Casey. The company was authorized to issue bonds to the amount of $1,500,000, and the State was required to guarantee the payment of 'the interest and principal of these bonds on condition that the company should deposit securities equal in value to the bonds issued, which securities, the act says, may be "bank indorsements or other good and solvent bonds!"

By an act authorizing a company to improve Bayous Portage and Yokeley, the State gave the company $100,000 by way of aid; and if the improvements should cost more than this sum, the company was empowered to lay a tax on all the lands benefited, to make up the inefficiency, and to sell for taxes any such lands whose owners had not paid after sixty days' notice. No limit was set of cost, and the company was made its own tax-collector.

A company chartered to improve Loggy Bayou and Lake Bisteneau received $50,000 State aid, and the people say, pulled out about twenty stumps for the money. A company chartered to improve Bayou Terrebonne received the exclusive privilege to improve Bayous Boeuf and Crocodile, and was authorized to receive $80,000, a sum asserted to be preposterously beyond the value of the service.

The Mexican Gulf Canal Company drew $36,000 in bonds from the State in aid of its enterprise, then abandoned it and merged with another company for a different purpose; got control of the drainage fund; fell into the hands of one man; and he, in the name of the company, is now doing a necessary work of drainage at a cost a hundred per cent, higher than responsible citizens stand ready to do it for.

The Legislature even chartered a company and gave it the sole and exclusive right to clean privies in New Orleans, and to empty their contents into the Mississippi River; made it obligatory on citizens to have this service performed at fixed intervals; and established a scale of charges much higher than that at which the service had long been performed.

Even the purchase by the State of the St. Louis Hotel, to be used as a state - house, was a swindling transaction. Several members of the Legislature and others were chartered as the Louisiana National Building Association. They got from the owners of the St. Louis Hotel an agreement to sell that building at a set price, and, this done, made a lease of it to the State for nineteen years at $50,000 a year and entire exemption from taxation. They overshot their mark, and the outcry raised against this act of extortion compelled the annulling of the lease. Thereupon the Citizens' Bank bought the same building outright for $84,000, which the Building Association had leased to the State for $50,000 per annum.

ST. LOUIS HOTEL.

The St. Louis Exchange Hotel
Demolished in 1915

The Louisiana Building Association was enjoined, and could not act under that title. They changed the company's name to the New Orleans National Building Association, bought the hotel for $149,000; and the Hahn Legislature, which met after the dispersion of the Wiltz body, in the spring of 1875, gave $250,000 for the building. These figures and other figures above are authentic. It is not always easy for men to cover up their tracks, and these men have not been careful to do so.

In 1870 the Legislature passed a law authorizing the improvement of the old City Park, a piece of ground which had been held for the purpose many years. During the year two politicians. South worth and Bloomer, got a written agreement from the owners of a large vacant piece of ground — the only large tract, except the old Park, near the city — to sell it to them at a fixed price — $600,000.

The Legislature of 1871 next amended the park improvement law so as to allow the commissioners to buy land for a new park, and made an appropriation of money to carry it into effect. The governor now appointed park commissioners, and one of these, by an odd coincidence, was Southworth, who was also at that time recorder of mortgages. Pinchback was another park commissioner, and Senator West another. Southworth and those interested with him next acquired title to the property they had held under agreement, but paid only $65,000 down ; the remainder of the purchase money was left on mortgage. Then, on the 15th of August, they sold to the city one -half of their purchase for $800,000, receiving $65,000 in cash and $19.5,000 in bonds, while $540,000 of debt was transferred from their shoulders to the city's.

It is the common street talk here, that, "after this transaction was completed, Antoine, the lieutenant-governor, went about complaining that Pinchback had cheated him out of $40,000, which he had in some way expected to get out of the affair." The park is still unimproved; it is used as a cowpasture; but the city is paying interest on its debt for a park.

I could go on indefinitely with stories of this kind, for I have only culled here and there out of the acts of the Legislature, and as I turned over the leaves of the books I met with dozens of petty swindles: ferry monopolies granted to members of the Legislature, oftenest at points where ferries already existed ; acts to remove a county-seat to some member's farm or plantation ; the creation of new counties; and acts incorporating a multitude of petty villages, some having less than three hundred inhabitants, afflicting their inhabitants with a city government, mayor, and administrators, authorizing these officers to lay taxes " not to exceed the parish tax;" and providing fees and salaries for the needless officers. Nor was even this the worst. I know some such little towns which have never, since their incorporation, been ruled by the officers they chose: on some pretext the elected men are rejected, and the governor then fills the vacancies thus created.

So severe has been the pressure of taxation, and so greatly has business been prostrated in the State by the long-continued misrule, that, according to an official report, in three years, 1871-'73, 47,491 tax seizures were made in the city of New Orleans by the sheriff; I have seen parish newspapers three of whose sides were filled with advertisements of tax sales — this not in parishes which prudently refused to pay taxes, as q few remote ones have done; and I have before me a statement, certified by the recorder, showing that from the 10th of November, 1871, to the 18th of November, 1873, 821 tracts of land and plantations in the parish of St. Martin were actually sold by the tax-collector for State and parish taxes. Yet, in spite of their exorbitant commissions, the official report of the State auditor for 1874 contains a list of defaulting tax-collectors containing twenty names, who are reported to be in default to the amount of $200,000.

Nor can it be said that the valuations are low, for in New Orleans the assessors receive by law five per cent, for their work, and the assessment is made annually. In the parishes, the tax-collectors, who have more or less to do with the assessments, receive ten per cent, of their collections, and in many cases it has been proved that they received taxes in greenbacks, and turned them in in depreciated scrip.

The city of New Orleans, being largely Democratic, has been afflicted with a double set of assessors and collectors — one for the State, the other for the city. The State's annual assessment of property in New Orleans cost, in 1871, $100,000. This wrong is so great that in the State auditor's report for 1872 I read, "Within the parish of Orleans two per cent, on the amount of the tax levied would be a fair compensation to the tax-collector, acting in the capacity of assessor; or, should the General Assembly so determine, an agreement with the city administration, at a nominal expense, to furnish complete copies of their assessment rolls, would thus make a further reduction of expenses without detriment to the interests of the State." And again, "Within the parish of Orleans assessors are paid in percentage upon the amount of their assessment rolls. As a consequence, experience has shown that great injustice is done by placing assessments very high — in some instances 150 per cent, above the true value of property. A large commission is thus paid by the State; and afterward, in many instances, the assessment is reduced by order of court or otherwise, thereby the State losing the compensation paid the assessor, besides the annoyance and expense it unjustly entails upon the tax-payer.

The assessment and collection of the State tax for New Orleans cost $175,000 last year, I am told. The result of all this is that property in New Orleans is almost worthless, and totally unsalable. Nobody likes to be a tax-payer. A house and lot assessed for $36,000 was sold in March, 1875, for $11,000. Good residence property has fallen since 1868 more than fifty per cent, in value. Rents produce very small net income.

Several years ago the Legislature was persuaded to pass a law that the parish tax should not exceed the State tax in amount, and a member of the ring here showed me this law to prove that the complaints of exorbitant taxation in the country parishes must be without foundation. He forgot to tell me of another law which allows the holder of parish scrip to sue the parish, and directs the judge, in the case of such suit, to lay a special tax on the parish for the payment of the scrip at par. This is continually done, and the business of buying up depreciated parish scrip, with the object of forcing the parish to pay it by getting a judgment against it, is so common that several tax-collectors have admitted to me that they had engaged in it. It is a perfectly safe speculation.

One can not study the politics of Louisiana and her politicians long without becoming aware that the Radical leaders are, as political managers, more skillful and adroit than the Conservatives. They understand the generalship of a partisan campaign ; and if they only had a little principle or a little of that wisdom which would teach them that misgovernment must have an end, some of them might even now rule the State for another term of years. Their difficulty is that they have so long used the worst arguments, and the most corrupt and corrupting means, that they can not stop without running a risk of losing their adherents. I believe Governor Kellogg would now like to make his administration honest; but he would also like to go to the Senate, and the result is that he will be no more efficient than those who control him will let him be.

The subalterns, the petty officers of the Radical army, are, as a general thing, a very poor set. With here and there an exception, they hang on to office with a tenacity which is almost pitiful; it is a sort of death-grip. A Radical member of the Legislature, whom I asked why he opposed the Wheeler adjustment, said, with a pathetic quaver in his voice, "Because if that is passed, it means that I shall go out."

I thought he meant that he would be driven out of the State, and asked him if he really feared violence.

He replied, " Not at all; you don't understand me; I mean that I shall have to go out of politics. If the Conservatives once get a majority in the House, they'll carry the State at the next election."

This man is a member of the Legislature; he had enjoyed three or four terms, but he wanted another. To "go out" seemed to him like dying does to common mortals, and his dolorous face was a study. It never occurred to him to think that the Conservatives had already carried the State, and were, in the adjustment, giving up a part of the majority they had fairly gained.

The strongest, and probably the most dangerous, politician in the State on either side is the United States marshal, Packard. He is reputed to be a man of unflinching courage, strong will, and no scruples. A citizen of Maine, he has lived in Louisiana since the war; he married there, became early known as a shrewd and successful political organizer; and was made United States marshal by General Grant. His body is large and somewhat heavy, and his mind does not move rapidly. His single idea is to keep Louisiana in Republican hands, and his only method is to mass the colored vote.

"Packard," said an honest Republican to me in New Orleans, "stands in our way in making a split in parties here, which it is so necessary for the welfare of the State to do. He always wants to mass the colored vote; he believes in the color-line. He discourages every attempt to bring the right kind of white men into our party, and always has something against a new man who would share our political fortunes — that he was in the rebel army, or something of that kind. I think but for Packard we might really make such a break and reorganization of parties as would give the State rest and permanent good government."

In Washington, last winter, Mr. Packard appeared as one of the strenuous advocates of the Habeas Corpus and Force bill, and his argument was that, if this measure were passed, he would guarantee to carry the State for the Republican party in 1876; but if it were not passed, he would promise nothing.

Here in New Orleans he opposed the Wheeler adjustment at first, and very strongly; and it was one of his adherents who amused me by denouncing this adjustment with a good deal of profanity, as "Sure to denationalize the Louisiana question."

Stephen B. Packard

Amidst the general demoralization and corruption, it is a part of Packard's strength that he is believed to be peculiarly honest. He has a little the air of a fanatic, but he is in reality an extremely

adroit and unscrupulous politician. They say he also wants to go to
the Senate.

As a politician he tolerates no rival near his throne. I was told
of a case where he imagined that a Republican was obtaining too
much influence in a parish. He sent up — it was last year — a steam-
boat with a brass band and some " organizers," and set up a rival
Republican organization, whose aim was to drive out the Republi-
can leaders whom he did not like. It was, as it happened, one of his
failures ; but it sufficiently shows that he means to rule.

The office of United States marshal in one of these Southern
States gives a man very extraordinary powers; for, so far from
Washington, and among a people whose complaints are not much
listened to, he is a kind of viceroy. Under the Enforcement acts he
may make summary arrests on frivolous pretexts; he may use the
army to do it; he is a peace officer with practically no superior, very
loosely defined powers, and small responsibility, particularly if he is
trusted by the President. That you may not think I overstate the au-
thority lodged in Marshal Packard's hands, I transcribe here part of
a general order to " commanding officers of posts and detachments,"
and issued from "Head-quarters, Department of the Gulf:"

"Whenever the United States marshal of the district in which
you are serving, or any of his deputies, shall make written appli-
cation to you for a detachment of troops to protect him or them in
the performance of their duties, or to aid him or them to serve legal
process, you will at once furnish such detachment, reporting your
action to these head-quarters."

Now, Mr. Packard is not only United States marshal, for he
unites with this office another of even greater importance — he is
chairman of the Republican State Central Committee.

That is to say, the United States troops in Louisiana are placed by
the Federal Administration under the orders of the chief manager
of the Republican party.

Every United States soldier in the State must obey the orders of the chairman of the Republican State Central Committee.

Such a situation, even if it were not abused, would be liable to suspicion, and must give just cause of complaint to the other party. Moreover, it is hardly possible that it should not be misused. For instance : It is in evidence before the Congressional committee that, just before the election of 1874, United States cavalry appeared in several parishes, armed with blank warrants of arrest issued in New Orleans by the marshal.

But why should a citizen, innocent of wrong, be alarmed at such things?

Well, because it is not a pleasant experience, which some of them have had at Mr. Packard's hands, to be dragged down to New Orleans from a distant country parish, put under bail, and then allowed to go home again at their own expense. I have heard from army officers several cases where such an arrest of a man against whom nothing was ever proved or attempted to be proved, caused great alarm and suffering to his family, which was dependent on his daily labor for support; and of other cases where men lay out in the woods for days, though conscious of innocence, out of a dread of Packard's blank warrants.

Moreover, while such warrants were sent abroad just before the election, none were sent out after the election, when, if ever, it might be supposed that offenses had been committed.

In a State where a political struggle of great bitterness and vital importance is going on, the chief of one party thus, you see, has authority to command at any time, at any place, and for such purpose as he may decide, the services of the United States army, and may and does use soldiers to arrest his political opponents. It is at least an Inconvenience to the other party. No doubt they would like to have troops, too.

The supervisors of registration are appointed by the governor, and are naturally, and in fact, partisans of the party in power. Fraudulent registration has been proved on several occasions; and I have before me a registration certificate now, blank as to name, date, and residence, but duly signed by the supervisor of Assumption Parish. The certificate is as follows:

"UNITED STATES OF AMERICA.

"State of Louisiana, Parish of ———, ———, 18—.

"I, ——— ———, do solemnly swear, affirm, that I was duly registered as a qualified elector of the parish of ———, in the month of ———, 18—; that a certificate of such registration was at the time issued to me by the supervisor of registration for the said parish, which certificate of registration has been lost or destroyed.

"I am —— years of age, ———; my occupation is ———; and I now reside at ———. I have no other place of residence. ——— ———.

"Sworn and subscribed to, this —— day of ———, A.D. 18—, before me.   E. E. GAURE,

"*Supervisor of Registration for the Parish of Assumption.*"

"DUPLICATE.

"[Original No. —.]

"UNITED STATES OF AMERICA.

"State of Louisiana, Parish of ———.

"I hereby certify that ——— ——— was on the —— day of ———, 18—, duly registered as a qualified elector on the original registry of this parish, No. ———, a citizen of the United States, and residing at ———, born in ———, age ———, naturalized in ——— Court, State of ———, —— day of ———, 18—. Now resides at ———.

"Witness my hand, this —— day of ———, A.D. 18—.

"E. E. GAURE,

"*Supervisor of Registration for the Parish of Assumption.*"

The nature of this instrument, which asserts a personal appearance of the applicant for registration, makes it, of course, impossible to be legally signed in blank.

Now, spurious registration papers would be of little value but for a peculiar clause in the election laws, which authorizes a voter to vote at any poll in his parish, or at any poll in the ward of his residence in New Orleans. A parish is a county. What is to prevent a man with a dozen registration certificates in his pocket from voting at a dozen polls in his county? Nothing, except the difficulty of getting to so many on the same day. This rule, which may have been made for good reasons — I don't know as to that — is in effect an invitation to fraud.

Finally comes the returning board for the State, named by the Senate, which sits at New Orleans and overhauls the returns, and, as was proved to the satisfaction of the Congressional committee this year, substantially does what it pleases with them.

Among other things it hears charges of intimidation, and, in order that every thing may be in readiness to bring forward such charges, these prudent Republicans print beforehand "intimidation certificates," to which ignorant negroes are persuaded to set their "+." marks. Here is an example, and on the other side of the same paper you will find a certificate of the same Narcisse Jacques, which also is sworn to before a notary public, and which also tells in detail quite a little tale of intimidation — but of a different kind:

"State of Louisiana, Parish of St. Martin.

"Before me, the undersigned authority, personally came and appeared Mr. Narcisse Jacques, a resident of the parish of St. Martin, who, being first duly sworn, declares and says that he is entitled to register and vote in the said parish of St. Martin, that he is a Republican, and that he would have voted the ticket annexed hereto, including for member of the Forty-fourth

Congress, had he not been prevented from registering by fear of personal violence from armed bodies of men who have been patrolling the country.

"His mark:
Narcisse + Jacques.

"Sworn and subscribed before me, this 27th day of October, 1874. Gustave Baker;
"Justice of the Peace.

"Before the undersigned authority, a justice of the peace of the parish of St. Martin, personally came and appeared Narcisse Jacques, a freedman of the parish of St. Martin, who, after being duly sworn, said and declared that the paper on which is written the affidavit on the other side was handed to him by Oneziphone Delahoussaye, the sheriff" of the parish of St. Martin, and that, though he affixed his mark to said affidavit, he was deceived as to its contents; that said affidavit is false; that he was not prevented registering, and so informed Gustave Baker, the justice of the peace, and Oneziphone Delahoussaye, Jun., the sheriff"; that said affidavit was signed by him in the Federal camp established at Breaux Bridge, in the parish of St. Martin, before and during the last election; and that he had previously been threatened by one Robert Allen, of the parish of St. Martin, a Radical leader, that, unless he registered and voted the Radical ticket, he (affiant) would be arrested, tried, hanged, or killed by the Federal cavalry then engaged in gathering negroes to the registration office. The threats of the said Robert Allen were made in the presence of Darmas Giudry, his employer, who told him to do as he wished and thought proper, and lent him a horse to go to Breaux Bridge; that the said Robert Allen told affiant's employer, Darmas Giudry, that he (Giudry) would also be arrested by the Federal cavalry.

"His mark:

Narcisse + Jacques.

"Witness to the above mark. Euo. A. Duchamp.
"Sworn to and subscribed this 2Sth day of December, A.D. 1874. Oscar Halphen, J. P."

It is a singular fact that in the greater number of parishes the registration lists of 1874 show that the colored registered voters are more numerous, compared with the colored population, than the white registered, compared with the white population, taking the census of 1870 as a basis. For instance, in Plaquemine Parish the registry lists show one white name for every seven and one-fifth of the total white population; but one black name for every three and one-eighth of the total colored population. But while I was in Plaquemine, out of a panel of forty-eight names drawn for jurors, from the registry lists of 1874, only twelve could be found. The other thirty-six were non-existent— that is to say, they were fraudulently registered names. In St. Charles the whites registered are one in three and a half, the blacks one in two and a half, of the respective population. In St. James, the white registry was one in four and a half, the black one in two and a half, of their population. In St. Landry, where it was pretended that there was intimidation, white and black both registered one in four and a half of their population. In Carroll, the whites registered five and one-third, and the blacks three and seven-tenths, of their population. In Terre Bonne, the registered voters stood — white, four and seven-eighths; black, three and two-thirds; and so on. In many parishes the proportions were reversed; but in the greater number the colored meu registered a larger proportion to their population than the whites to theirs. This does not look much like intimidation.

Finally, the vote of 1874 was uncommonly full. "The whole number of votes registered was 167,604. Of these, 146,523 voted. This is a larger proportion of registered voters than usually vote in any of the Northern States." So say the Congressional committee.

"When a man marries, his troubles begin," says an old song. In Louisiana, when a man votes the Conservative ticket, his troubles begin. He must prove that he voted, and that he did not frighten some other body from voting; and when ho has done that, then the returning board may, after all, turn him out.

I have gone into this detail to show you that it is no joke to carry an election against the Republicans in Louisiana. If the party in power were united, and had the Federal Government to support them, they could easily, with all this machinery, from Packard to printed intimidation certificates and returning board, remain in for a century.

But, 1st. They are no longer united. A portion of the Republicans certainly desire honest government. They are a small minority of the party, but they are hopeful.

2d. The negroes are becoming a nuisance to their corrupt white allies. Under the jurisdiction of Pinchback and other ambitious colored leaders, they begin to grasp after all the offices. "We have the majority," they say: "we cast the votes; the offices belong to us; we do not need you." They are ready to give judgeships to the whites; but the Legislature, the sheriffs' places, the police-juries, (county supervisors) — all the places where money is to be spent or appropriated — they demand, in those parishes where they are the majority.

"I was very glad of the affair of the 14th of September in New Orleans," said a Republican to me. This was the affair in which M'Enery took possession of the government.

I asked him why, and he said, "We have a very heavy colored majority in my parish. We have always managed honestly, and vigilantly protected the blacks in all their rights; but we have given the important places to intelligent and honest whites. Last summer I suddenly found that some colored leaders were quietly getting up an opposition to our management, and were determined to turn us out, and put in an entire colored set of office-holders. All our white people were uneasy; for an ignorant and corrupt policejury and sheriff might run us into heavy debt. The blacks would not listen to arguments or appeals from us white Republicans, who had always been their allies and protectors. Just then came the 14th of September; the news of M'Enery's success flew up to our parish; it was believed that the Federal Government would recognize him; the negroes were alarmed; they flocked around me again, and were very ready to heed the good counsels of those of us who had been for years, as they knew, their safe guides and advisers, but whom just before they had been quite ready to throw overboard with contempt."

JOHN F. M'ENERY.

This incident will give yon the key to an important part of the situation in Louisiana and in Mississippi as well. The blacks are not wise enough to resist the allurements of their own corrupt leaders. Office has great temptations for them; and the strongest Radicals have confessed to me that the blacks have no shame about bribery or corruption, no sense of the dignity of office. I speak of them, of course, as a class. There are exceptions.

You will see that no tax-payer, no matter of what party, can afford to give up entirely to the colored voters.

The Conservative politicians have not been wise. They have too often been ruled by their tempers. For instance, under the natural irritation of misgovernment, much of which is truly blamable to the ignorant blacks whom the Radicals have brought into power, the Conservatives in State convention last year at Baton Rouge, adopted a resolution declaring that they would nominate no colored men to any office whatever. It was seen by themselves to be so foolish an act, that no sooner had the convention adjourned, than in thirteen parishes the same men did actually nominate colored men on their tickets. But they were too late. Their adroit opponents made full use of the Baton Rouge platform, and in most instances prevented the break which the wiser part of the Conservatives had sought to make.

An intelligent negro in one of the country parishes expressed to me his disgust at the bad character of the men nominated and elected by the Radicals in 1874 in his parish.

"But," I said, " if you knew that, why did you not vote for the compromise ticket, which also had colored men on it, and honest, intelligent ones, I am told?"

He replied, "It came too late. The Radical organizers had already been around among our people; our ticket was nominated and our people pledged to support it, and the Baton Rouge platform made them feel angry." And so they voted for men whom they knew to be corrupt.

It is not nice; but it is a sample of Louisiana politics.

The real embarrassment in the future lies with Packard and Pinchback. They believe in the color-line, and Pinchback is an unscrupulous, and, with his own people, a very influential, politician.

The colored people, unfortunately, are very susceptible to such influences as his. They are — their best friends and most zealous supporters openly confess it — incapable of independent political action. They require a leader. This is so true that the office of "organizer" is one of the most important in the Radical machinery in Louisiana. He is a person sent into country parishes from New Orleans some weeks or months before election, to gather up the colored vote; to appoint and hold meetings; to instruct the local leaders, who are mostly preachers and school-teachers, and to organize the party.

"We had a light colored vote in our parish," said a Conservative to me; "but there was no intimidation. The organizer came up late, and fell sick as soon as he got there, and the negroes had no one to drill them and tell them what to do."

Now, Pinchback understands organization. He has at this time a propagandist of his views in many parishes, and it is said he means to make himself, if he can, master of the colored vote. I believe he can not do it; but he can do much mischief.

It is a grave misfortune for Louisiana that in her crisis she has so weak a governor. I believe that Governor Kellogg has a sincere wish to do right; but he has no force of character; he has no influence over those who rule with him. He lacks the iron grip which is needed to bring reform. He himself complained to me in New Orleans, after the adjournment of the Legislature, that the State Superintendent of Public Instruction (a colored man) had just appointed two notoriously corrupt men to be president and treasurer of the school board of a parish. I asked him how he came to permit such a wickedness. He replied, "The colored Senator Blunt demanded it. Brown, the superintendent, weakly gave in to him. I am sorry — but what am I to do ?" One listens with contempt to such an excuse, which no man would make who really commanded his administration. By law the superintendent appoints; but a governor

who was a strong man would know how to resist such action. The
good Kellogg only drifts, and hopes he is drifting toward the United
States Senate. But, so drifting, he fatally impedes reforms; he allows
things to be done which imbitter the passions of men, and make
them hopeless of reform; he really bands together the white men,
who have all to lose by continued bad government, and all to gain
by good, and the great mass of whom would to-day be happy and
content with good government on any terms.

Many of them, indeed, would vote to make General Grant Presi-
dent for life, and Louisiana a province, because, as a very respect-
able and intelligent man said to me but the other day, "In that case
we should at least have equal protection, and could appeal direct to
Caesar for justice, and against robbery." It is not pleasant to hear
such, words from an American citizen.

The only sure remedy, I am persuaded, lies in the absolute non-
interference of the Federal power. If to-day it were known that the
Federal Government would not interfere in the affairs of Louisiana
on any account except for rebellion against the Federal Govern-
ment, the influence of those Republicans who sincerely desire good
government would be increased a hundred-fold. They would be
able to extinguish at once the power of the colored demagogues; for
the negro dares to be politically corrupt only because he profoundly
believes that the Federal arm will protect him in his acts; he has
always seen it do so. Take away the constant menace of Federal
interference, and the whole body of corruptionists will at once sink
out of sight, as they did in Arkansas.

Nor do I believe that any serious disorder would happen in
the State. The good people would know that they could hope to
control the government by fair and peaceable means, and would
have its help in controlling the disorderly whites. There is not the
least disposition to fall into trouble with the Federal power. There
is no hostility to the Union or the Government. The negro laborers

are too valuable to be abused; for free labor is a very great and universally acknowledged success.

The spirit of Louisiana is not bad; he who says it is has, I do not hesitate to assert, some bad motive.

There are a few parishes, like Franklin, where human life is held cheap, where ruffians rule, and where one might, without exaggeration, say that, under the careless sway of the Republican rulers, outlaws have mastered society. But even in these parishes, of which there are but two or three at most, no one pretends that murder is practiced for political purposes.

Franklin, for instance, was the refuge of deserters and outlaws during the war; it is thinly populated, contains but few blacks, and, I think, from what I have heard from both Democrats and Republicans, it has substantially no law except that of the pistol and knife. "The people are getting very tired of it," said a Democrat to me. "Property is unsalable; nobody goes there; and they would welcome law and order if they could get it."

I said there were perhaps two or three such parishes, but I know of only this one. Its condition is probably worse than that of some of the coal counties of Pennsylvania, but not much worse. Neither Warmouth nor Kellogg has done any thing to improve it.

But the great body of the white people of the State are good citizens, and they have learned a terribly severe lesson of the importance of justice, peace, and order in the last ten years. They have learned to respect the rights of the negro, and they and the blacks ought to be trusted with self-government. There is no other way to reform abuses in the State; and, what is still more important, a continuance of the Federal protectorate will speedily result in making life intolerable even to the white Republicans, or, at least, to that part of them who have property in the State; for, as I pointed out before, it is the worst class of colored demagogues who are now coming to the surface to take command.

The agricultural industry of Louisiana divides itself broadly into two parts — sugar and cotton. The upper part of the State is mainly engaged in cotton-culture; the lower, in the production of sugar. But, as in some of the northern and western parishes stock-raising is also practiced, so on the low alluvial lands intersected by the Mississippi, the Atchafalaya, and the numerous bayous which lead out of these streams, rice is a considerable and profitable crop as well as sugar; and latterly the small planters begin to set out orange orchards, the few orchards now in bearing being very profitable. This tree requires ten years in this climate to come into full bearing, and is liable while young to be cut down by frost. It is not a sure crop here, is subject to the scale insect, and the orange-planter needs to select with some care the site of his orchard, and to seek protection against the cold north winds of the spring season. But the tree bears well, and has much less care than it should have; and the crop finds a very ready sale for cash, the orchardist usually, I bear, selling his fruit on the tree, and at a gross valuation made when the oranges are ripening. The flowers, also, have a market value.

A few large sugar-planters are beginning the systematic culture of the orange; and where the situation is favorable to the tree, it makes a very profitable crop. At twelve years after planting it should yield one thousand dollars an acre, with a trilling cost for cultivation and care.

Along the river or the bayou there is usually a strip of land from half a mile to a mile deep; back of that come forest and swamp, and beyond that, probably, the face of another bayou. The land is flat, but falls a little from the river toward the swamp; so that when a rise of the waters comes, the plantation is overflowed from the back first, unless, of course, the levee in front breaks. Many plantations have a back as well as a front levee, and often you see a pumping wheel and engine, which are needed to get rid of the rain-water. They say of Florida that the water is so close to the surface that you may dig down anywhere two feet deep and go a-fishing; and these sugar and rice lands are at this season not much drier. The banks of the stream are fringed with live-oaks, and in the shade of these the plantation-house is usually placed, with the sugar-house near-by, and the cottages of the laborers beyond that. On some of the bayous which are quite narrow, the plantation lines extend on both sides, and the fields are connected with the sugar-house by floating bridges, which are swung to one side to allow a steamboat to pass. On the Mississippi the high levees partly conceal the buildings, and from the deck of a steamboat the view of roof-lines above the levee gives the landscape a very quaint appearance.

In many places rice is the crop of the small farmers — men with one hundred or two hundred acres of land. It requires less capital than sugar, and is sufficiently profitable. It depends, of course, on the waters rising succinctly high to flood the laud at the proper time. To accomplish this, flooding ditches are cut, and water is let in through the levee by simple flood-gates. About Point á la Hache such ditches and gates are found at intervals of every few hundred feet for miles of the river-front. In a good season the yield, I am told, is from twelve to fifteen barrels per acre, which ought to bring five dollars per barrel. The expense is about twenty dollars per acre, which includes taking off" the crop. In some parts the people continue to cut it with a sickle, and I have seen it threshed out by driving horses over it in a large circle. But reapers and steamthresh-ers are coming into use, and the rice country bas always mills to which the farmers take their rice to get it bulled. In the rice-fields the colored laborer receives one dollar a day, and feeds himself

In some places, as on the Atchafalaya and about Grand Lake, live-oak timber is cut and shipped to different parts of the world. One of the important petty industries of Lower Louisiana is the collection of the moss which bangs in long festoons from all the trees, particularly from the oak. Negroes and white men alike devote themselves to this, and the quantity brought to New Orleans annually is quite large. On the sugar-plantations, when fire-wood is cut the moss is usually the perquisite of the colored men, and they understand bow to prepare it for market, and make some pocketmoney in this way.

Sugar, however, is the main crop of Southern Louisiana. Various causes make it just now a precarious crop; and sugar-plantations in some of the best locations in the State could be bought in the spring of 1875 for less money than the machinery of the sugar-houses cost. I was surprised to find that a large number of Northern and North-western men have come down there since the war, and bought sugar-estates. Some of these manage their plantations with the help of overseers, and live here only in the winter; others manage their own places. As you pass up a bayou on the steamboat, the white-washed cottages and neater culture generally tell you that here a Northern man has settled with capital enough to carry on this business to advantage. Many of the plantations are still in the hands of the old planters, and often these have a dilapidated look, which shows that their owners are in embarrassed circumstances.

The bad condition of the levees has brought serious loss to many planters, especially in the Atchafalaya and Teche country; and there is a general complaint of high taxation and wasteful expenditure of public money.

The planters, without exception, so far as I have heard them speak, are thoroughly satisfied with the colored man as a laborer. I do not mean to say that they have no fault to find; but they say that the negroes are orderly, docile, faithful to their engagements, steady laborers in the field, readily submitting to directions and instructions, and easily managed and made contented. This applies to cotton as well as sugar planters, and all is summed up in the phrase I most frequently heard used, "We have the best laboring class in the world."

Their faults are mainly of carelessness with such property as mules and farming-implements, and killing cattle and hogs. As to the first, several planters told me they had found it useful to give the charge of animals entirely to a special person, who fed and cared for them. But it appears to make no difference whether the mules belong to the planter or to the laborer; the latter is as conscientiously careless of his own as of another's property. It is part of the heedlessness bred of slavery, and it will take time to be bred out, as it was bred in.

As to killing cattle and hogs, this is a custom which arises, in part, out of a slovenly way of letting animals run half wild in the woods without that care which marks special ownership. It is a matter which the planters are meeting gradually by letting the laborers keep stock of their own, and thus making it to their interest to put down the indiscriminate theft. A Northern man, a planter, told me that he had brought from the North thirty-four cows, and all had been killed but two, which, for safety, he now kept within the door-yard of his dwelling. I asked if his laborers were generally dishonest, and he replied emphatically, no ; he would trust any one of them, he said, with ten thousand dollars to carry to town, without fear of loss ; he had never missed any articles from his house, where he had colored servants, and where the women from the quarters often came. But he could keep chickens and turkeys only with the utmost difficulty and care; and as for cows and hogs, it was entirely out of the question.

The laborers on the sugar-plantations receive from thirteen to fifteen dollars per month; a cottage, usually of two rooms, and a garden patch near it; a ration of pork and corn-meal, rather more than enough for a hearty man; and a corn patch, which the laborer cultivates for himself on Saturday afternoon with the planter's teams. About their cottages they can keep chickens and pigs, if they like; and often they have a horse, a cow, and even an old carriage of some kind, in which they drive out on Sunday with great satisfaction, crowding in wife and children.

The planter usually has on his place a store where necessaries and luxuries are sold? and among the former whisky is reckoned, I am sorry to say. They tell me the blacks will have it, and it is better to sell it in moderation on the place than to compel them to go to a distance for it. As the sugar-plantations are all situated upon navigable streams, they are exposed to a serious nuisance in the shape of peddling boats, which sail up and down with a license from the State to sell various matters, among which whisky is prominent. These anchor opposite a plantation for a day or two, and carry away, not only all the spare cash, but chickens and other "truck" which the colored people may have raised.

The negro is fond of credit. Few of them, I find, are sufficiently forehanded to deal for cash. They have credit at the store; and it is the planter's object to so manage the laborer's account that he shall have a pretty little sum at Christmas, which he thereupon mostly spends during Christmas-week with very great satisfaction. If he has been allowed to draw out all of his account beforehand he is dissatisfied, and likes to remove, thinking that he has not done well — no matter how clearly he is shown that he was wasteful during the year. Only a very few lay by money ; but occasionally a negro was pointed out to me who had several hundred dollars ahead.

One thing greatly pleased me: the black man pays his debts. All the petty shopkeepers, of whom the country is full, are ready to give credit to the negroes. It was a question I asked very often, and always received the same reply, "They always pay up." Among the rice-planters, where the blacks work by the day, they frequently hire cottages, and the owner of some of these told me he would rather have negroes than whites for tenants, because they paid more promptly. A country store-keeper said to me, "Ninety per cent, of my sales are to colored people, and ninety per cent, of my bad debts are owed by whites."

I had read somewhere in the North a complaint that the planters refused to sell land to the negroes. The case I found stands thus: In the sugar country the negro does not aim to buy twenty or forty acres, and plant cane for himself. He would need to have the cane ground; and the business is too hurried at the close of the season to get this done with certainty and at the proper time. But they like to own au acre or two, on which they place a cabin ; and this home-stead makes them contented. Unluckily, they do not improve their places; invariably I have found them in the roughest and most dis-orderly condition. Now, naturally, no man likes to sell a corner of his estate to such purchasers; and the planters very justly and very generally refuse to sell such little patches to negroes. Some would divide their estates into hundred-acre tracts, but there are few pur-chasers for such parcels. Many others hold on to their large estates, even when they have not capital enough to work them; and I have seen some plantations which were not worked at all, but on which the owners paid the taxes, and waited for better times. For my part, I do not much blame them. Nobody, except a land-speculator, likes to sell land; especially where it has been his home. And these people are not land-speculators.

It is not uncommon, however, for a speculator to buy a hundred acres near a town, and divide it into two-acre tracts, which are readily sold to colored people at a great advance. I have seen several such villages, and certainly the regular rows of neatly whitewashed cabins on the plantation look, and arc, far more comfortable.

In the cotton country it is not very uncommon to find negroes owning twenty or forty acres; and they can always buy land if they want to. The great majority, however, as yet, prefer to cultivate the laud on shares, either furnishing their own teams or only their labor; and in the rich Louisiana bottoms they make handsome returns in this way.

The sugar-planter lies, in all countries where he is found, under a practical disadvantage, because ho combines two callings very different in their nature — he is both a farmer and a manufacturer. I found this recognized in the Sandwich Islands, where one or two of the shrewdest planters have tried the experiment of inducing the natives to raise cane and bring it to their mills to the ground. In this way the risk of the crop is divided; and this is so great that a large sugar-planter maybe fatally embarrassed by the loss of a single crop, or by a trilling fall in the price of sugar. There are undoubtedly some difficulties in the way of dividing the business; but in several of the sugar counties of Louisiana planters are making the attempt to turn the mere raising of cane over to laborers and small farmers, and with a promise of success.

In Plaquemine, Mr. Dymond, of New York, has begun to buy cane and grind it at his mill, and with profit to himself and to those who raise the cane. One farmer told me that the experiment last year, which he made only because his own sugar-house had burned down, was so far successful that this year he was putting a part of his land in rice, and over two hundred acres in cane. He sold last year one hundred and seventy-five acres of cane for five dollars a ton — he cutting it, and loading it on the barge which carried it to the mill; and he thought the returns satisfactory.

In Terre Bonne I found an intelligent young planter, a Louisianan, who was trying a different plan, and, as he thought, with the promise of success. He has made a contract for five years with his laborers, under which they take of him on an average ten acres per hand, he furnishing seed-cane, cane land, houses, fire- wood, fences, and land for a corn patch; they supplying teams, tools, labor, and feeding themselves, and taking half the crop. The men work in squads of half a dozen. "When the cane is ready to cut, the planter takes charge, and uses all the teams and men for the common purpose of getting the cane in and the sugar made. At this time also he hires extra hands, and the tenants pay half the cost of these. The planter advances all the money needed, and, in fact, makes advances of food and other supplies also to the tenants, which is the evil custom of the country. The cost of taking the cane from the field and turning it into sugar is about twenty dollars an acre.

Under this system this planter told me that the men worked more zealously than ever before. He had even sold them teams on a credit of three years; and the result of the first year was that the tenants lived, and paid one-third the cost of their teams; and of eleven squads, the members of seven came out at the close of the season one hundred dollars per man ahead. As for himself, he said he had lost money for several years; but last year he made money, and he attributed it largely to the new system. I ought to add that most of his tenants were white men, but a squad of colored men did as well and made as much money as any of the others.

I found a Southern man in charge as superintendent of a railroad which employs a large colored force as track layers and menders, etc. The men receive one dollar and fifty-seven cents a day, and pay sixty cents a day to their foreman, a colored man also, for food. They are "the very best of laborers, always willing, zealous, and faithful, and will work very hard and in the most disagreeable labor for any one who treats them well." So said the superintendent. One large gang was pointed out to me, which for some years had labored in the swamps through which a part of the road runs. They composed a little independent community, having a justice of the peace of their own, who maintains order and decides disputes.

Where sugar-planters keep no store for their hands, it is customary to pay the hands half their wages at the end of the month and the balance at the close of the year; and I imagine those who make advances in goods try to keep their men to about the same limit.

Very few cotton-planters in Louisiana pay wages. The colored man prefers to take the laud on shares, and it is by far the best way. Where they rent land in the rich bottoms, they pay from six to ten dollars per acre, or, which is more usual, eighty pounds of clean cotton. In some cases the planter furnishes land, house, fuel, a corn patch, teams, tools, and feed for the animals, and takes half the crop. If the colored tenant wants to undertake corn as well as cotton, that, too, is planted at halves. They usually work in squads, and undertake about fifteen acres of cotton and ten of corn to the hand.

Cotton will average three-quarters of a bale to the acre, and I judge that the laborer with a fair crop may live through the year, and have one hundred and fifty dollars in cash at the close of the season, neither he nor his family having suffered for any thing in the mean time. The returns are very satisfactory to the laborer, and Northern farmers, who save as well as work, could easily grow rich on the Mississippi and Red River bottom-lands.

Every body tells me that the colored men save but little. In one cotton-parish a Republican who has taken great interest in the welfare of the negroes said, in answer to my question, "They are not worth a dollar a head of the population to-day." "That man had one hundred and fifty dollars due him last Christmas for his cotton," said another planter to me: "he spent it all in ten days, and bought the greatest lot of trash you ever saw; but he and his wife and children were satisfied and happy, and when I reproached him, he said, 'What's the use of living if a man can't have the good of his labor?'"

New Orleans has a considerable number of colored mechanics, who are spoken of as skillful and competent men. Elsewhere in the State I have seen colored men working as masons and carpenters, and occasionally shoe-makers, and they are skillful blacksmiths. I am told, in the towns a considerable proportion of the colored people own the houses in which they live, and they all have a strong desire, as I have said, to own small lots of land. But in a parish which has a negro population of over twelve thousand, a planter who has taken much interest in the colored people told me he knew not more than twenty men who owned farms, and some of these he thought would not make their payments on the price, by reason of improvidence. This was in the cotton country, where the colored people can readily buy laud, and at a reasonable rate.

The women do not regularly work in the fields. They receive from eight dollars to ten dollars a month as field-hands, and in the cotton-picking time women and children turn in to this work. In the sugar country, too, the planters employ women in the fields at certain seasons. If the colored laborer is forehanded, he prefers that his wife shall not work in the field.

Of schools most of the parishes have a sufficient number, and the colored people are generally better supplied than the whites with free schools. This arises in part from the fact that school-teachers are made use of as politicians.

The notion that the negro race is dying out is absurd, and one never hears it mentioned here. The whole country is full of hearty, shiny little pickaninnies, fat, quiet, generally nicely dressed; and in the towns and villages the larger children look very neat and happy as they go to and from school or Sunday-school.

The colored people are almost universally, I am told, anxious to send their children to school, and in my conversation with them the most frequent complaint I heard was of the mismanagement or inefficiency of schools. I never heard any complaint of a lack of schools, though some outlying parishes are not well supplied. In a country parish on a Sunday, I fell into conversation with three colored men whom I met in my walk. One had his little children with him. He complained that the school was not kept open — "not more than one day in the week. It was a shame, when they had a good schoolhouse; but the teacher was of no account." I said they ought to cure that by choosing good officers at elections, and one replied that they always got cheated. The Republican office-holders were as bad as Conservatives, and he would just as soon trust one as the other. "And if we put our own color in, somebody comes along and shoves money in their pockets, and makes them forget their own people."

As to churches, in the cotton country the colored people are mostly either Methodists or Baptists, and they have their own churches and preachers of their own color. The meeting is a curiosity. The preacher is almost always so far illiterate that he uses large words in a wrong sense; but he freely denounces the sins of the congregation. Then come screams, violent contortions, jumping, dancing, and shouting — but not more violent or ghastly than I have seen in Western camp-meetings among white people, in my younger days, I must own.

You hear it commonly said that the preachers are not good men, and do not live up to their calling, but I doubt it. They arc politicians— as preachers, lawyers, and doctors are commonly among white men. But even though the form which Christianity takes among these people is repugnant to my colder nature, I found no upright, thoughtful planter who did not acknowledge that the Church is a restraining influence upon them; and in one case where I put the question the planter told me that he had noticed that almost all the crime, lawsuits, and troubles generally, in his parish, which came before the courts, originated on those plantations where there was no meeting-house. "As for me," he said, "I think it an economy to support both church and Sunday-school among the colored people on my plantations." In Southern Louisiana a large part of the colored population are Catholics, and have not separate churches.

The colored people are the main working force of the State. It is not fair to say that they are the only workers, as is sometimes rashly asserted, for there is a considerable population of white farmers scattered over the State. In the Acadian country these people, who are called "Cadians," are industrious and prosperous. They speak French, and retain many of their old French customs. They live a good deal among themselves, and do not even care to trade with the Americans, whom, though they have occupied the country ever since the acquisition of Louisiana, the Acadian still regards as interlopers. In other parts of the State there is a population of white farmers who cultivate the thin uplands. They have been much neglected, and are not very highly thought of by their neighbors in the lowlands.

To conclude, the industrial prospects of the colored people in Louisiana are satisfactory. They work, and they receive a fair and even handsome return for their labor ; and working so largely on shares, they have incentives to faithful work which day-laborers in the North are often without. Louisiana is an extraordinarily rich State; millions of acres of the most fertile soil lie uncultivated, and may be obtained at a price so low that an industrious man may pay for a farm from the savings of two cotton crops. These lands are open to the colored people, and when time and a longer experience of liberty have taught them self-denial, economy, and business habits, they will more largely become independent farmers.

It is my belief that they ought now to be finally — in this State — left to themselves, so far as the political interference of the Federal Government is concerned. They know how to help themselves, and it is, in the opinion of the best Republicans I met in the State, a danger to social order that the negroes, preyed upon as they are by demagogues of both colors, shall any longer have cause to believe that the Federal power stands behind them to protect them against the results of their misconduct, or to maintain them in places for which they are, by lack of education and of training and experience, unfit.

7

Mississippi in May, 1875

Mississippi is, politically, in a melancholy condition.

The State is unnaturally fertile and rich; the people work; the means of prosperity and content are at hand. Nor can it be said that there is actual disorder or violence. Mississippi is still, even more than Arkansas, a frontier State, with frontier habits. Men, and even boys of fourteen, go about with pistols in their pockets, and murder is not a crime if the murderer can "get a continuance" — that is to say, if he is not lynched, and his lawyer succeeds in delaying his trial. But, except in Vicksburg last year, there has been in two or three years but little political violence and murder in the State. The evil passions which raged after the war, and continued too long, are subsiding ; the State debt is trifling; the schools are in a tolerably good condition; the Civil-rights Act is submitted to; there has been little occasion for the interference of the Federal Government under the Enforcement acts, except at Vicksburg, for at least eighteen months or two years; the State is in the main at peace.

And yet it is neither prosperous nor happy. It is the prey of two political factious of the worst type, who, on both sides, aim to create and maintain excitement, bitterness, suspicious, fears, and hatred. On the one side stands an unscrupulous and. determined band of Democratic politicians of the worst kind — the pistol and bowie-knife stripe, namely — who, in newspapers and by their daily conversation, excite the white Democrats who listen to them to unreasoning and unreasonable fury, and at the same time alarm the timid negroes and bind them together. Arrayed against these Democrats stands another equally unscrupulous band of Republican politicians, with Governor Ames at their head, who have "captured" the colored vote, and mean to hold power and plunder by its means.

Between these contending factions stand the mass of honest Republicans and honest Democrats, moderate and conservative, but unable, it seems, to control the bad elements; unable, at any rate, to unite and take control into their own hands.

Here are two examples which do not badly illustrate the state of affairs in Mississippi.

Knowing that I am interested in schools, some one in New Orleans sent me a letter of introduction to the State Superintendent of Public Instruction here — a colored man named Cardozo. On asking for him I found he had gone to Vicksburg "to look after an indictment " found against him; and when I myself went there, I discovered that Cardozo was not merely indicted, but, as an indignant Republican told me, "shingled all over with indictments" for embezzlement and fraud, and likely, if justice is done, presently to be sent to State-prison. "What a lovely and improving sight for the children of the State, white and black!

Yet this man is one of Governor Ames's confidential and influential advisers.

Here is the other side. The postmaster, ex-Senator Pease, while I was in Vicksburg, was stopped in the street by a person who, I was assured, is "one of the most respectable citizens " of the place, who said to him in a loud voice, "I hear, sir, by God, that you are going to appoint a damned nigger to be a clerk in your post-office !" Pease replied that he certainly was going to appoint a colored man to a clerkship. "Then, sir, I tell you it's a damned outrage, and this community won't stand it, sir!" said this "most respectable citizen" in a blustering tone. Pease replied, "You will have to stand it," which is perfectly true. And as they have a colored sheriff already in Vicksburg, and colored officials in many counties, this bluster seems to be as foolish as it is wicked. At the same time, a hack -driver was furiously driving his hack up and down the main business street, shouting, "Pease is going to put a nigger in the post-office!" Now, see what follows. The next day's *Vicksburg Herald*, the Democratic organ, remarks:

"Pease puts Milton Coates at the general delivery of the post-office as an insult to our people. He says the people ' must stand it.' They may not stand even Pease very long. Our people have a rather summary way of disposing of men and measures sometimes."

And another article in the same journal says:

"Pease was remonstrated with yesterday upon the assignment of a negro to the ladies' window. A gentleman modestly suggested that the men of Vicksburg would not submit to have a negro assigned to the duty of waiting on their wives and daughters at the post-office, when the insolent scoundrel replied, 'They will have to stand it!' The appointment is a deliberate insult to the ladies of this city, and the alleged Jersey school-house burner may find that he is not quite so potent as he imagines. He may find that he has made a blunder, and he may yet live to realize that a blunder is worse than a crime. He may convert the post-office into anything but a bed of roses."

The mayor and police of Vicksburg, who are Democrats, took no notice of the disorderly hack-driver, whom they ought to have summarily arrested. The insulting words of the "respectable citizen" are approved by a considerable part of the Democratic citizens, and

those the most prominent politicians. The colored man whom Mr.
Pease has made clerk in the post-office is a young man of education,
acknowledged integrity, and quiet, gentlemanly demeanor, whom
several Democrats praised to me. The hackdriver who objected to
him never objects to taking a fare from a negro, and a citizen
of Vicksburg told me he had seen him repeatedly driving negro
prostitutes about the town. The "most respectable citizen" is agent
for a steamboat line, daily sells tickets to colored people, and never
refuses their money. The whole affair would be a farce, if it were
not so likely to become a tragedy.

Mississippi has a colored majority in its voting population of
probably fifteen thousand, and possibly twenty thousand. To these
must be added about nine thousand or ten thousand white Republi-
cans, of whom at least two-thirds are natives of the State. About five
thousand negroes arc counted on to vote the Democratic ticket.

The Ames faction in the Republican party contains but a small
part of the white Republicans— a majority of the petty office-
holders and the camp-followers; but it controls the colored vote.
In the anti-Ames wing of the Republican party, I found a number
of men, Northern and Southern, who have a substantial interest in
the State; who are men of culture, upright, wise, and good citizens
in the best sense of the phrase; such men as Judge Tarbell, of the
Supreme Court; Judge Luke Lea; Mr. Musgrove, late State Auditor;
General M'Kee, a member of Congress; Judge Hill, of the United
States Circuit Court; G. W. Wells, United States District Attorney
for the Northern District; and many others.

The large majority of the Democratic party also is composed of
men of moderate and conservative views, who would prefer peace,
harmony, and good government, but who are influenced to a large
degree by a small but fierce band of fire-eaters whose head-quarters
are at Vicksburg, and who control a number of presses in different
parts of the State, and keep the people in a ferment by their violent

language and their exaggerations of evils which are great enough in fact, but not nearly so great as they pretend, nor by any means entirely blamable upon the Republicans. Through the appeals of these persons the people of Mississippi have been led to believe themselves outraged and oppressed in some ways in which they are not; partisan bitterness has been maintained to a degree which leads the ignorant Democrat to unite in the same denunciation honest and dishonest Republicans; and so intense is the feeling kept up that the material interests of the State suffer by reason of it — confidence is shaken, values are depressed, and even industry is disturbed. Meantime these Democratic demagogues strive to lead the people away-from the legitimate and natural means by which they could rid themselves of corrupt rulers and establish a sound government, based upon the union of the best men of both parties.

Governor Adelbert Ames

That there have been wastefulness and corruption in the government of Mississippi there is no doubt. I am so weary of official grand and petit larceny that I do not mean to go at any length into Mississippi finances. It is enough to say that the State debt is trifling; there have been no great railroad swindles; a constitutional provision wisely forbids the loan of the State credit. But there has been gross financial corruption in many counties; officers with high salaries have been needlessly multiplied; there have been notorious jobs, such as the State printing; and the ruling powers, the Ames Republicans, have unscrupulously used the ignorance and greed of the negroes to help them in their political schemes. Controlling the negro vote, and using it as a solid mass, they have put into such offices as county supervisors and treasurers, as well as into the Legislature, negroes who were often not only unable to read and write, but who were notoriously corrupt and corrupting demagogues. For instance, the late treasurer of Hinds County, in which the State capital lies, was a negro who could neither read nor write, and who was killed by another negro a few weeks ago for a disgraceful intrigue. In the last Legislature were several negroes who could neither read nor write. It has happened that the members of a grand jury were totally illiterate. A city government was to be elected last August in Vicksburg, and the Republicans nominated for mayor a white man at the time under indictment for twenty-three offenses, and for aldermen seven colored men, most of them of low character, and one white man who could neither read nor write, the keeper of a low groggery. This ticket was denounced by General M'Kee, Republican member of Congress, in a public speech, and, with the help of the Republicans, was beaten. Of the present supervisors of Warren County (Vicksburg), the president and two others can not read. It is a notorious fact that Governor Ames has appointed to judicial places men ignorant of law, and that he has used his appointing power to shield criminals, who were his adherents, and to corrupt the judiciary of the State.

These are serious matters; but, on the other hand, it must be said that the Democratic demagogues have repeatedly urged the negroes to nominate only colored men for office. They say they " would rather have a Mississippi nigger than a carpet-bagger;" and, moreover, in the notable cases of corruption, both in State and counties. Democrats have in many cases shared the plunder, and in some have got up the scheme. Now, on this head the Democratic leaders are silent. They cry out that the State is ruined, which is not true; but they have themselves helped to rob it, and it is at least a doubtful question whether, if some of those who so loudly denounce corruption had power, they would make an honest government.

There is, for instance, a loud outcry about the enormous debt of Vicksburg; but of the money spent for street improvements, Democratic contractors got the most; and the money given to railroads was voted by Democrats and Republicans alike.

Such men as Barksdale, Wharton, Lamar, and hundreds of other prominent Democrats, have clean hands and are men of honor; but there is an undoubted propensity to corruption among some Democratic as well as among Republican leaders. For instance, Vicksburg has been, since August, under Democratic rule; but the expenses, of the city government, I am told, have increased, and order is not as well maintained under Democratic rule as formerly.

Nor, if the Democratic leaders were fair, would they omit to tell their people that the expenses of State and county governments have necessarily increased, for the colored people being free give business to the courts and the officers and institutions of justice; they must have schools; and in other ways the cost of government is increased. That a very large balance of waste and theft and high taxation remains, is perfectly true, and of that all may rightfully complain, as well as of other and graver wrongs which I have mentioned above.

It is a complaint, also, of the Democrats that their opponents have, for corrupt purposes, maintained the color-line in politics. It is true that the Ames men cultivate the negro vote by corrupt means; but it is also true that the Democrats have helped them. In Arkansas and Louisiana, I do not remember having once heard of the negro except as a part of the body politic, ignorant, to be sure, but a good worker, and, as was often said to me by Democrats,

" not to be blamed that he went wrong under bad advice." But in Mississippi the commonest topic of discussion is the "damned nigger." A dozen times, at least, prominent Democrats told me he was a peculiar being, not possessing the virtues of the Caucasian race, and not fitted by nature to vote, or to sit on jury, or to bear witness — a creature admirably fitted to make cotton, and so on. I have heard such discussions going on in the presence of colored men, who naturally listened with all the ears they had.

Now, the negro is not an idiot. He would be if he voted for and with men who habitually call him a "nigger," and often a "damned nigger," and who openly assert his incapacity by nature to perform the functions of a citizen. When the "most respectable citizen in Vicksburg" blustered about the postmaster appointing a "damned nigger," he was heard by at least twenty-five colored men and women Yet, in that very town leading Democrats groan about the impossibility of breaking the color-line. One would have a contempt for such politicians were not their course a constant injury to the State in which they are so foolishly noisy, and in which the quiet, sensible, and orderly people seem to have almost entirely resigned the power and supremacy which belong to them.

The thing which was oftenest said to me in Mississippi by Democratic politicians was this: "Our only hope is in the Democratic success in the next Federal election. The Democratic successes last fall gave us our first gleam of light." But when I asked how a Democratic administration could help them, the reply was, " Because then we can disorganize the colored vote. They will not vote without white leaders to organize them." And when I asked one of the white leaders of the "white-line" movement, whose object is to draw the color-line strictly, how he could hope to get all the white people, with their strongly diverging views, into his movement, his reply was, "We'll make it too damned hot for them to stay out."

Now, to me this does not look like the American way of carrying an election. It is a method of bluster and bullying and force. The honest Republicans whom I asked whether the white -line movement could possibly draw in all the white voters, all replied in the affirmative. It would silence opposition at any rate, they said.

At present there is vigorous opposition to the "white-line" movement among the more sensible Democrats. The party policy is to be decided in a meeting of a State committee on the 17th of May, and the opponents of the "white line" profess to be confident that they can defeat the extremists.* But in the mean time they do not attack the corruptionists and. extremists in their party, and, what seems to be more deplorable and fatal still, they have nothing to say against the brutal intolerance displayed by Democratic demagogues, either toward colored men or toward the honest white Republicans. All Northern men are united in one general and fierce condemnation as "carpetbaggers." But many of these men thus condemned and held up to hatred have lived in the State since 1865-'66; they are men of means, and have all their means invested in the State; many of them are large planters; against the honesty and high character of many of them no one can say a word. It is charged that some of these hold office; but why should they not? They are citizens of the State in every sense of the word, and worthy, capable men, whom no one charges with peculation or oppression. They are as strongly opposed to the misrule and corruption of Governor Ames and his faction as the Democrats themselves. [1]

Only a little wisdom on the part of the Democrats would lead them to conciliate these men, to win them over to co-operate with them. But nothing of the kind is done. They are sneered at as "carpet-baggers," and made to feel that the Democratic leaders will have nothing to do with them. So, too, with Southern men who have chosen to join the Republican party; they are at once denounced as "vile renegades," entirely regardless of their actual character. Thus Judge Niles, who represented a Mississippi district in the last Congress, is habitually spoken of as " that renegade Niles." Now, Mr. Niles is a man of singular purity of character, a quiet scholar, an old resident of the State. No Democrat pretends that he is dishonest, or that he tolerates corruption. But he is a Republican, therefore a "vile renegade," not fit for the society of decent men.

The same course is pursued toward the colored voters. They have among them some — a few — men of education and honest desires for good government. But these are denounced in common with the whole herd of ignorant and easily corruptible black voters, who are the prey of designing and unscrupulous white politicians.

On the other hand, a man ceases to be a carpetbagger the moment he becomes a Democrat. For instance, a former sheriff of Warren County, then a Republican, a Northern man, has recently become a Democrat, and is at once made a " respectable citizen." Yet it is notorious that he came to the State poor, has been an office-holder, is now worth over one hundred thousand dollars, and does not own a dollar's worth of property in the State. He keeps his means in bonds and other securities, and, it is said, pays no taxes in Mississippi. But the Democrats do not hesitate to accept him, while they cry out "carpet-bagger" against men who have invested all their means in the State, and are large tax-payers.

THE "STRONG" GOVERNMENT 1869—1877.

Now, "you can't catch flies with vinegar." The natural result of this stupid intolerance among Democratic leaders is that honest Republicans are driven to, and kept in, the Republican ranks. They have no other place. They must either remain silent, or vote the Republican ticket. It is not an exaggeration to say that the unruly part of the Democrats of Mississippi themselves keep up the color-line of which they so bitterly complain. It is their folly and ignorance which mass the negroes, and fling them into the bands of Ames, and make the colored voters what they really are — a real danger to the State. This folly goes on in the face of the fact that the negroes have a numerical minority in the State, and that without intimidation or conciliation it would seem impossible for a "white-line" party to obtain political control of the State.

Lest I should give you a false impression of Mississippi, I must tell you that there is no wish or hope among her politicians or people for the least trouble with the Federal Government, no expectation or desire for the re-enslavement of the blacks, or the change of any constitutional amendment; not the least wish for a "new rebellion." No one can truthfully say the reverse of this. The disease which afflicts society and politics in Mississippi, and which threatens serious effects, is of a different nature entirely. The honest and sensible men have to too great an extent abandoned their duties as citizens, and tolerate crime, misconduct, violence, which could not exist but for their too tame submission.

While I was in Jackson both the State and Federal courts were in session, and I bad thus an excellent opportunity to see prominent persons from different parts of the State, and used it to inquire as to its general condition. The substance of what I heard from both Republicans and Democrats is, that peace and order prevail in all the counties of Mississippi; that there is a better feeling than formerly between the whites and blacks; that the colored people who labor on the plantations, and who, here as elsewhere in the cotton country, usually work on shares or rent the land, have made their contracts and gone to work earlier this year than heretofore, and are laboring more steadily than in any year since the war; that but few cases occur where they are wronged in their settlements, and these only among poor farmers, who sometimes take advantage of the negro's ignorance to make a hard bargain with him; that there is a strong disposition among planters to get the colored man to buy land, in order that he may become a tax-payer, and thus feel the burden which ignorant black supervisors lay upon property; that a considerable number, though small in proportion to the aggregate negro population, have actually bought farms; that numbers of colored men are continually moving into the State from Alabama and Georgia, and mostly settle on the bottom-lands, where they raise cotton; that they are brought in at a small expense — ten or eleven dollars a bead — by agents who fill the orders of planters; that real estate is almost unsalable, and industry has been much disturbed, partly by high taxes and financial mismanagement, and partly by "politics;" and that the great fault of the State is, that the courts do not punish murder, either of white or black.

Life is not held sacred, as it is in the North. Every body goes armed, and every trifling dispute is ended with the pistol. Nearly all the disorder and crime is caused by the lower order of whites and by negroes; for these latter have, it seems, generally taken up the fashion of carrying arms, and in their quarrels among themselves use the pistol or knife freely. The respectable people of the State do not discourage the practice of carrying arms as they should; they are astonishingly tolerant of acts which would arouse a Northern community to the utmost, and I believe that to this may be ascribed all that is bad in Mississippi — to an almost total lack of a right public opinion; a willingness to see men take the law into their own bands; and, what is still worse, to let them openly defy the laws, without losing, apparently, the respect of the community.

It is the most serious crime which any one can charge upon the Republican politicians who have ruled Mississippi since 1868, that they have not dealt with this lawless spirit. Instead of that, they have been engaged in plundering the State, and in demoralizing the colored people, encouraging them in demanding and taking places of responsibility and trust for which their absolute ignorance unfitted them, and using the .colored vote to further the personal ambition of leading "men, and the greed of their hangers-on." Governor Ames is one of the most guilty in this respect. He is not accused of peculation, but it is notorious that his personal adherents are among the worst public thieves in the State. He has corrupted the courts, has protected criminals, and has played even with the lives of the blacks in a manner that, if this fall a good Legislature should be elected, ought to procure his impeachment and removal.

The Vicksburg riot shows so clearly the condition of the State and the faults of both the political factious, which between them tear it to pieces, that I will tell here the prominent points.

Crosby, an illiterate negro, was chosen sheriff and tax-collector of Warren County, which has a large negro majority, and which contains Vicksburg. Thereupon the Democratic fire-eaters began to create an excitement, and charged that Crosby's bondsmen were not good, which is probably true. There was a legal way of testing this question, and if, after twenty days' notice, ho did not make approved bonds, he was, by that neglect, out of office, and incapable of performing its duties.

Nor could it be pretended that he could evade the law, for the prosecuting attorney was then Judge Luke Lea, a man of spotless honor, against whom no Democrat in the State has a word to say. But this lawful way was despised by the Democrats. A public meeting was held in Vicksburg, and, against the advice of some respectable men, a crowd violently rushed to Crosby's office, and extorted from him, with a half-hour's delay, a written resignation.

Crosby thereupon went to Jackson, to lay the case before Governor Ames.

Ames was urged to go in person to Vicksburg, and by his presence calm the tumult, which, I am assured by prominent men of both parties, he could have done. He refused.

Then several prominent citizens, some in high official position, offered to go themselves as a committee, being confident that they could arrange the affair, quiet public feeling, and prevent further disturbance.

Ames declined their services; but told Crosby to return to Vicksburg and summon, not the posse comitatus, as would have been proper, but the negroes from the surrounding country, whom, I am told, Ames had some time before armed with State guns, as he had a right to do, they being part of the militia.

Crosby did as he was told. On Sunday, the colored preachers, under his instructions, told their people that on Monday morning they were ordered to Vicksburg, and those who had them were to carry their guns.

I can not blame the people of the town for being greatly alarmed and exasperated at this proceeding, which became known to them during Sunday. If the sheriff of Westchester County should one day, finding his title to his office disputed, summon the most ignorant part of the population to come pellmell into Yonkers with fire-arms, the people of that town would also be alarmed. Nor do I greatly blame the white mob for what followed. A mob is uncontrollable; and here were two mobs running tilt against each other. There were sensible and brave Democrats in Vicksburg who moderated the fury of the whites as soon as they could, and thus saved many lives that otherwise might have been sacrificed.

Having dispersed the negroes and defeated Crosby, the Democrats now coolly proceeded to hold a new election for sheriff, which had no warrant or authority in law, and installed one of their members in the sheriff's office.

Thereupon, Governor Ames, still "placid," as he declared himself, instead of asserting his authority as governor of the State, and calling on good citizens to help him, called on the Federal forces, who put out the pseudo-sheriff and restored Crosby.

This being done, the Democrats began to bargain with Crosby to become his bondsmen, on condition that one of them should run the office as his deputy, and share in its profits. Before the bargain was completed, a native Republican from an eastern county appeared, and with him Crosby made this arrangement.

This is the brief story of the Vicksburg riot. Begun by lawless Democrats, it was continued and brought to a bloody climax by an unscrupulous Republican governor. To complete the story, I must add that Crosby's accounts have been found entirely correct, so that the Democrats were without the least excuse for their violence; and that Governor Ames has never instituted any investigation into the riot or attempted to bring the rioters to justice.

One incident of the stormy period remains to be told, as its most instructive lesson. Before the riot, the negroes of the county, who are in a great majority, had insisted upon putting forward for office a black ticket, containing the names of some notoriously corrupt colored men. After the killing of so many colored men on the fatal Monday, and when the victory apparently remained with the whites, honest Republicans in Vicksburg told me the colored leaders came to them greatly humbled, and acknowledged that they bad been badly advised, and promised that in future they would heed the counsels of good men, and allow honest and intelligent candidates to be nominated.

But when, at the instance of Governor Ames, Federal troops removed by force the Democratic pretended sheriff, and re-installed Crosby, all these pious intentions were thrown to the dogs, and the old spirit of defiance of good advice at once re-appeared among the negroes.

You will remember, perhaps, a similar story of misconduct in a Louisiana parish by the colored men, which was cured by the M'Enery affair of the 14th of September.

The colored people are, in their ignorance, the prey of demagogues. They are only too ready to follow bad leaders, but only when these leaders appear to have the Federal power at their back. It is an undeniable fact that to the negro the Federal support seems every thing, and be bas been persuaded that the power at "Washington" will uphold him in whatever be chooses to do. The moment be sees reason to doubt this be falls back, and is glad to be guided by honest counselors. Men like Pinchback, in Louisiana, and Cardozo, Crosby, and others, in Mississippi, are dangerous to the commonwealth by the power they have over their people; but they are dangerous only while they can make it be believed that the Federal power will sustain them. Governor Ames lost influence among the negroes after the riot in which be suffered so many of them to be killed; but when at his call United States troops came to reinstate the negro Crosby in his office, then they beheld in Ames the direct representative of the United States Government, and they were ready again to rally to him, and to do his bidding and follow corrupt leaders.[2]

Surely such incidents most clearly show that the interference of the Federal Government, at the demand of State authorities, in such a lawless manner as bas been practiced in New Orleans and in Vicksburg, tends only to harm, and to a mischief so grave as to threaten society, because it encourages contempt for good government in a very numerous and still very ignorant part of the population. The problem of black citizenship is sufficiently difficult, without muddling it by extraneous and arbitrary interference. It is the opinion of honest Republicans whom I met in Mississippi, that the Vicksburg riot could have been entirely prevented, and the dispute peaceably settled, bad the governor done his duty.

The truth is, the Enforcement acts have been used in the last year or two, in all the Southern States I have seen, almost entirely for political purposes; and they are very dangerous and effective tools for this purpose. But to right personal wrongs they are slow, ineffective, and almost useless. There was, I believe, a time, four or five years ago, w-ben the Enforcement acts were valuable, by enabling energetic Federal officers to promptly suppress Ku-klux organizations. But at present these laws are mere political and partisan instruments; and they demoralize the Southern Republican State governments, because these turn over the administration of justice, which is of right their business, to Federal officers, and take to stealing and political intrigue themselves. When I see to what base uses the Federal power is put in these States, even under the Enforcement acts, it is plain that the proposed Habeas Corpus and Force Bill would have been, in the bands of such men as Marshal Packard and Governor Ames, only a monstrous engine of oppression and political intrigue.

In my letters from Arkansas I spoke harshly of the Republican rulers of that State, but, compared with those of Louisiana and Mississippi, they were respectable men; for they did use the power they had — they governed the State which they ruled; they held it in an iron grip, and crushed disorders with so stern and severe a hand that the lawless class were really awed, and the decent part of the community gained courage to assert themselves. They created a wholesome public opinion, adverse to violence. These others have in reality encouraged violence by omitting to punish it, and I wonder that Louisiana and Mississippi are as orderly as they are. It shows that there is a predominant love of order among the mass of the white population.

The Democratic politicians of Mississippi have, however, succeeded in affecting the people with an unreasonable discontent. You hear everywhere that the Federal power oppresses them, and that it maintains the color-line. As to the color-line, from what I have told you it is plain that the Democrats themselves keep it up quite as much, even more, than the Ames Republicans. A candid Democrat said to me, "The negroes whom I employ will always come to me for help in their troubles; they deposit their money with me; they think I am the best man in the world. But when it comes to election they will take the word of the most notoriously low-lived vagabond who calls himself a Republican before they will mine. "It is all our fault," he added, "because we were so foolish as to oppose their rights in the beginning. It has cost us more to support their paupers and criminals than it would have cost to educate and train them for political life. "We made a great blunder, and we are paying for it now." This sensible man, unfortunately for his State, does not control public opinion. He is not a noisy blusterer.

It is not unnatural that the white people should be even unreasonably discontented, for in the planting counties the emancipation swept away the greater part of the accumulated wealth of the whites, which they had constantly invested in slaves. But it is a pity that they have not men wise enough to tell them that courage and hopefulness are more useful than despondent grumbling; and to explain to them that a part, at least, of the taxes laid since 1868 has gone to build school - houses, to repair public buildings, roads, and bridges, to make good the public losses of the war.

Nor ought they to forget that violence and a lawless spirit inflict serious blows on property. Meridian, in Eastern Mississippi, was a flourishing and prosperous place some years ago; but since the riot there it has languished, and many of its houses now stand empty. The Vicksburg riot was a severe blow to the prosperity of that town; much of its traffic has gone off to Edwards Station, which has grown in a few months to be a large and busy place.

The negro is the principal producer in Mississippi, and since the war he has become a large consumer also, for he almost always spends all he makes. The men who have the negro trade all get rich. But a riot frightens the colored people. They are timid, and avoid blustering whites, and they are quite able to transfer their traffic to new points, and do so. This is what has built up Edwards Station, where the colored men do not hear so much talk about the Caucasian race and the "damned nigger" as at Vicksburg.

I must tell you something more of the causes which make a union of the good men of both political parties, for the purpose of electing an honest Legislature and responsible county officers, difficult in Mississippi.

One is the extreme and bitter intolerance of the Democratic politicians, which jealously interferes to keep the members of the two parties apart. A Northern man, being a Republican, is therefore a "carpet-bagger," no matter whether he is honest or dishonest. His children hear themselves called "Yankees" at school, his wife finds her church relations unpleasant. He is looked on with aversion, and this though he may have brought capital into the State, may have all his interests there, and have lived there since the war.

"I have found in Mississippi some of the pleasantest and nicest people I ever met in my life," said an excellent Northern man to me. "My wife and I have made many of the most delightful and conge-nial friendships of our lives here among the natives of the State. But they are people who live quietly on their plantations, where they welcome us with true hospitality. They do not mix in politics. The moment I touch political circles, that moment I am repelled as only a 'Yankee and a carpet-bagger.'"

Now, to be a lawyer, and meet, as you enter the court, only a stony glare of hatred or repulsion; to be a merchant, and know that your neighbors will go a block or two further rather than trade with you; to be conscious as you walk the streets that men are cursing you for being a Northern man, and asking themselves, "What the ---- makes him stay here?" — this is not pleasant for honorable men, who pay their taxes, do all their duty as citizens, and add materially to the prosperity of the State; and who know, besides, that this hatred is not the sentiment of the mass of honest people, but only of some politicians, who encourage it among the baser class of whites, whom they influence.

On the other hand, the negroes and those who control their vote form a close corporation, bitterly jealous of opposition, transacting all political business by the tyrannical rule of the caucus, and ready to persecute any Republican who dares to be independent. At the first symptom of opposition to the decisions of the caucus the opposer's name is taken down; it is sent around in his county or district as that of a " bolter," and every colored voter is solemnly warned to beware of him, as though he were a rattlesnake. Men are as gravely "read out " of the Republican party in Mississippi as though it were a church ; and the act of excommunication fixes, with the ignorant blacks, a stigma upon him as though he were a traitor or a murderer; and white Republican demagogues encourage this spirit of intolerance.

Thus, the two factions play into each other's hands; both conspire to make independent political action and reform almost impossible.

As for the colored voters themselves, the testimony is universal that they are incapable of independent political action. They must have white leaders and organizers; and, under the circumstances, it is inevitable that they should fall a prey to the lowest and least scrupulous political vagabonds and demagogues. These teach them to take up the trade of politics for a living, and tell them that, as they cast the most votes, so they are entitled to the most offices.

Some of these men have not even a residence in the State. O. C. French, for instance, was at one time chairman of the Republican State Executive Committee, was appointed by Governor Ames commissioner to the Centennial Exhibition, was a representative in the Legislature from Natchez; and yet, when search was made for him the other day by a Federal law officer to enforce the penalty of a bond, he had not, so far as could be discovered, a residence in the State; and it is said and believed that he lives in Ohio.

Others are mere place-hunters, as, for instance. State Senator Price, who is also public printer for the judicial district in which he lives; his wife is postmistress, his nephew county superintendent of education and deputy- collector of internal revenue; his son-in-law chancery-clerk; and he himself was lately asking to be appointed sheriff and tax-collector. Again, the President of the Board of Supervisors of Hinds County, in which Jackson lies, is reported to be a partner of the State printer, and he has the job of printing for the county. The other four supervisors are ignorant colored men, easily imposed on.

The Democrats complain loudly of Republican rascality, and with reason ; but their own skirts are by no means clean. There are Republican counties in which county warrants are at or near par; and there are Democratic counties where the warrants are at a heavy discount; and this measures the variety of maladministration. In Vicksburg the Democrats got up a tax-payers' league, but were made a laughing-stock when it was discovered that one of the officers of. the league had charged the town five hundred dollars for removing a safe from the landing to the court-house.

It must be added that while the Federal officers in the State are in some cases excellent men, the later appointments are in many cases persons despised in the community where they live. The recently appointed collector of customs at Vicksburg I heard spoken of by colored men as " Polecat Hall," and was told by Republicans that he is held in general contempt in the community. I could mention others.

As I have spoken frequently of the bitterness of political feeling in the State, I ought to tell you that I have heard of no complaints from Republicans of intimidation or violence at any general election held in Mississippi since 1868. Nor do the Democrats complain of registration and election frauds. The laws are far better than in Louisiana. The canvass is usually conducted in what would seem to us a rough way; but the Republicans are very outspoken. They give as good as they get; they assert their rights, and "do not scare worth a cent." The only cases of political fraud and intimidation of which I have heard occurred in Vicksburg last August, and at a local election in Columbus last December. So far as I have heard, these did not attract the attention of the Republican State authorities.

In the Vicksburg city election the Republicans put up so vile a ticket — described elsewhere — that only three white men voted for it, and a threat to refuse employment to any negro who supported it was, I think, clearly justifiable. I certainly would neither trade with nor employ a man, white or black, who would vote to inflict upon me a notoriously corrupt set of city officers. But in the face of the fact that the leading Republican in the district, General M'Kee, denounced the ticket in a public speech at Vicksburg, and that it had no white Republican support, such silly advertisements as the following were printed in the Democratic papers and applauded:

"AMERICA! AMERICA! "

The firm of George M. Martz & Co., No. ISS Washington Street, are making a splendid stock of every thing in the confectionery line for Christmas. They have no *European* or *Northern* workmen, but have the best in the country, and home folks at that, who understand their business to perfection. The public are invited to come and judge for themselves if this is not so."

In the Columbus city election, held in December, 1874, there was undoubted and public intimidation of the kind denoted by the document I give you below, and it was without excuse, because the Republican candidate for mayor, Mr. Eggleston, was an honest man, against whom I am assured no charge of corruption or incapacity was made; and as there had been some trouble, the leaders of the two parties had agreed that there should be a fair and free election. In spite of this, the following handbill was circulated and posted before election. I have an original in my possession:

" [This means Business.]
"BREAD OR NO BREAD.

"At a large meeting of the citizens of Columbus it was
" *Resolved*, That the colored man who votes for Eggleston will, as certain as fate, vote meat and bread out of the mouths of his wife and children; that we pledge ourselves to employ no man who has been discharged by a member of our club who fails to bring a recommendation that he has been discharged for no fault.

"You have driven the white man to the verge of ruin, and he has determined to draw the color-line, and if you can stand it, he can.

"Now, hunt for bread and meat among those whom you support.

"We will know who you are, and it will be brought up to you the first job of work you ask for.

"Any colored man who votes for Joe P. Billups, S. C. Plunger, and J. H. Sharp will be protected in every sense of the term, and every proper assistance afforded him in the power of the white men of Columbus.

"December 8, 1874."

After the election a private circular was sent around to leading Democratic business men, of which also I have an original :

" [*For Private Use.*]

"Stand to your colors,
Hew to the line."

" WORTHY.	UNWORTHY.
George Simonton.	Robert Gleed, merchant.
Ellick Valentine.	Braxton Littlejohn, merchant.
Henry Watts.	Parson Dickson.
Henry Glover.	Parson Proctor.
Granville Brothers.	Parson Boulden.
Henry Cheatham.	

WORTHY.	UNWORTHY.
Johnson Wade.	Wesley Hodges, black-smith.
Allen Collins.	
Frank Meek.	Eli Hodges, blacksmith.
Charles Timberlake.	Dick Ammons, carpenter.
Sidney Wilson.	Henry Lovely, "
Randle Thomas.	Jeff Kirk, "
Green Bell.	Robert Hall, "
Riley Gilkey.	Orange Baskerville, "
James Downer.	Davy Christian, "
John Jones.	Lewis Goodwin, "
Lewis Oliver.	Ruffin Eckford, "
Wilburn Johnson.	John Green, "
Thomas Anderson (dead).	Pressley Green, "
Henry Powell,	Allen Marquess, "
Billy Billups.	Henry Baker, "
A. L. Williams.	Armstead Jones, "
Ed. Humphries.	Warren Baker, "
Titus Gilmer.	Stephen Evans, "
Cæsar Perkins.	Ellick Latham, shoe-maker.
Henry Spann.	
Nathan Fields.	Charlie Williams.
Johnston Williams.	Rochester Gregory, apple-stand.
Solomon Williams.	
Ottaway Ridley.	Davy Humphreys, apple-stand.
William Skipwith.	
Perry Richardson.	Joe Baker, cabinet-maker.
Colly Harrison.	Lewis Alexander, loafer.
Robert Billups.	Henry Harrison, mer-chant.
Otho Sherrod.	
Dig Blewett.	Boston Witherspoon, mer-chant.
Billy M'Neal.	
John Evans.	Harold Blewett, steward, hotel.
Bill Williams.	
Granville Topp.	Guy Powell, waiter, hotel.
Ned Harrison.	Jim Moore, clerk at Gaston's.
Asa Sykes.	
Frank Young.	Simon Mitchell, ex-police-man.
Beck Covington (doubt-ful).	
Moses Crusoe.	Peter Anderson, Selig & Hedle's.

Martin Baker.

Jupiter Stallings.

Andrew M'Cann.

Tom Banks.

Jones Baskerville.

Jack Gilmer.

Ben Green, carpenter.

John Henry.

John Miller, sexton at cemetery.

Bud Sykes.

Armstead Billups.

Squire Ross.

Solomon Brown.

Granville Butler.

Phil Irion.

Aaron Cobb.

Richard Clay.

Thomas Walley, *alias* Tom Sykes, livery-stable keeper.

Sargent James (voted for Billups, but is under Lewis).

Jim Munroe.

Mark Brownlee, captain negro company.

Ben Gordon, laborer.

William Henderson, very bad.

Henry Carrington.

Ellick Harris.

Anthony Baskerville, orator.

Paul Harrison, cabinet-maker.

Governor Whitfield.

Christmas Lipscomb,

Morris Hamilton, gardener. Says, 'Let the white man go to hell.'

Scott Crusoe.

Richard Harrison, ex-magistrate.

Aberdeen Stallings.

Austin Jones.

Harrison Barry, wood-chopper.

Elzy Richards.

R. F. Sturdivant,

Munroe Jones, awful.

Jim Graves.

Mack Bartee, brick - mason.

Ham Blewett, fruit and vegetable peddler.

Reuben Covington, gin-house builder.

Cato Daves.

Luck Blewett, wood-chopper at Loeb's.

WORTHY.	UNWORTHY.
	Robert Jackson.
	Ben. O. Young, captain negro company.
	Bill Pulliam.
	George Bailey.
	Josh Hairston.
	Ben Moore.
STREET-WAGONS.	**STREET-WAGONS.**
Wilburn Johnson.	Gid Sims, street-wagon.
Tom Sykes.	William Witherspoon, street-wagon.
Perry Richardson.	Ephraim Curry.
Henry Spann, H. L. Atwater's driver, two horses.	Lewis Whitfield.
"By order of the Club."	

The main object of the " white liners " is to demoralize the negro vote by depriving it, so far as possible, of white organizers. If they can do this fairly I suppose it would be justifiable; but I do not see how it can be done. The attempt, made in the temper in which these Democratic leaders live, would not affect the Ames men, whom it is their desire to drive from power. It could silence only the honest Republicans, whom the Democrats, if they were wise, would conciliate.

It remains to speak of the negro as a laborer. The universal testimony of the whites of both parties is, that the colored people are industrious, but not economical; and that they appear to be less interested in politics and more steadily at work this year than ever before. Mr. Richardson, who is the largest planter in the State, told me that the most energetic colored men rent the bottomlands at ten dollars an acre, having, of course, besides the laud, house, fuel, fencing and some other and minor privileges, as that of keeping stock. At this rate, a renter, he said, would make in a good year two hundred dollars, clear of expenses. The renters raise corn as well as cotton, and where they plant on shares and furnish their own teams and implements, the land-owner receives one-quarter of the crop, whatever it may be.

There is no reason to believe that the large planters wrong the negroes in their contracts or settlements; but the improvidence of the colored people, which has led them into a vicious system of requiring advances of food and other supplies from the planter, naturally brings them a loss, in the higher prices which credit always requires, and which in a country like Mississippi, where interest is high, must be considerable. A planter near Jackson, who pays cash for his supplies, told me that while be was buying bacon at fourteen cents, a neighbor, who required a credit, was charged twenty-one cents, and did not hesitate to buy at that rate.

There is no doubt at all that on the share or renting system, as practiced in the rich bottom-lands of Mississippi and Louisiana, the colored laborer is able to make handsome wages, and yet secure greater independence than the day-laborer usually enjoys elsewhere. Nor is the planter's share too large; for he must give careful and constant supervision, and he has fences and cabins to repair, a gin -house and mill to furnish, and must have capital enough to keep on hand supplies for the renters on his land, from the sale of which, however, he of course makes a profit.

Mr. Richardson, of whom I spoke above, has engaged a part of his capital in a cotton factory in Southern Mississippi, where he now employs two hundred and fifty hands. It is so successful that he is about to double its capacity. The operatives are all whites, and mostly taken from the population of small farmers, to whom this additional chance of employment is a great boon. He told me that the saving in transporting cotton alone secures a handsome profit; but he has also very cheap fuel and a large and steady home market for the goods he makes. He said he had been surprised to discover how large a working capital such an enterprise demanded, and thought that the chief reason why so many Southern factory enterprises had failed was, that those engaged in them had not a sufficient working capital, and were cramped and destroyed by the necessity of raising money at high rates of interest to keep the mills going.

Notes:

1. Since this was written, Colonel Lamar, in the Democratic State Convention, brought forward and carried a platform denouncing the color-line as an injury to the State ; and thus the "white-liners" have failed to carry their point. During the canvass going on as I write this note, several political meetings have ended in disturbance and riot; the canvass is probably the most exciting the State has experienced for some years; Governor Ames has called for Federal interference: but ex -Senator Pease, above mentioned, a radical Republican, has telegraphed to the President that a posse of citizens can be got in any county to keep order, and that Federal inter-ference would be an injury rather than a help. I have left my letters unchanged; they give my impressions in May, 1875.

2. Since the above was written, Crosby has been shot, in a bar-room brawl, by his deputy, a white Republican.

8

Alabama in May, 1875

The Alabama Registration and Election laws, made in 1868-'9, and unchanged until last -winter, formed one of the most perfect machines for political fraud that I have ever heard of. It is amazing to me that the decent people of the State, of both parties, did not unanimously and loudly protest against them long ago.

A complete registration of the State was made in 1868-'9. The lists then made were, by law, placed in charge of the probate judges in the counties, and these were obliged thenceforth to place every one's name on the registry who applied for the purpose, and took oath that he was a citizen of the State and county, and had the requisite qualifications; and such application might be made at any time.

No provision was made for any revision of these registration-lists to strike off the names of voters who had died or removed; new names were added from year to year, or rather from day to day, for there was no set time for registration; it was possible even for a man to register under several different names. Moreover, lest any voter should neglect registration, it was provided that an inspector of election must register him, if required, on the day of election; and the names so registered were afterward sent to the probate judge.

It is easy enough to see that registration lists so prepared, and never revised, were mere instruments to conceal fraud. That is to say, they would have been the cloak for frauds at election if they had ever been used.

For fear that they might, under some conceivable circumstance, be used to detect fraudulent voting, an amendment to the Registration Act, passed by the Legislature, March 3, 1870, enacts this astounding provision: "That it is the intent and meaning of this act (namely, the Registration Act) that no registration-lists shall be used by any inspector, or any other officer of election, on the day of election for the purpose of determining who may or who may not vote; and any person attempting to interfere in any manner with any other person who may desire to vote, shall be deemed guilty of a misdemeanor, and punished in the same manner as now provided for in the election laws."

Lest you should think, as I confess I did, that this was only a bad joke or a blunder of the Legislature, I show you here that it was a law actually obeyed. The clerk of the Circuit Court of Wilcox County, one of three officers who officially count the vote of the county and make the certificates of election to the secretary of state, was asked, a few weeks ago, " As supervisor of elections, would you count a vote that you knew was not properly registered?" and answered, " Without any further knowledge of the law than I now have, I would." Again, "Are the names appearing in the poll-lists duly registered according to law ?" He replied, " I do not know."

Another returning officer of the same county being asked how long it would take to compare the poll-lists of the county with the registration-lists, thought it would take at least six months.

"Poll-lists " were lists made at the polls of the names of those who had voted. Now mark: The voter in Alabama could, until the present year, vote at any poll in his county. As he was not required to show a registration certificate; as it was impossible to tell whether or not he had registered; as an act of the Legislature expressly prohibited any one from preventing his voting, even if he had not been registered ; and as he might vote at one of a score of polling-places in the county, and evidently under any name he chose to give, it is quite clear that the election law was as great a sham as the registration law.

The whole thing was simply a huge practical joke, or would have been, had not the consequences been too serious. I can imagine Warmoth, Packard, and the other Louisiana "worthies gritting their teeth at the thought that they were not up to such a trick as this.

Naturally, "repeating" was carried on on a scale which would make even a New York political manager blush. In the Congressional district which includes Mobile and Selma, an investigation has been going on this spring into frauds which involve the seat in Congress claimed by F. G. Bromberg, against a colored man, Jeremiah Haralson. Such an investigation is a formal affair. Due notice is given of the witnesses to be heard by each side, each candidate is represented by counsel, and the witnesses are subjected to a severe cross-examination. Haralson had for his counsel the Republican candidate for attorney-general of the State, an able lawyer. The testimony will be laid before Congress.

Since the recent Democratic success in this State a number of the Republican leaders and managers have quarreled among themselves, and some of them have, so to speak, turned State's evidence. Among others, one Squires, a political manager in Mobile, was brought up before the committee, and, under oath, testified that he was chairman of the Republican Union Club in Mobile; the club met almost every night for some time before the election; it had about two hundred and fifty members. "Its object," he testified, "was to increase the Republican vote of the county — first, by voting themselves; second, by inducing their friends to vote; third, by voting for their absent friends, those who are dead, and others who never had any existence."

The club was divided into squads of ten men, for each of which a trusty leader was selected. They were regularly instructed how to evade the election laws. "Explanations were given how persons who repeated could escape the consequences."

Finally, sham elections were actually held in the club-room, "in which," said this witness, who was confirmed, by-the-way, by other witnesses, " members were drilled in the actual business of election-day; some were judges of elections, some inspectors, others deputy-sheriffs and deputy-marshals. The members were divided into two crowds, representing Republicans and Democrats. Some were quiet citizens, standing around the polls; others were noisy and disorderly, and were arrested; others, yet, were quietly putting in their work. They would come up, vote, pass away, retire, change their clothes, return, and vote again."

Observe, all this was not real; it was a sham election — a training-school for repeating, and I am quoting sworn testimony, all the essential points of which rest on the independent evidence of several persons.

"If a man was challenged and objected to, and was fearful of arrest, he would retire without voting, and forthwith assume some other and better disguise. Each crowd were shown how they might deceive the members of the other by pretending that they were vot-ing tickets, when in reality they were not. For instance, Republicans would receive their tickets from those representing Democrats, and, while pretending to deposit such tickets in the ballot-box, really deposited them in their pockets or in the lining of their hats, sub-stituting therefor Republican tickets. They were taught that those who go quietly about on election-day are very little noticed; and that while one party was certain that such persons were voting for them, and the other party was more certain that the same persons were voting for them, they need fear no interruption. This fact had been thoroughly proved by the personal experience of many there present at that sham election. A majority of the members had been admitted on account of their well known Republicanism — by their zeal displayed in previous well-fought campaigns, and their enthusiasm and determination that the Republican party should triumph in the elections of 1874." I quote this from the sworn testimony.

In addition to these sham elections, arrangements were made for preparing fraudulent lists of registered names for use on the election-day. The majority of these names, though properly registered, were only creations of the fancy. The persons for whom these names appeared on the registration lists never had existence. Some three thousand names were thus prepared. It was proposed, that the squads before mentioned, under the control of competent and energetic leaders, should assemble on the election-morning early, and, having been fed, should proceed, on previously designated routes, from poll to poll, voting as often as possible. They were instructed to avoid detection and arrest by various means: "first, to vote names that were properly registered; second, to change their personal appearance by various disguises ; and as there was "but little danger of their arrest by Republicans, that, if it should appear expedient, they should deceive the Democratic managers at the polls into believing that they were voting the straight Democratic ticket, while in fact they were industriously engaged in voting the straight Republican ticket. These instructions were given in such a way that no member could faithfully say that he was advised, commanded, or instructed directly to vote more than once. Nevertheless, the leaders of the squad and men in whom confidence was reposed understood the whole matter." "It was further suggested that it might be expedient for some members to carry Democratic tickets in their hands, and thus appear to be voting such tickets, while their pockets were stuffed with an ample supply of Republican tickets, which they were rapidly depositing in the ballot-boxes. Also, the leaders were privately instructed to keep a, careful record of the number of Republican tickets deposited by these squads, so as to get an approximate estimate of the vote. On the night before election, at the clubroom, after the members had gone, and when only the leaders of the squads remained, two thousand Republican tickets were laid out and folded. Persons were appointed to distribute tickets, also food, and some to keep account of the reports made by squads. As far as possible the route of each squad from poll to poll was designated beforehand, so that there might be no confusion and no assembly of several squads around one poll on election-day. Instructions were also given by which reports were exchanged, from time to time, of the progress of the work, so that the precise locality of each squad at any time, and also the number of votes up to that time deposited by each squad, might be known. * * * No regular account of the number of votes polled was kept after one o'clock on election-day. The aggregate returns, after making all allowances, was over one thousand votes cast. About two hundred members went out on this work on election morning. * * * I saw all the squads at work on election-day — some voting; others were waiting for their turn to vote; others passing rapidly from one poll to another. They reported up to one o'clock that the work was going on with vigor. After that time, as we found we were beaten, no further accounts were kept."

The scheme broke down because the Democrats had horsemen moving rapidly from poll to poll, following the squads of repeaters, and exposing them.

Squires's testimony is fully corroborated by a number of witnesses, members of this club. One testified that if the plan had been carried out, two hundred men could have cast fifteen hundred votes. Another, after speaking of the "drill" and sham election, said that he thought the club had polled about one thousand votes, and that they did this "for the promotion of the interests of the Republican party by voting early and often." Another testified that they "were drilled to repeat, then change hats and go back again, but be smart enough not to be caught." Another testified that two thousand names were written for the use of the repeating squad, ten names on a slip; and so on.

This was one of the districts in which bacon was distributed by order of Congress, and at the expense of the Federal Government, ostensibly for the benefit of sufferers by the overflow of the Alabama River in 1874. This bacon was made a means of scenting Republican votes; the negroes were told, in some instances, that it was sent them direct from General Grant, and it was reported and understood that the receiver of Government bacon must vote the Republican ticket, under penalty of losing all his "rights in law," a fearful threat to the ignorant blacks.

J. S. Perrin is a Republican politician. In the canvass of 1874 he was at the same time Republican candidate for the Legislature, United States deputy-marshal, chairman of the Republican county committee. United States supervisor of election, and, besides this, had charge of the distribution of bacon appropriated by Congress for sufferers by the overflow of the Alabama River. He is the same person who recently confessed before the Spencer Investigation Committee that in the canvass of 1872, being then United States deputy -marshal, he shot a hole through his own hat, and thereupon immediately called for Federal troops to protect Republican voters against Ku-klux.

Perrin was made United States deputy marshal again on the 12th of October, 1874, at the request of the chairman of the Republican State Executive Committee; and on the 27th of October he called for United States troops. The use he made of them appears in his testimony, thus: The ostensible object was to enforce writs of the

United States courts; but, says Perrin," said writs had no existence." He adds, under oath, "The real object of these troops was to quarter them in the most central portion of the district, and intimidate Democratic voters by causing reports to be circulated that the deponent had warrants for the arrest of a large number of whites for alleged violation of the Enforcement acts and National Election Law; also for persons who had failed to pay colored men their full wages. Many persons who had taken an active part in the Democratic nominating convention, and some who had had personal difficulties with colored men, were led to believe the report was correct, and rather than be arrested and arraigned before a United States commissioner's court, with unscrupulous witnesses to testify against them, and in order to avoid the expense and trouble of a trial, prepared to leave, and did leave, the county. This action incited and encouraged the more partisan and turbulent negroes to unite the colored crowd against the whites, and enabled me to vote them as I chose."

As to the use made of government bacon, Perrin testified: " I issued the bacon for Monroe County. Previous to doing so, a report was circulated among the negroes that in order for them to obtain bacon they would have to vote the straight Republican ticket; and if they received bacon, and afterward refused or neglected to vote said Republican ticket, they would forfeit their rights in law. As I was a candidate for the Legislature upon said ticket, I did not consider it necessary to correct this report.[1] It was extensively circulated through Monroe, Conecuh, Clarke, and Wilcox counties that a barbecue would be held at Monroeville on election-day, and that all negroes who would attend and vote the Republican ticket would receive bacon enough to last them a year. This induced many to come from adjoining counties to Monroeville and vote on said day. The barbecue was held, and largely attended. I could not prevent these illegal votes had I been disposed. All strangers were challenged, and, having taken the oath, were permitted to vote. This was the law of the State. At least five hundred illegal votes were cast there for the Republican ticket."

The Federal soldiers were on election-day "stationed directly at the polls under arms;" and Perrin testifies positively that of the nine hundred legitimate votes cast at Monroeville for the Republican side, eight hundred would have voted the Democratic ticket but for these tricks and promises, "as the colored people were getting along so well with the whites" in their business and planting relations.

In Dallas County, where bacon was also distributed, an ingenious Republican politician to whom this bacon had been confided caused the negroes who applied for it to make affidavit that they had been overflowed, and for witnessing these papers he charged each twenty-five cents. He gave to each man about two pounds of bacon, and he could have bought nearly three pounds for a quarter of a dollar. He really "made a good thing" out of the negroes, and could have afforded to go into the bacon business on his own account.

Dallas is one of the heaviest negro counties in the State. It has suffered from the control of low white and black demagogues, and in this county there is the most positive and abundant testimony of intimidation of black voters by the colored Republican leaders, both before and on election-day.

At one precinct, Orville, Haralson, the Republican candidate for Congress, a colored man, said, in a speech, that any negro who voted the Democratic ticket ought to be swung from the limb of a tree, and called on the men and women present to hold up their hands in approval of this sentiment. He then appealed to the women in the audience, demanding if any of them would live with a husband or have a sweetheart who would vote with the Democrats.

Forze, a colored man of remarkable ability, who rents and himself manages one thousand four hundred acres of land, testified that the negroes were put under a general apprehension that if the

Democrats succeeded they would lose their right to vote; and the more ignorant, he says, believed that they would be re-enslaved.

At Bellevue precinct a Republican candidate openly threatened all blacks who should attempt to vote the Democratic ticket; and a number of colored men testified that those who were suspected of such an intention were driven away from the poll.

At Warrenton precinct a colored man who had been detected voting a Democratic ticket was seized by a negro mob, who dragged him off, and from whom he escaped only by the intervention of -white men, -who concealed him, and, later, set him on a horse, on which he escaped.

At Pleasant Hill, just before the election, Walker, candidate for clerk of the Circuit Court, violently denounced all negroes who should vote with the Democrats, and declared they should be killed.

At Portland a large number of colored men complained after the election that they had been individually threatened if they should vote with the Democrats ; and Cyrus B. Warner, a colored justice of the peace, elected by the Democrats, testified that the fact that he had been mobbed and nearly killed in 1872, by negroes, for supporting the Democratic ticket, was remembered, and prevented, to his knowledge, a number of colored men from voting with the Democrats.

I could go on at great length with such and even more forcible evidence, but this is enough. In this county, Haralson, the Republican candidate for Congress had, in writing, positively charged intimidation by the Democrats; but the testimony of Republican violence and intimidation was so overwhelming that before the commission he confined himself to efforts to prove that there was no intimidation on either side, but a fair and peaceable election.

Nor did the candidates confine themselves to verbal intimidation. One circulated an "order" to the colored people to vote for him, signed "U. S. Grant, President." Another, J. S. Diggs, now and at that time county solicitor, and in May arrested under criminal indictment by the grand jury for embezzlement and bribery, circulated through the county a printed warning against his opponent:

"REPUBLICANS, BEWARE!

"Any one found with tickets with the
BOLTER SILSBY'S NAME
on it will be prosecuted, and sent to the Penitentiary. "
"-J. S. DIGGS, *Solicitor*, Dallas County."

The solicitor is the prosecuting attorney, who represents to the colored man the majesty and terror of the law; and this threat was so effective that Silsby received but one hundred and fifty-five votes in the county.

The financial condition of Alabama is bad, but it might be worse. The State debt is heavy, and will probably have to he scaled. Its exact amount is as yet unknown. Matters have been managed so loosely that the governor told me the other day it would take him several months to discover the entire State indebtedness. Auditors and treasurers have kept their accounts with such lack of method that their reports are untrustworthy. The governors since reconstruction— two Republican and one Democratic — seem to have spent, invested, exchanged, and generally manipulated the State funds and bonds with extraordinary carelessness. So far as ascertained, it is believed the debt amounts to about twenty-eight million dollars.

The condition of the counties is not bad. In only a few has there been serious financial mismanagement. There has been no such wholesale plundering as was suffered by the people of Arkansas, Louisiana, and Mississippi. Generally I find the majority of supervisors have been white men and property- owners, and this has often been brought about by persuading, or even by bribing, negroes to give up their offices —this in the black counties. But in at least a third of the counties the whites have the majority.

The Democrats complain unreasonably, as it seems to me, of Republican misrule. The truth is, the State has been misgoverned and the State debt increased under Democratic as well as under Republican administrations. From 1868 to 1870 its governor was William H. Smith, Republican. Him followed, 1870-72, Lindsey, Democrat. His successor, 1872-74, was Lewis, Republican, followed now by Governor Houston, who strikes me as a moderate and well-meaning man, who is determined to keep the peace and to restore order to the finances.

Now, so far as I can discover, the Democratic Lindsey was little, if at all, more economical than either his predecessor or successor. The Democrats say he was an honest blunderer; but the Republicans say that Smith and Lewis were also honest blunderers. All, by-the-way, were Alabamians, and the State has suffered less from "carpetbaggers," so called, than any of the other three I have seen. The native Alabamian, under the tuition of United States Senator Spencer, who is a carpet-bagger, has shown himself very capable of misrule, and particularly of the most unscrupulous political trickery.

It must also be said that where conspicuous, financial jobbery took place. Democrats have, oftener than not, been parties in interest. For instance, in Dallas County, which has a largo negro majority, complaint is

made that the blacks, -who do not pay one thousand dollars of the total yearly tax, by their votes saddled the county -with a subscription of one hundred and forty thousand dollars to a railroad; but some who complain of this fail to tell you that the directors of the railroad were all prominent Democrats ; and that they advocated the subscription, and even paid the railroad fares of negroes to bring them from the county into Selma to vote for it.

Again, while the finances of Dallas County have been mismanaged, and the assessment and collection of taxes have been for years fraudulently performed by Republican officers, you find that in the adjoining county of Montgomery the only defalcation which has occurred in recent years was by a Democrat, appointed by the Democratic Governor Lindsey. This collector robbed the county of thirty-five thousand dollars, and the State of fifteen thousand dollars, and, I am told, now conducts a Democratic newspaper in Texas.

It is not fair, therefore, for the Democrats to blame the financial mismanagement entirely on the Republicans, or to speak of these as having robbed the State. But there is no doubt that dishonest Republican leaders have been guilty of most flagrant and shameless political debauchery. I have already given some account of how they carried elections. But the character of candidates was often of the lowest.

For instance, in Dallas County, last year, Haralson, colored, himself candidate for Congress, was president of the Republican county nominating convention, and renominated for tax-collector a man who was then under eleven indictments for malfeasance in office. He was " triumphantly " re-elected ; and the grand jury, composed of six Republicans and ten Democrats, with a white Republican foreman, an excellent citizen, while I was there brought in ten new indictments against this Republican tax-collector, who was at the same time county superintendent of education— but was removed for drunkenness — and was also member of the Common Council of Selma.

Haralson, himself a "smart" negro, who holds the certificate of election as Congressman from the district, which includes Mobile, was indicted in 1872 for stealing a bale of cotton; and the man from whom the property was taken, in a civil suit actually proved ownership, and got the bale, which was found in Haralson's cotton

-house. The criminal suit was dropped by a Republican solicitor (Mr. Diggs), who is now himself under indictment.

There is a good deal of complaint of high taxation, but I doubt if the Democrats, now in power, will be able to reduce it much, and their revenue bill of the last session is very unpopular in the State, and some of its features have been declared unconstitutional by their own attorney-general. Undoubtedly there have been numerous abuses in the State and local governments, such as — to give an instance — the letting-out of convicts to their own relatives; the needless increase of petty officers, and a generally wasteful administration.

But the most serious charge that can be brought against the Republican leaders in Alabama is, that they have secured power by corrupting the negroes, and enjoyed it without enforcing the laws. It must be added that they appear to me to have systematically and grossly misrepresented the condition of the State as to peace and order, with the view of getting the use of United States troops and courts for the punishment of offenses which the State government ought to have taken in hand, or, oftener yet, for the intimidation of white voters, and with the object of keeping up irritation and a division between the whites and blacks.

Alabama is, in parts, still a frontier State. In some counties there are bad and lawless men, but they do not preponderate; they are nowhere so numerous that the State authorities could not, had they been energetic, have repressed disorder and maintained peace. Unfortunately, the readiness of the Federal authorities to interfere demoralized the Republican State rulers, who, when a disturbance took place, supinely turned the matter over to the United States marshal and Federal troops. Here, as in every other Southern State I have visited, I have found the Federal interference under the Enforcement acts not only unnecessary, at least for the last two years, but an absolute and grave injury, because it has demoralized the State governments, and led them to abdicate their proper functions.

As an example, take the Barbour County riots of last year. The Republican governor at the time took, so far as I have been able to hear, no measures at all to punish the authors of a very cruel outrage — the shooting into a house at Spring Hill, by which a little boy was killed — or to investigate the riot at Eufaula. On the contrary, he acted as though it had been none of his business. The -whole matter was turned over to the United States Court, and, as Judge Bruce has chosen to put off the trial of accused persons until the Supreme Court decides upon the constitutionality of the Enforcement acts, if any one is ever punished for these crimes, it -will he more than a year after their commission.

A more recent instance has been treated by Governor Houston (Democrat) in a different way. In Etowah County three masked ruffians broke into the jail some weeks ago at night, took a negro out, and shot him. The people of the county, who are mostly Democrats, met at once, and called for a special term of the County Court to investigate this murder, and asked the governor to offer a reward for the discovery and conviction of the criminals, which he did immediately. The better class of Republicans in the State, so far as I have seen them, without exception, told me that the Enforcement acts were needless, and ought to be repealed. In their opinion. Federal interference irritates and imbitters feeling between the races, makes the Republican party odious, and is used mainly by corrupt politicians to intimidate the whites, and to encourage the worst black as Avell as white demagogues.

There is a different opinion, which you hear freely uttered by some Republicans; but these men are disappointed politicians, and in Alabama I have found this class to be men of low character, who are demagogues rather than politicians. These would like to see the Enforcement acts retained, and they universally praise General

Grant for his readiness to send troops and allow of Federal intervention. Also these people speak dolorously of the "poor negro," and in general they resemble those Arkansas politicians who haunted Washington last winter, and who swore solemnly that they would not dare to return to Little Rock unless Garland were overthrown and the Force Bill passed, but whom I found two weeks after the adjournment of Congress walking about Little Rock with cheerful faces, declaring that every thing was lovely and peaceful.

The agitation of the Congressional Civil Eights Bill did more, even, than Republican misrule, to give the State to the Democrats last fall. Alabama has a large population of whites — small farmers, collected in the northern counties, where there are but few negroes. These people, who had pretty generally voted the Republican ticket in previous years, became alarmed at the prospect of "negro equality," which has greater terrors, it seems, the less likely it is to become a fact; and last fall, under the representations of adroit and earnest Democratic speakers, they went over in a body to the Democratic party. The passage of the absurd Civil Rights Bill by Congress has probably allayed their fears, because it is now found to be substantially a dead letter. The blacks do not attempt to have it enforced, and it is probable that its only use will be to annoy the Republicans in Northern States, and in regions South where there are but few negroes, and where the Democrats propose to arouse the race prejudice by hiring negroes to board at hotels, and to otherwise insist on the enforcement of the law during the next year's canvass.

The Democratic victory has brought to the victors, I suspect, more cares than pleasures. The reformation of the State's finances is not an easy task; the Legislature proved to have among its Democratic majority some embarrassing simpletons; the Republicans did not fail to annoy their opponents, as only demagogues solicitous for party success rather than for the good of the State know how

to annoy; some imprudent promises made by the Democrats, such
as a reduction of taxation, could not be fulfilled; and, altogether,
the Democratic party does not stand so well in the State as it did
immediately after the election.

The governor is a good man, with experience in legislation and
administration; and it is at least probable that he will be a governor,
and not a mere political figurehead. In his inaugural address, he
said: "With a firm determination to respect and maintain my oath
of office, which shall be a seal to my conscience, I unhesitatingly
undertake to perform such duties as it imposes; and I will regard
it as one of my highest and most sacred obligations to see that
the laws 'are faithfully executed,' and the rights of all citizens, '
without regard to race, color, or previous condition,' duly guarded
and protected." Governor Houston assured me that these were not
empty words, but that he was solemnly determined to enforce the
laws, and to maintain peace and order, and protect alike all the citi-
zens of the State. The immediate results of the Democratic success
in Alabama are: first, a strong tendency in the white politicians to
re-arrange parties, and to split in such manner as to break up com-
pletely the color-line. You must understand that the Democrats, as
is but natural, resist this with all their might. They want to keep
together the white vote, and to attract to themselves some part of
the colored vote. But there are, naturally, two factions among the
whites. The line between Whigs and Democrats is not so strongly
drawn in Alabama as in Louisiana and Arkansas, but it exists; and,
besides, there are more ambitious men than there are offices in the
gift of one party.

At several places in the State the local elections this spring have
developed differences among the Democrats. At Opelika the result
was odd enough, the Democratic candidate receiving a majority of
the black vote, and the independent man a majority of the white.
At Montgomery over four hundred colored votes were cast for

the Democratic candidate, who was chosen over his independent competitor; but the latter "was not a competent person, as some of his supporters confessed to me. I hear, however, that in this place Democrats bought up, at two dollars a piece, the registration certificates of colored men to the number of over two hundred, and these were carefully retained, except in cases where it was quite certain that the original holder would vote the Democratic ticket. Under the new law a voter must produce his registration paper, so that if he parts with it, he loses his vote.

At Opelika, by-the-way, I am told, the Democrats managed to capture a whole colored church, minister and all, by a moderate subscription to the church-fund. It was a Republican politician who told me this, on the authority, as he explained to me, of a "colored man, a member of the Legislature, whose brother lives here, and keeps a bar and a gambling-place. The legislator is a gambling man himself, but an honest fellow so far as his politics are concerned." This description gives one a curious notion of Alabama colored legislators, and of the moral standard among the Republican leaders.

The Republican party in this State has some excellent men among its members, but they are, unfortunately, men of little influence in the party councils. If they could get rid of most of the Federal office-holders, they might hope to re-organize, and become a valuable and effective political force in the State. But the present Republican leaders are, in the main, meu of little character or power. There are but two insignificant Republican newspapers in the State, both owned by one man, and apparently published for the sake of the post-office and other Governmental advertising, which is their pap, without which they would perish, and which Senator Spencer secures them.

The Democratic success has had a good effect on the colored voters, or, rather, on the demagogues who controlled them. It has moderated their ambition. The negroes themselves begin to think of "splitting the vote." In two places I was told that the proposal had been made by negro leaders, as an act of prudence, to divide their vote hereafter.

Immediately after the election, ignorant colored people were much alarmed, thinking they would be deprived of some rights, and, perhaps, even reduced to slavery. This fear is dying out. It grew out of the declarations made before the election by Republican demagogues, who appealed to the fears of the poor negroes, in order to secure their votes to the Republican ticket. But, now that they find themselves unharmed and justly treated, they begin to lose their fear, and even to think of voting with the Democrats. While I was in Selma, a colored man was defended in a suit in court by one of the best lawyers in the State, General Pettus. He had six black witnesses; his opponent, who was white, produced six white witnesses; the jury were all white; but the colored man gained his case: the jury gave a verdict for him. It produced a great effect upon the negroes, who saw that justice was done regardless of color, and this after a Democratic political victory.

I think it probable that the negro vote in the next election will fall off heavily, and this not through intimidation, but partly because the baser white men who have lived off the negro vote are discouraged, and will not take so much pains to "organize" the black voters, and stimulate them by inflammatory addresses and the exhibition of United States troops; partly because in many counties the blacks have been for some time disgusted with their Republican leaders, who have promised many things, such as the famous "forty acres and a mule," which have not come to pass; and partly, also, because the new law which requires a voter to vote in the precinct in which he lives, and no longer allows Lira to vote anywhere in the county, makes the election-day a comparatively tame affair. Formerly all the negroes of the county used to march into the county town to vote, where they saw each other and made a grand holiday.

No doubt, too, the Democrats will do their best to persuade those negroes who would vote the Republican ticket to abstain from the polls, and there are legitimate ways to do this. In Louisiana colored laborers on the railroads, who lose a day's pay if they go off to vote, often, in 1874, did not vote at all. The check which all this will set to the negro's ambition to hold office will be an undoubted advantage to him and to the community, lu the last Legislature there were three colored members who could neither read nor write. In some counties the majority of the supervisors are illiterate blacks. Matters are not nearly so bad in this respect in Alabama as in Mississippi; but, of course, a law-maker or a tax-levyer who is illiterate is not fit for his responsibilities. Some of the Republicans complained to me of a law adopted by the last Legislature obliging office-holders to procure the proper bondsmen within the counties in which they serve ; and I was told that in Dallas County, for instance, there are not more than a dozen Republicans who own property and can become bondsmen. But it seems to me that the rule is a sound one, and can inconvenience mainly only a class of men who ought not to hold important offices. At any rate, it is of no permanent importance, because when the color-line is broken property-holders will be found in both parties.

I do not think that I have anywhere found the negro vote more wickedly or thoroughly manipulated than it was in Alabama. It was systematically compacted. A "bolter" was not merely denounced, but held to be no better than a criminal. In the black counties there were colored demagogues who had a clientage of voters whom they con. trolled; and more than one Republican told me that such fellows would go about in the beginning of a canvass and "coax a man to run for office, in order that they might sell him the vote they could carry." Such fellows were hired to make the canvass of a county. A Republican politician said to me, "I have sent a negro on a hired horse, paying him days' wages, over the county, to advocate a measure, and when election - day came, every colored vote was cast for it." Perrin, a Republican manager, defeated Sheats for Congress by simply telling the blacks that he, Perrin, thought him unfit. Negroes testified that they would have voted the Democratic ticket if Perrin had told them to.

Alabama was not in the old times famous for schools, but it is now better provided than Mississippi, or even Arkansas. In Mobile, Selma, and some other places, an admirable school system is found for both colors. In Selma, ten per cent, of the city revenues is set apart, by a Democratic council, for school purposes, and divided among both colors. Mobile, Montgomery, Selma, Birmingham, and Huntsville, all have graded schools for both colors, and at Huntsville there is a colored normal school. The State school-fund yields one dollar twelve and a half cents per head for all the children in the State; and, besides this, the poll-tax is given to the school-fund in each county. Unfortunately, the poll-tax has not been fully collected. In Lowndes County, for instance, not a dollar of poll-tax was collected last year; and the tax-collector, being a candidate for re-election, urged, as a point in his favor, that " he had not troubled them about the poll-tax." The State superintendent told me that fewer black than white children attend school, in proportion to the population.

It is the universal testimony of men of both parties that the colored people are working better this year, more steadily and effectively, than ever before since the war, and also that, on the whole, they are requiring smaller advances, which means that they have corn left over from last year. It may be said that the people generally, white as well as black, in all parts of the State, are more steadily laboring than in previous years. Alabama has had three successive poor crops, and the planters and farmers are generally poor. This year, so far, promises well, and a good crop would put both parties in good humor.

The State has lost a considerable part of its colored population by emigration to Mississippi, Arkansas, and Texas. Now that its political affairs are settled — as I believe they are — it is possible that the tide may turn. Its immensely rich mineral resources in coal and iron are as yet almost untouched ; but it is a singular fact that iron is already sent from here, not only to Ohio, Missouri, Kentucky, and other Western States, but even to England, where the tenacious, soft iron of Alabama begins to be used in the manufacture of car -wheels. If high protective duties had not caused the establishment of too great a number of ironworks, and an oversupply of iron in the country, the Alabama iron region would be rapidly developed. If the tariff on pig-iron should be considerably lowered in the next few years, furnaces would be set up in great numbers in this State; for here iron of the finest quality can be produced at so cheap a price that it requires no duty to protect it against foreign competition.

As in the other States I have visited, cotton and corn are usually planted on shares, the planter receiving a moderate share of the crop as rental on his land. This plan is satisfactory to the colored people; but they, as yet, lay by but little of their earnings, and show a very slight disposition to buy laud.

Note:
1. Other witnesses swore that Perrin was the author of the report.

9

North Carolina in June, 1875

North Carolina had, according to the census of 1870, 678,470 white people, and 391,650 colored. The Republican estimate of voters here in Raleigh is that, of a total voting population in the State of about two hundred thousand, between seventy thousand and eighty thousand are colored.

The State was heavily Republican in 1868. This means, of course, that a considerable part of the white population then supported the Republican ticket. But in two years this majority was so fur frittered away by the people's disgust and alarm at the corruption and maladministration of the Republican rulers, that the Democrats, in 1870, carried the Legislature, and they have held it ever since. The governor, however, has been, and remains, Republican.

I need not recite here the story of the North Carolina era of railroad grants, and other official and party corruption and maladministration. Its results still remain in a State debt, the interest of which is not paid, and which the rulers of the State evidently do not know how to manage. The total State debt amounted, last November, to very nearly $30,000,000, which includes heavy arrears of interest. The State debt in 1860 was only $8,37-2,900, in addition to which $1,128,000 of bonds were issued during the war for internal improvement purposes. The pastdue interest on all the State debt has been funded several times, and the interest on that is not paid.

The Republican rulers between 1868 and 1870 managed to issue over $12,000,000 of bonds for railroad and other purposes, the greater part of which was wasted or lost in stock-gambling in Wall Street; and it was this which caused their overthrow.

In 1872, Caldwell, the Republican candidate for governor, was elected by about one thousand eight hundred majority. The governor in this State holds office four years. In 1874 a State superintendent of public instruction was chosen, and the Democrats in this vote carried the election by about eight thousand majority. The agitation of the Civil Rights Bill caused the greater part of this change in the two years; but it is confessed by the Republicans that they lose strength constantly, the fact being that no new white voters join their ranks, while they lose constantly by death, removal, and desertion.

When the Democratic Legislature of 1870 came into power, it carefully gerrymandered the Senate and House districts, so as to secure a permanent, though not large, Democratic majority in the General Assembly. There has been some complaint among the Republicans on this head; but the leading men of that party, who are mostly candid men, confess that they can not complain, because they set the example of gerrymandering in 1868, when they were in power; and, no doubt, if they should carry the Legislature they would do it again.

North Carolina is at peace. I tell you this on the authority of the ablest and foremost Republicans in the State; and, indeed, there is no pretense here to the contrary. "The Democrats mean no violence, no wrong to anyone, no hostility to the Government; there is no political crime in the State; there is no intimidation by the Democrats; they mean only to defeat the Radicals and keep them down; and they dislike negro rule." This was said to me by one of the foremost Republicans in the State, a Federal office-holder", and it was confirmed by not less than a dozen others, all zealous and some bitter Republicans, and by leading colored men also.

Those to whom I put the question unanimously said, too, that the Enforcement acts are of no use or importance any longer in North Carolina. There is no necessity for such laws in the State. "They were once useful and necessary, but the time for them has passed." They are now only a reproach to the Republican party, and a handle for the Democratic politicians.

The Republican testimony is unanimous on these heads. It is confirmed by the attitude of the two parties toward each other. There are, here and there, extreme and bitter men on each side ; and in a few counties where the negroes have a large majority, and where they have been used by corrupt white and black men to keep in power wasteful and corrupt local rulers, there is, naturally, strong feeling. But even there there is no violence, and the best men of both parties cooperate together to maintain order. There is but little estrangement of families on account of politics; it is not uncommon, for instance, to see a Democratic and a Republican lawyer partners; and the Democrats try to relieve themselves of the undoubted, and by the Republicans generally acknowledged, evils of negro supremacy in the few counties where the blacks are predominant, by the exercise of ingenuity in framing charters, and gerrymandering city wards. Of this I will give some account hereafter when I describe the conduct of the negroes in politics, which has not been entirely lovely.

The Republicans admit that the Civil Rights Bill has nearly broken up their party in the State. It was the predominant issue in the canvass of 1874, and caused not only their defeat, but a partial disorganization, which the Democratic leaders, if they had been wiser than they are, could, I believe, have made entire.

The Republican party of North Carolina is composed of the great body of the negroes, and of a large mass of the poor whites in the western, or mountain, districts. But these small white farmers dislike the negro, whom they know little about, and are easily alarmed at the thought of social equality with him. The Democratic politicians very naturally worked upon their fears on this point, and thus found their best argument put into their hands by those Republican leaders in the North who insisted upon this measure.

Nor was this the worst result, even, of the Civil Rights agitation. There is no doubt that the Democrats had begun to make up their minds to conciliate and, if possible, gain over a part of the negro vote — to break up the color-line. The best and wisest of them acknowledged to me freely that the only permanent political settlement in the State lies in this direction — a reformation of parties, with an extinction of the color-line in politics ; and they looked forward to this as not far off. But, said these same Democrats:

"When the Civil Rights Bill came up as a prominent issue last year, we dared not conciliate or ask for the colored vote. To do so would have alienated from us the great mass of the white vote, for our people were naturally and deeply excited on this question. Hence, in the canvass of 1874 we addressed ourselves entirely to the whites, and were forced to let the negro vote go where it would. It would have aroused our own people against us, had we made any overtures to the blacks. Oar efforts were all turned to gaining over white Republicans, and we did so pretty effectually."

These men were right, of course, as politicians; and I find that their appeal to white Republicans was strong enough to gain over in Wake County, for instance, which has a negro majority, and is usually Republican, 499 votes, all whites, who in 1874 voted the Democratic ticket because of the Civil Rights Bill.

A prominent colored man with whom I spoke, a politician of some note in the State, and an able man, told me that he was persuaded the Civil Rights Bill had done serious harm to his people. He added that no sensible colored man favored it; they were opposed to it, but the bad and ignorant negroes were excited by it; and this largely because bad white men, who use the negro vote in such counties as New Hanover (in which Wilmington lies) took pains to advocate it; the object of these white men being — said this colored man to me— to keep themselves in profitable offices by pandering to the ignorant negro vote.

I asked him why, if he and others of his race saw this, they did not go to Washington, and remonstrate with the Republican leaders in Congress, and explain to them the mischief they were doing.

He replied, " Some of us did speak our minds privately to Senator Morton and others, but it was of noise."

" But," I said, " you should not have worked privately. Why did you not get up a public remonstrance?"

"Ah," he replied, "we did not dare do that. It would have been said at once among our people here that we had sold out to the Democrats; that we were bolters; and all our influence would have been gone from that moment. The difficulty with our people is that they do not read. The moment one of us tries to oppose the working of the bad whites or corrupt black leaders, these send out runners all over a county or district to tell the colored people that we have sold out, and then they will have nothing more to do with us, and we are gone up." That is to say, the mass is so ignorant that it is controlled very easily by a few designing knaves, whose personal interest in controlling it is so great that they can afford to take extraordinary pains. This is one of the main difficulties with the whole Republican party in North Carolina. Its honest members have no means of forming a public opinion in the party which would enable them to reform abuses, to turn adrift corrupt and incompetent leaders, and to make the party useful and strong.

The poor whites who commonly vote the Republican ticket are but little less illiterate than the blacks. It is believed that not more than twenty-five thousand newspapers are taken in the whole State; but of this small number, seven-eighths are taken by Democrats. Some Republicans to whom I submitted this estimate, which was made by a Republican for me, remarked that, in their opinion, the Republicans did not take even so many. The party has no daily newspaper in the State, and only six or seven weeklies, all small, and edited with little intelligence. They tell a story in Raleigh of the owner of the official organ of the party two or three years ago, a prominent Republican, who determined to wind up the paper, and being asked to continue its publication, remarked, "Do you think I'm a d — d fool, to print a paper for a party that can't read?"

A political party composed so entirely of a mass of ignorance is, of course, easily deceived and misused by designing men, and it can scarcely look for the respect or the confidence and cooperation of the intelligent and property-holding class; especially where, as is fully acknowledged by the honest men in the Republican party, these find themselves with too little influence to guide or control the mass, and are, for the most part, subordinated to corrupt and incapable leaders.

In spite of all this, the State is by no means certainly Democratic. It would be, I am persuaded, if the Democrats had not among their politicians a number of men of little brains, who make foolish speeches in the Legislature, and appeal to the old prejudices among the people. The blunders of such men alienate a good many sensible whites from the Democratic party. For instance, in the last Legislature they carried through a usury law, with the result, now seen and generally made known to the planters and farmers, of forcing the banks and other owners of money to send it out of the State into other States where no usury law exists. North Carolina needs more capital, for the State is rich in mineral and other natural resources; and being at peace, there is no reason why its natural wealth should not begin to be developed. But money is worth from one to one and a half per cent, a month in neighboring States, and capitalists naturally prefer to send it there, rather, than accept seven per cent, at home. Of course the Democratic party is rightly held responsible for this blunder.

Again, the last Legislature forced upon the people, after long caucusing, and against the better judgment of the wisest Democrats, a constitutional convention. It is generally acknowledged by both parties that the constitution requires change in one or two matters, especially in the article relating to county courts, which in a blundering manner fixes the number of these courts in such a way that in the wealthier and busier parts of the State they are entirely taken up with criminal business, to the exclusion of civil cases, whereby justice is seriously impeded. But the opponents of a constitutional convention urge that the required amendments could easily have been submitted by the Legislature to the people; that this would have saved the expense of an election and a convention to a State which already does not pay the interest on its debt, and which is not prosperous ; and, further, that it is impossible to tell what a constitutional convention will do or attempt. It is by no means certain that the Democrats will carry the convention, and, with a Presidential election to come next year, they have put themselves into the dilemma of either being beaten at the convention election in August, or, if they are successful, of having the responsibility of a convention in which it is pretty certain that ignorant men will bring forward some injudicious and perhaps alarming measures.[1]

Also, some of the changes which they propose are not popular, and will arouse opposition. Such is a proposition to abolish the system of townships, established for the first time in 1868, under which justices of the peace are elected by the people, and return to the old system, under which the Legislature appointed an unlimited number of men in every county justices of the peace or magistrates for life or during good behavior, and gave to a certain number of these, selected by the whole, the duty of holding quarter sessions. Of course, the present justices of the peace, their friends, and all who have come to favor the township system, will oppose the change, and this includes a number of Democrats. The object is to relieve the "black" counties of colored justices of the peace, which seems reasonable enough; for some of these negro Dogberrys are amazingly ignorant, and they are, unfortunately, always likely to be corrupt.

The error of the Democrats lies, it seems to me, in endeavoring to adapt the constitution to a transitory state of political affairs; for it is quite certain that the political color-line will presently be broken; and when that happens, when the body of intelligence and wealth in the State is pretty equally divided into two political parties, and the negro vote is also split, the colored men will no longer be put into offices for which, by lack of intelligence and character, they are unfit.

Meantime the Republicans acknowledge that, if they are defeated in August, their party organization will be pretty thoroughly destroyed.

In the last election (1874), the white Republican vote was very greatly reduced, and the civil rights agitation strengthened the color-line, as I have said. But the blacks have acted very well under the law. Here and there one hears of a colored man trying to enforce it; but the public opinion of the best colored men is against it, and the law is a dead letter.

The Republican party of North Carolina, as at present constituted, is not a useful body; and the sooner it disappears and makes way for another, the better for every interest in the State, and especially for the colored people, who are now, in the main, the creatures of bad white and black leaders, who only keep up irritation against the race by their corruption. This, I have reason to believe, is the opinion of many honest and sincere Republicans in the State — some of them colored men — and also of a large number of conservative Democrats, who feel themselves now without influence in the Democratic party, but who will not, and can not, act with the Republican party as it is at present constituted.

North Carolina had formerly a peculiar constitution. Under it the State Senate was chosen by freeholders owning fifty acres of land or more, and a State senator must hold three hundred acres in fee. The justices of the peace were a numerous body in each county, recommended by the governor, and appointed by the Legislature during good behavior. They chose in each county certain ones of their own number to hold the county courts. There was no township government such as is now general in the United States, and as obtains also at present in North Carolina.

Some of the Democratic citizens desire to return to the old system, believing that property ought to be represented in one house of the Assembly, and wishing also to take away from the people the election of local magistrates.

If the color-line were to be perpetual in the State politics, probably some change guarding property against the attacks of a mass of ignorance would be expedient. But as soon as the intelligent and property-owning citizens cease to act with only one party, and become distributed by the mutations of politics somewhat equally in both, the ignorant voters will cease to be dangerous; for there can be no doubt that the negro will, in such a state of things in the South, for many years to come, vote with his employer if he treats him justly, and against him if he cheats him.

Of course, there are Democratic politicians who tell you that they think it best to keep the white vote together, and massed against the black vote. "Thus we may hope to control the State, and the west and middle can protect us in the east, or sea-board:" so said a Wilmington Democrat to me, and made me smile, because, not an hour before, a Republican had said to me that it was "best to keep the black vote together; for thus, with the help of white votes, the State could," he thought, "be controlled by the Republicans." And while such politicians dream, both parties are splitting to pieces; and if Congress will only stop legislating about the South, or threatening it with Force bills and Civil Rights bills, no power on earth can keep them in their present condition after, and hardly until, the nest Presidential election." North Carolina is the first Southern State I have visited where men are discussing some public question other than reconstruction, the negro, and civil rights. There is a strong hard -money element in the present Democratic party, and I heard a good deal of disgust expressed by some respectable Democrats at the platform of the Ohio Democrats. The adoption of a usury law by the Legislature has also raised discontent and discussion. Of course, the party leaders discourage such opinions. They want "harmony," and "a firm front to the enemy;" but the people are really thinking of new questions, and tired of the old.

The State is not as prosperous as it ought to be. A large part of the planters are heavily in debt, and have even fallen into a way of mortgaging their crops in advance. They work, mainly, a thin and worn soil, which needs manure, and they adhere, to a greater extent than in any of the South-western States, to the system of paying wages, which I do not believe to be the best or most satisfactory, either to the planter or the negro laborer.

I have noticed that, when a cotton-planter is embarrassed, in debt, and not making money, he is very apt to think that "the negro don't work," and this you may hear occasionally hereabouts.

But wherever I have found a planter who managed well, and had sufficient capital to carry on his operations, he was successful, and was also well satisfied with the negro. The answer I oftenest received from planters and others whom I asked about the negro as a laborer was this: "If you pay him regularly, cash in hand, and do not attempt to sell him any thing, but let him trade elsewhere, and if you deal fairly with him, he is the best laborer you can get, and you can always keep him."

In the cotton country a few negroes rent land outright, I judge mostly on the richer soils, and then pay from three to seven dollars per acre. The commoner way is to rent twenty-five acres, for which, on strong land, he pays sixteen hundred pounds of lint, or unginned cotton. Others plant on shares, and give the planter one-third of the corn and one-quarter of the cotton. In this case the negro has his own mule. If the planter furnishes the mule, the negro receives sometimes one -third or one -quarter of the crop and a meat ration. Where they serve for wages, they receive from ten to twelve dollars a month and a ration, consisting of five pounds of bacon and a bushel of meal. Where the negro works for wages, he tries to keep his wife at home. If he rents land, or plants on shares, the wife and children help him in the field.

It is odd that the blacks will not eat beef or mutton. They say "it don't stand by them." The meat ration is always of pork. An intelligent planter told me, after some consideration, that he thought if you took a, thousand colored people, men, women, and children, now, working in cotton, they would produce one -quarter less than when they were slaves. He was, however, not certain of this ; nor had he ever thought which was the cheapest, free or slave labor. Slavery, he said, was enormously profitable by reason of the rapid and sure increase in the slaves, which made a man wealthy in the course of some years, even if he produced only enough to feed and clothe them. He told me that in this State, before the war, a full-handed laborer could be hired for one hundred and fifty dollars per annum, with rations, clothing, and medicine. At this rate slave labor was probably, for this region, very little, if any, dearer than free.

An intelligent Republican told me that ho thought not one in ten of the agricultural negroes owned a working mule. This shows them to be poorer than their fellows in the South-western States; but they have here a much poorer soil, and have to spend some money for manure.

A good hand in the tobacco country receives fifteen dollars per month. In all cases they have a cabin, land enough for a vegetable garden, and usually Saturday afternoon to work it, with the use of the mule and plow. Some planters believed that at least half the agricultural force (negro) in the State work for wages.

There are many colored mechanics, and they are all thrifty people, and very commonly own the houses they live in, and often a town lot besides. In the cotton country, an increasing number of colored men own farms of from forty to a hundred acres, but many of these were free before the war. In the towns and villages the colored people have a prosperous look ; they dress neatly, and very commonly live in frame houses. On the whole, their condition appears to me very comfortable and satisfactory.

They have everywhere in the State, I am told, their fair proportion of schools; and here in Raleigh the colored people are, in general, more anxious to send their children to school than the poorer whites. The school system of the State is not in a very good condition. There are 369,960 children between six and twenty-one years, according to the school census of 1874, of whom 242,768 are white, and 127,192 black. There were in that year 4020 public schools open, attended by 119,083 white and 55,000 colored children, under 2108 white and 767 colored teachers. I believe whites teach in some of the colored schools. The schools cost during the year $278,000. At Raleigh there is an excellent colored academy, and this is in part supported by contributions from citizens of other States. There were, in 1874, 2350 white and 999 colored schools.

I have spoken above of the lack of prosperity of the planter class, and I must add that the farmers, on the contrary, are generally prosperous. The tobacco farmers have made good and very remunerative crops for some years, and in general the small farmers, I believe, were never better off than now. The towns, too, are growing ; there are more shops, and there is more demand in all the arming parts of the State for mechanics. More money circulates in the community, I am assured, than ever before, and it passes through more hands. Here, as elsewhere in the South, the retail dealer is prosperous; and the surplus capital or savings of the people, which were formerly invested in slaves, now take the shape of houses and shops and valuable improvements of all kinds. If the credit of the State were restored, there would be an opportunity for the development of its rich and almost untouched mineral resources. New enterprises of this kind are needed to give more profitable employment to the poor white class, which in some respects lags behind the negro.

The colored man, having no pride of race to contend with, has one advantage: he can do any kind of honest work without losing public respect — black boots, run errands, or perform house-service; and I imagine that the civilizing influence of house -service, which brings the colored people in contact with the better class of whites, not only enables them to live better, but also to acquire better and more elevating ideas than the children of the poor whites, who often live in poverty and in wretched hovels.

Note:

1. Since the above was written, a constitutional convention has been chosen, with but two Democratic majority.

10

Georgia in July, 1875

"Georgia," said a Federal office-holder to me, a Republican, and long resident in the State, "is still a rude community. In the country districts the people are what you would call careless of law, and apt to take revenge into their own hands." And he instanced to me two acts of assassination which had occurred within six months at no great distance from Atlanta, the victims being old citizens, prominent, and Democrats. One was waylaid and shot on the road, the other was shot while sitting in his house at night. "Politics," said this Federal office-holder, who is a strong Republican, "has nothing to do with such crimes. Such things occur not unfrequently, though by no means constantly; but they happen because our people are, in the main, not much above them. If a man offends or wrongs another, this other takes the law into his own hands."

"There has been no political crime, properly so called, in this State for two or three years," said another Federal office-holder to me, also a zealous Republican, and in a position where he had the opportunity to know whereof he spoke. " There is a good deal of crime in the State, but it is not political. The general community is apathetic; the magistrates often are not active in ferreting out criminals, for fear of taking harm themselves. Matters are improving; but still rude men in the country districts are too apt to take the law in their own hands. Negroes are generally more openly attacked than white men when they become the subjects of dislike by others, but otherwise there is no difference. The negro, usually, will not defend himself, and thus encourages attack. The white man is more formidable, and so his opponent lies in wait for him."

He gave me, as an example, the case of a negro who complained to a United States officer that a white man had beaten him over the head with a stick. The negro's hog had got into his white neighbor's garden; whereupon the beating, and the request from the black for the interference of the United States Government. " "Who saw the man beat you?" " Nobody, sah." "Were you and he alone ?" " Yes, sah." " And you stood still and let him beat you?" was the officer's pertinent question. "Now," said he to me, "you see, this black man was then and there openly beaten. If it had been a white man, his antagonist would have lain in wait for him after night and done him some severe injury. But it is not political."

On the day I came to Atlanta news came there that a United States deputy-marshal had been shot through both legs, and had had his horse shot, in a northern county. This looked a good deal like Ku-klux, and I have seen such cases reported as Ku-klux outrages. But the marshal told me his deputy was engaged in ferreting out illicit distilleries. He had just captured and destroyed two or three, and the enraged owners took their revenge on him. This business of illegal distilling is followed to a great extent in the mountain region of Georgia and North Carolina, and by Republicans as well as Democrats, of course; and these people hate the sight of a deputy-marshal, and do not hesitate to shoot at him, regardless of politics.

Petit larceny is here, as in other cotton States, the principal and the most vexatious offense of the plantation negro. "They are an excellent working force," said more than one planter to me; "but they will steal cattle, hogs, and many other things." This crime is very severely punished in Georgia — they are relentless toward it — and it results that negroes are sent to the penitentiary and the chain-gang for very long periods for it. The severity of the sentences. would be with us inhuman; but the crime is so serious and frequent, I am satisfied that it must be checked with a strong hand. I was amused to discover that in many cases employers refused to prosecute their servants for theft, on the ground, as in more than one instance they frankly but privately confessed to me, that they " did not like to be the cause of such severe punishment;" and this feeling will, I suspect, work its effect by-and-by, in causing milder punishments to be favored.

There are only very few counties in Georgia in which colored men are drawn for jury duty. The constitution of the State, made by Republicans, declares that "the General Assembly shall provide by law for the selection of upright and intelligent persons to serve as jurors. There shall be no distinction between the classes of persons who compose grand and petit jurors."

This seems to me an admirable regulation, but I do not think it is fairly administered. There is no doubt that it properly excludes the great mass of the negroes, and also a great many whites; and I am told that juries are generally carefully selected. But there are certainly in the large towns a few colored men who answer to the definition of "upright and intelligent," and these ought to be included in the jury-lists. In Atlanta, the other day, the colored people made up a list of one hundred and fifty names of men of color whom they regarded as fit jurymen, and presented it to the Ordinary, that he might select from it some names for the jurybox, which, as I understand, is drawn for two years' service. They now assert that no attention was paid to their request. I spoke on this subject with an uncommonly intelligent Georgian, a planter and business-man;

he said that in his county the negroes complained of their exclusion, but be thought it wise. "The most intelligent of them are often the worst," be said; "and to the negro the jury-box, with its handsome daily pay, seems heavenly. They would all like to serve on juries."

This last is true enough. The plantation negro naturally likes jury duty; and the pay, two or three dollars a day, seems to him princely; while, of course, be is shamefully unfit. Nevertheless the wholesale exclusion is neither right nor wise; and it is one of the causes why so many negroes have emigrated from the State. Of course, the most intelligent leave first.

You bear a good deal of complaint, both among planters and in the cities, about the unsteadiness of the negro as laborer or houseservant. I was a little puzzled at this at first, because in other States I heard but very few such complaints. But a number of planters and citizens later explained to me the cause. "Whoever pays his black laborers regularly and honestly can get as many as he wants at all times, and they will work faithfully," said a South Georgian planter to me — a rough man, whose conversation in some respects impressed me unfavorably. "Come down into my country," be added, "and I'll show you plantations standing idle, whose owners will tell you that the nigger won't work; and I'll show you plantations right along- side of them where one hundred hands work faithfully year after year, and don't think of moving away. All you've got to do is to pay them honestly and sell them nothing, and you won't complain. I don't keep a store. I make the niggers go off to the village. That's what they want, and I pay cash — that's all they want; and I can get one hundred extra bauds whenever I like; and I'm not an easygoing man, either."

The same story I beard from citizens. "Where a man complains that his servants leave him, you'll find that his wife has paid them in driblets — a dollar now, and half a dollar another time. They don't understand accounts; they are spendthrifts; and at the end of the mouth, when they have but little due them, they think they have been cheated, and go off" dissatisfied. I suffered in this way for a while; but now I pay them their whole month's wages punctually at noon on the day their month is out, and they never leave me. Punctual and honest pay is all that is needed to make them faithful and steady servants." Similar testimony I received from a number of persons of both sexes. Irregularity of pay, and often the failure to pay wages, have been another fruitful cause of the large negro emigration from the State.

A law of the State deprives a man of his vote at an election who has not paid his taxes for the year previous. There is a polltax of one dollar. "This," said a Republican to me, "works badly against our party, because the negroes evade its payment, or are careless about it, or lose their tax -receipts, and then their vote is rigorously challenged, and they lose it."

"Half the negroes in Georgia are disfranchised for non-payment of their poll-tax," was the assertion of another and a zealous Republican, a leading man in the party. "Many whites do not pay either," he added; "but the Republicans do not challenge as rigorously as the Democrats."

A number of Republicans complained of this law to me as though it were wrong or unfair; but I think, on the contrary, it is just and right. If a voter neglects or refuses to pay his poll-tax, certainly he is not fit to cast a vote. By-the-way, a Republican in North Carolina owned to me that so remiss were the colored people there in paying their poll-tax, that if failure to pay there forfeited the vote, two-thirds of the negroes in the State would be disfranchised.

Aside from this perfectly just reason for disfranchising a voter, I am persuaded that in Georgia other means have been used to overcome the colored vote — means not at all justifiable. In some cities, for instance, as in Atlanta and Savannah, insufficient voting-boxes are provided, and the negro voters are crowded out and prevented from casting their fall vote. A candid planter whom I questioned upon this subject — he living in a county which had a black majority, but had been for some years ruled, honestly, I must add, by Democrats — said, "We had white Republican county officers, natives; we discovered that they were corrupt. They kept the county offices for themselves, but were ready enough to let a negro go to the Legislature, where the Democratic majority left no chance for stealing. As we could get no county reform by arguments or appeals to the negroes, who were as three and a half to one white voter, we made up our minds to buy the black leaders, who fooled their people with imitation Republican tickets. Later, we bought over also some of the white leaders, and others we put in jail when we could prove corruption against them. "We have had a struggle for it, because some oven of our own men proved corrupt, and wo had to pitch them overboard. But we have managed to maintain a pretty good government."

In another case I was told, "We can always elect a Democrat to the Legislature. There is no stealing there, and neither the negro leaders nor the corrupt whites care to go there. The struggle is over the county offices. In my county and in others, I do not doubt there has been ballot-box stuffing. This was unknown among us before the war, and it is one of the bad things that will be left here, arising out of the new order of things. I don't justify it, and I very deeply regret it; for, once introduced, it will continue to be practiced ; but where the blacks are in a large majority, they are the means of very serious robbery, and men are apt to think that any thing is justifiable to save themselves from such gross misgovernment."

In yet another case a planter said to me, "The Republicans began in my county with Union Leagues, and these became quickly the prey of vagabond and corrupt whites, almost without exception, natives, for we have had few carpet-baggers in our local politics. You could not buy a member of the Union League; but we found we could easily buy the leaders, and this we did do. These leagues are now almost entirely broken up. The negroes have discovered that the white leaders were corrupt; but they stick to their black leaders, some of whom are sharp but generally unscrupulous men."

I give these statements, because they describe pretty accurately what has been done in many counties where the negroes have a majority of votes. The whites have been determined to keep the local governments in their own hands, and they have used means which the better class do not attempt to justify, except upon the plea that no other means were available to save themselves from the hands of thieves. That the negro voter has been, to an extraordinary degree, the prey of demagogues and scoundrels, wherever in the South he has had a considerable majority, no one can doubt who has examined the question. His ignorant attachment to the Republican name, and his readiness to follow black leaders, who are easily corruptible, and low whites who flatter him, have made him the tool of robbers. That the whites, wherever they can, should protect themselves, even by counter-frauds, is lamentable but natural. I wonder it has not been more universally practiced in other States. That intimidation and crowding out at the polls should be practiced is not at all remarkable, under the circumstances.

Governor Smith seemed to me to speak sensibly when he told me that these evils could be cured only by a division of parties off the color- line, which he thought must, before long, come about.

The other means used, however, have, I believe, made actual intimidation rare in the last two or three years, except here and there in some uncommonly rough and lawless county, -where it would be practiced upon whites as well, if the white vote were divided. Georgia has a few such counties, where society is not in a pleasant condition, where violence is frequent; and here the negro suffers probably oftener than the white, because he does not defend himself. But emigration is emptying these counties of the negroes. It is a sure cure, moreover, even in these counties. I have been told by Republicans of some cases where the perpetrators of violence upon an unoffending negro found the public sentiment, to their surprise, so changed of late that they thought it prudent to leave the State. I believe this better sentiment is caused, in part at least, by the fact that planters in such localities see their laboring force removing to other States.

It may seem to you that the condition of the negro in Georgia is not happy, under all these circumstances ; and yet here is proof that such a judgment would be mistaken. It is not difficult to hear of instances of abuse; but the best and conclusive proof that these are only sporadic cases, and that, in general, the colored people are safe in their lives and property, is found in an official report of the comptroller-general of the State, for 1874, giving the character and value of property and amount of taxes returned by colored tax -payers for that year. The number of colored polls listed was 83,318. These returned an aggregate value of taxable property amounting to $6,157,798, on which they actually paid $30,788 in taxes. They owned 338,769 acres of agricultural laud, and city and town property to the amount of $1,200,115.

Now, remembering that these people were slaves only nine years before; that they owned, when they obtained their freedom in 1865, absolutely nothing except what they stood in; and that they have not only acquired all this property in seven years, but lived, spent a great deal of money in foolish ways, and lost, I do not know how many thousands, in the Freedmen's Savings-bank, I think it clearly establishes that, first, they have labored with creditable industry and perseverance, and, second, that they have been fairly protected in their rights of life and property by the Democratic rulers of the State. I do not think the colored people in any other State I have visited own half as much real estate, or, indeed, a quarter as much, as those of Georgia. Surely this says a good deal for the effective justice and protection given the negro in this Democratic State.

At least twenty- five thousand colored people have left the State in the last five or six years. In Atlanta I had some conversation with a negro who had been one of the leaders in this movement, and he gave me a number of instances where colored farmers had removed to Mississippi or Arkansas, taking with them mules and farm-tools, in some cases enough to fill two or three cars. This man remarked to me that when he was younger, and during slavery times, he had noticed that many white people, even planters' sons, removed from the State, and when any of them returned for a visit home, they proved usually to have prospered by the change. " I thought if it was good for the whites, it would be good for our folks too," he said; "and so I always encouraged all that wanted to try it."

He had started a son-in-law to Louisiana, where, after two years, he found him prospering. He had visited Arkansas and Mississippi also, and confirmed to me my own observations that in these States the colored people thrive, and are generally secure in their rights. He thought Arkansas the best of all the States for his people, but showed me also pamphlets recommending certain parts of Mississippi, which he was distributing among his people.

I do not know, by-the-way, what better evidence one can have than this of the generally satisfactory condition of the colored people in those States. The testimony of a colored man — a sufficiently shrewd fellow I judged him, who had traveled through the regions he spoke of, and whom I saw, from his conversation, to be a stickler for the "rights" of his people — ought to go very far to satisfy Northern people. Such disorders as are now happening in Mississippi will injure that State, but they are strictly local and sporadic.

He told me, what I knew otherwise also, that emigration agents come into Georgia from different counties in the three States I have named in search of laborers. I know myself a single county in Northern Louisiana which has drawn in the last seven years not less than four thousand colored people from Georgia and Alabama. These agents make known the fact that rich lands lie open in the sections they represent, and, not unfrequently, they are ready to pay the expense of a family's removal. The late fall and winter, after the crops are made, is the season of removal; and the man I speak of thought, from what he knew, that not less than five thousand would leave the State next winter. This, bear in mind, was long before the so-called insurrection.

I confess that, to me, this readiness to better their fortunes by emigration seemed one of the best signs I saw in the South of the real independence of the negro ; and I found it most fully developed in the very State where, according to the commonly received reports of Southern Republican politicians, the negro is still in a condition little better than slavery. If this were true, of course he would not be moving away, for he would be tied to the soil.

Nor do I believe that Georgia will sustain a serious loss by this emigration. It will make room for white emigrants; and Georgia is peculiarly fitted to receive and utilize a white farming and manufacturing population. It is not properly a planting, but a manufacturing, State.

I recur for a moment to the remarkable return of over six millions of property owned by the negroes oˆ Georgia, to say that it is the only official report of the kind I have found in any Southern State. Arkansas, Louisiana, Mississippi, Alabama, long under Republican rulers, yielded me no such information. Only in Democratic Georgia had the rulers sufficient intelligent curiosity to ascertain what practical progress the negro had made under freedom.

The result is, of course, very gratifying and surprising. It speaks well for the negro's industry, and his growing power of accumulation, and it speaks well for the justice and fair dealing of the whites toward the blacks.

Georgia has at this moment but one Republican journal, and that is a weekly — the National Republican — printed in Atlanta. From that I take the following editorial comment on the condition of the colored people. It seems to me a little harsh, but it comes from a Republican:

"What is the record of ten years of freedom? In the matter of temperance has there been   progress? Nay, in this respect the freedmen are a thousand per cent, worse off than they were in slavery. Rarely do we find a strictly temperate man. Very nearly all drink, in town and out, young men and old, and the women too. Thousands spend a dollar for whisky through the week, and on the Sabbath put a nickel or nothing in the contribution-box. The freed-men of Georgia spend in a half-year for liquor as much as they have paid for schools since emancipation. Is this a matter of which they should be proud ? To whom is the infliction of this wrong due? What has been done for schools? A little money has been raised, but not a hundredth, if a thousandth, part of what has been spent for tobacco, and shows, and shot-guns, and flues. One show here last winter is said to have carried away $3000 of the colored people's money— more than their voluntary contributions to schools in this city since 1865. In ten years not more than one in nine or ten has learned to read in the State; or out of 550,000 not more than 60,000 or 70,000; and these very largely through the aid of Northern missions. This year taxes will be paid on an aggregate of $7,000,000 of property, or less than $13 a head. This is the showing of a decade of freedom and fair opportunity. For it, in some measure, the whites may be responsible, but the responsibility lies chiefly with the people themselves. They have probably earned from $35,000,000 to $45,000,000 a year, and out of it should have saved a large percentage. But there has been improvidence and waste on every hand. Not quite, but very nearly, as poor and ignorant are the freedmen to-day as when emancipated; and their ignorance and their poverty, quite as much as the 'prejudice and hate' of the whites, serve to keep them where they are and what they are — hewers of wood and drawers of water."

If a Democratic journal had said these things it would have been called prejudice, and I should not have thought of quoting it. They are the words of the Republican and colored organ.

While I am speaking of the Democratic management of the State, I think it right to call attention to the satisfactory financial statement, which compares remarkably with the condition of Louisiana, Arkansas, and other Southern States which have been under Republican control. The State debt is but $8,000,000, and the credit of the State stands high in New York and abroad. In January of this year there was a surplus in the treasury of over $1,000,000. The total cost of the State government for 1874 was but $776,000, while the mileage, per diem, and contingents of the Louisiana Republican Legislature in 1871 cost $958,950; and- the State printing cost $431,000 in one year.

The counties have no debts of any consequence. The cities have some, but not a very heavy indebtedness.

It is altogether such a showing as these Democrats need not be ashamed of. It has one weak spot only — the expenditure for schools. Georgia had no free schools before the war, and the system makes but slow headway in the State. The present superintendent of public instruction (a Democrat) is a zealous and efficient officer, and he looks forward to better days.

There was apportioned by him for the support of schools in 1874 only $265,000, and the schools are open, in general, less than three months in the year. For the present year the. school-tax will yield only $270,000. Last year there were 135,000 children in the public schools — an increase of 50,000 over 1873. In 1873 there were actually attending school only 63,922 white, and 19,755 colored children; in 1874 the numbers stood 93,167 white and 42,374 colored children. This was out of a total of 218,733 white, and 175,304 colored children within the school ages.

There is still in many counties some prejudice against colored schools, but it constantly decreases ; and you will notice that more than twice as many colored children attended schools in 1874 as in 1873. Atlanta has a colored university, and the Legislature appropriates yearly toward its support $8000 — the same amount which is given to the old State University. The governor and superintendent of schools both desire that this appropriation shall be diverted to a colored normal school; and there is some ignorant prejudice in Atlanta against the teachers in the university, on the ground of their sitting at table with the colored students, which is thought to promote "social equality." It is not denied, however, that the school does good work; and I imagine the teachers can best instruct the pupils in the minor morals by eating at the same table with them.

One can not help feeling a little contempt for the people who here in the South make themselves needlessly unhappy about "social equality." I was amused at a sensible planter — a Democrat, and a native Georgian— who said to me, "It is absurd in us to make such a fuss. There is scarcely a man of us whose children are not suckled by negro nurses ; our playmates were negro boys; all our relations in the old times were of the most intimate; and, for my part, I would as soon ride in a car with a cleanly dressed negro as with a white man. It is all stupid nonsense, and makes us absurd in the eyes of sensible people."

The feeling takes the most ridiculous forms, too: for instance, in Atlanta and Augusta colored people are allowed to ride in streetcars; in Savannah they are forbidden. Why the difference? Is a Savannah negro less clean, or is a Savannah white man a more noble being, than those in the other two cities?

As showing the relations of the two races, I found on a wall in Augusta a poster giving notice of a colored railroad-excursion to Port Royal, stating price of passage and time required, and at the end a notice that a special car would be provided for such of the white citizens as would like to take advantage of this opportunity to see Port Royal, and special accommodations for their comfort would be at hand. The whole affair was under the conduct of colored men.

The superintendent of schools told me that there was less prejudice against colored schools in the southern counties, where the negroes are the most numerous, than in the northern part of the State.

The negroes in and near the cities and towns are usually prosperous. There are many colored mechanics, and they receive full wages where they are skillful. Near Atlanta and other places they own small "truck-farms," and supply the market with vegetables. There are fewer black than white beggars in the cities; and a missionary clergyman surprised me by the remark that the blackberry crop, which was ripening, was "a blessing to dozens of poor white families whom he knew," who lived half the year, he said, in a condition of semistarvation. He explained that these people would not only sell blackberries, but that in the season they largely lived on this fruit. These are the kind of people to whom factories would be a blessing.

In the cotton country the planter usually pays his hands ten dollars a month, by the year, with a house and ration. The ration consists of three pounds of bacon, a peck of meal, and a pint of molasses per week. The laborer has also a "patch" of land for a garden, and Saturday afternoon for himself, with the use of the planter's mules and tools to work the garden. They work from sunrise to sunset, and in the summer have two and a half hours for dinner. The cotton-pickers receive fifty cents per one hundred pounds in the seed, and are fed; or sixty-five cents per one hundred pounds, if they feed themselves. The ration costs about fifteen cents a day.

Most planters keep a small store, and sell their laborers meat, bread, and tobacco on credit, the general settlement being made once a year. The women receive for field work six dollars a month and a ration; and I was told that they insist on receiving their own wages, and will not let their husbands use their money. They form an important extra force for pressing work.

One of the most intelligent planters I met in the State told rue that his laborers cost him about fifteen dollars a month — wages and ration. He added (what surprised me) that the best planters prefer to pay wages rather than let their land on shares, and that the wages system was growing in favor also with the negroes. I found this confirmed by other testimony. It is very different in the other States I have seen, except, indeed, North Carolina; and I imagine the poverty of the soil is a main reason for it. In Mississippi, Louisiana, and Arkansas, the planters told me it would be poor policy to pay wages. Certainly, it is the poorest system for the negro.

Where the negroes plant on shares, the planter furnishes the land and mules, and feeds the mules. The negro furnishes labor and feeds it, and gets one -third the crop. He pays for one-third of the fertilizers. The planter gins the whole crop. Where negroes rent land, they pay seven hundred and fifty pounds of lint or ginned cotton for thirty-five to forty acres of land — as much as they can cultivate with one mule — and they keep up the fences, and pay for the fertilizers. "On this lay," said a planter to me, "I know one man who made two hundred and fifty dollars clear in a year over and above his support, and another who lost one hundred and fifty dollars." He added that the negroes, on the whole, preferred the wages system; and this is mainly, I imagine, because the artificial manures are costly, and an uncertain element in making the crop. This means really, of course, that it costs more money to make cotton in Georgia than in the other States I have named. A third of a bale to the acre is the average crop in Georgia, but in Mississippi they expect to get from three-quarters to a bale per acre without manure.

A planter from one of the "black counties," where the negroes are most numerous, told me they were a most quiet and docile population. "I live in the midst of several hundred," he said, "with no white family within several miles of me, and my people are never in the least alarmed. I have not a fire-arm in the house half the time. Treat them honestly," he said, "and they are all right."

This man amused me with some stories of how the blacks were deceived by a set of white rascals for some years after the war. Among other things, these fellows brought red and blue sticks, which they sold for one dollar each to the negroes, wherewith to "stake off" the land which the Government was to give them. The blacks used also, when they went to the polls to vote, to bring halters with them, for the mule which General Grant was to give them. I would like to know what graceless wretch it was who spread all over the South, among the blacks, the story of "forty acres and a mule," which has caused bitter disappointment to many thousands of credulous negroes, and appears to have been used mainly to induce them to vote the Republican ticket. In Louisiana, several negroes told me that General Butler, they understood, would make them this gift; but usually it is from General Grant that they expect it, and they are very ready to vote for him.

The planter of whom I speak told me that the young negroes who had grown up since the war worked less steadily than the old hands. He added that, in his county, some blacks owned as much as two hundred and fifty acres of land, and many were doing well on their own farms. "If it were not for petit larceny, they would all do well." He kept a colored school on his own plantation. The black people liked it, he said. They are fond of hoarding coin, especially since the Freedmen's Bank failed, which caused loss to many of them, and they are quite ready to buy gold and silver coin at a premium.

The negroes in Georgia have some, but slight and lessening, causes for dissatisfaction. The fact that they will pay taxes on over seven millions of dollars this year, all acquired since 1866, and by a class notoriously unthrifty, shows that they have suffered no serious wrong or injustice. The fact that over twenty-five thousand negroes have emigrated from the State, shows also that they know how to better their condition.

But their dissatisfaction does not arise from wrongs; for the whites also are dissatisfied, and an equal number of them have removed to other States. The chief difficulty in Georgia is that it is an old State, with worn lauds, whose near neighbors, Mississippi, Arkansas, and Louisiana, invite its people to come and take possession of new and fertile soils, where they need no manures, and can get greater returns for their labor.

Georgia and North Carolina differ from the other Southern States I have seen in this: that much of their land is thin and worn, and will not produce a crop, even in the cotton region, without the use of expensive manures. This, of course, makes cotton planting less remunerative than it is in the rich bottom-lands of Mississippi, Arkansas, and Louisiana. Moreover, judging from appearances, I should say that even in the old times, before the war, Georgia must have been a less wealthy State than those west of it.

One evidence of a general lack of prosperity in this State I came upon even before I entered Georgia, is the considerable number of emigrants of both colors, who are leaving the State for Arkansas, Texas, and Mississippi, and parties of whom I frequently spoke with at railroad stations. Georgia has lost in this way, since the conclusion of the war, I have been told by good authorities. Democratic citizens, at least fifty thousand people — half of each color.

The fact is that Georgia, though it is still essentially an agricultural State, has its greatest future as a manufacturing region. It has a great deal of valuable water-power ; also coal, iron, and other mineral wealth ; it has a great deal of land better fitted for small farms and varied agriculture than for either cotton or corn ; and it has ready to the hands of manufacturing capitalists a numerous population of " poor whites," whose daughters make excellent factory operatives, and to whom the offer of this species of labor is a real rise in the scale of civilization.

The cotton-planters are not, as a class, either wealthy or prosperous; but the few cotton-factories are, even in this day of general depression, very remunerative. The iron and coal works are in a good condition, and the farmers of Northern Georgia are said to be doing well in all respects. I have been surprised by the unbroken prosperity of the cotton-mills in Georgia. The Augusta mills have paid a yearly dividend of not less than twenty per cent, since 1865, and the stock is quoted at 168 to-day, and none is for sale. The product is 275,000 yards per week. The Eagle and Phoenix mills of Columbus, built since the war, with a capital of $1,000,000 and 25,000 spindles, have paid an average dividend of over eighteen per cent., and have a considerable surplus. No stock can be bought. The Graniteville cotton-mills, which lie in South Carolina, just across the border-line of Georgia, were not fairly started until 1867; and since then, I am told, have paid off a debt of $75,000, increased their capacity from 15,000 to 23,000 spindles, built over forty houses for operatives, and have meantime paid an average dividend of over twelve per cent.

But all these mills have done a more important work besides; for all of them give employment to the girls and women of the poor white class, to whom such labor is, as I have said, a real and very important step in civilization. They make excellent operatives, I am told, and the factory life not only improves their own condition in a remarkable degree, but adds greatly to the comfort of their parents; and is, perhaps, the only means of redeeming this large population from a somewhat abject and degraded condition.

I think I can see that the cotton-manufacturer has several important advantages in this State over his rivals in the Northern States. He needs no such solid and costly dwellings for the work-people; land is still cheap; lumber for building is cheap; fuel is unusually cheap; the operative class is, I suspect, more manageable, and more easily made intelligent, than the rude, imported labor now used in the North; food is, and must long remain, cheaper; the mildness of the winter is certainly an advantage, and there is an air of comfort and contentment about these Southern factories which is very pleasing. The operatives are usually very nicely lodged in cottages, and are evidently happy and pleased with their life.

It is among the factory workers and the small farmers of Georgia that one finds the chief prosperity of the State. Here there is little or no debt; money circulates rapidly; improvements are seen; and there are patient, hopeful labor, thrift, and enterprise, which affect, as it seems to me, the whole population. I heard here and there of instances of poor young mechanics working steadily and earnestly, in a New England way, at their trades, making labor respectable, accumulating property, and taking honorable places in their communities ; and some such men talked to me of their past and their future, of the hopeful change which the extinction of slavery had produced in the prospects of their class, in language which showed me that there is a new-born hope of better things in the poor white people of the State.

When yon strike the cotton region, affairs are not so happy. In the first place, the cotton farmers and planters — the large land-owners, less energetic than the population I have spoken above — have suffered from two bad laws which fostered their lack of business capacity and love of ease. The Homestead Law reserves to a land-owner a homestead of the value of three thousand dollars in gold, exempting this from seizure by creditors. Of course, in an agricultural region, so large an exemption can be easily made to cover a very considerable amount of property. To this was added a lien law — fortunately repealed by the last Legislature — which enabled the planter to borrow on or mortgage his unplanted crop ; the factor who furnished him tools, manures, food, and clothing having, by this law, the first claim on the crop. Of course, he also secured the handling of it. I have seen the evil operation of such a law in Louisiana in the slavery times, and in the Sandwich Islands more recently. It is ruinous, for it offers a prize to incapacity and unthrift, enables men to undertake planting with insufficient capital, and deranges the whole industry. In Georgia the Homestead Law doubtless increased the evils of the Lien Law ; and between the two it resulted that many of the planters fell over head and ears in debt. These were regularly a year or more behindhand; and if the crop — which is more precarious in this State than in some others — failed, or fell short, the factor took all; and the laborers, employed to a great extent on wages, sometimes lost all their pay, except what they had consumed during the year.

I do not doubt that in some cases such loss and wrong fell upon the negro laborer through the recklessness or dishonesty of the planter; but I am satisfied also that much oftener the planter would have honestly paid if he could, and that he, as well as his workman, was the victim of a bad business system and of his lack of capital and of business thrift. It was one of the incidents of the reorganization of labor on a new basis in a State where the culture of cotton is less certainly remunerative than in more fertile regions.

To show you how the Lien Law worked, here is a statement made to me by a planter of the charges which he had known to be paid for advances made by a factor. He instanced to me the case of a planter who required from his factor a loan or advance of five thousand dollars to make his crop. For this he paid one per cent, per month, to which I was assured seven per cent, per annum were sometimes added, making really nineteen per cent. Then the arrangement was that the factor should buy all the planter's supplies for him; and for this service he charged him two and a half per cent., and billed the goods to him at "time prices," which added eight or ten per cent, to their cost. Then the factor sold the planter's crop, and charged for this two and a half per cent, again.

I should not have believed such a system possible, had I not seen precisely the same thing regularly done by the sugar -planters in the Sandwich Islands two or three years ago. Of course, no business except the slave-trade could bear such a drain. Some planters complained to me that they could never get advances from the banks, which preferred to lend to the factors; but this will hardly surprise any business man. The profits were great enough for the bank and the factors to divide.

One of the natural results of this system has been discontent among the negroes — the laborers — who sometimes lost their wages. At least twenty-five thousand of them have left the State; and this emigration, which last year already began to alarm the planters, has not ceased. It has been increased by other causes; but I am satisfied, from conversation with leading colored men, that the lack of prosperity here, and the well-founded belief that they could do better elsewhere, have been one of its main causes.

The repeal of the Lien Law has, of course, left the poor and improvident among the planters without credit, and they are naturally in poor spirits. But they will presently see that it is their salvation. Already they are planting more com than ever before. They see that to raise bread and meat enough for their laborers will keep them out of the hands of the factors. More corn will be harvested in the cotton region of Georgia this year than in any year since the war.

I have given this statement of the industrial condition of Georgia because it is certain that many of the incidents of Georgia society grow mainly out of the fact that the planting region is less prosperous than the cotton region of Arkansas, Louisiana, or Mississippi; and is so mainly for the reasons I have given — the poverty of the soil, the precariousness of the crop in the far southern counties, where it is peculiarly exposed to the attacks of insects, and the poverty and unthrift of the planters. That you may not think I have overstated this lack of prosperity, I give you here some figures from a mercantile report, which I find in an Augusta journal. The business failures in the State amounted in the last six months to the sum of $2,956,215. This is a greater loss by far than is reported from any other Southern Stater; greater even than in South Carolina, as the following figures show:

Alabama	$523,000
Arkansas	211,000
Florida	235,000
Georgia	2,956,000
Louisiana	630,000
Mississippi	1,045,000
North Carolina	263,000
South Carolina	2,042,000
Tennessee	325,000
Texas	1,153,000
Virginia and West Virginia	1,383,000
Total	$10,766,000

The liabilities of Georgia amount to nearly one-third of the liabilities of the twelve States; the liabilities of Georgia and South Carolina together amount to nearly half the liabilities of the entire

South. Georgia compares as follows with other larger and wealthier States:

```
Indiana.............................................. $1,860,000
Iowa................................................     436,000
Kentucky............................................   2,456,000
Missouri............................................   2,328,000
Ohio................................................   2,594,000
Georgia.............................................   2,956,000
```

Now, you must remember that, unlike Ohio, Indiana, or Missouri, Georgia is almost entirely an agricultural State, and that her factories and other purely business enterprises have been, almost without exception, prosperous. These figures show the condition mainly of the planting interest and of those businesses intimately related to it.

I conclude my account of Georgia with a few remarks about the political condition of the State.

There is no Republican party worthy of the name in the State. There is but one Republican newspaper, and that is a weekly. One of the most zealous Republicans in the State said to me, "The Republican party, so far as its white members are concerned, consists mainly of Federal office-holders and men seeking office — mostly natives of the State." He added, "There are not more than a hundred active white Republicans in Georgia who are honest, and out of office." Another zealous Republican said to me, "The white Republicans of Georgia are made up almost entirely of Federal office-holders whose aim is to keep their places, and of men who are trying to get these places. There is substantially nobody else, white, in the party." Another said, " White men put themselves forward for Congress on the Republican ticket, knowing they will be beaten, with the sole object of rushing to Washington as soon as the election is over to set up a claim for a Federal office on the ground of their defeat." "The Civil Rights Bill killed the Republican party in this State," said a Federal officer to me; " it put us back to 1867."

Less than five thousand whites voted the Republican ticket at the election of 1874. In 1872, a Republican told me, at least tea thousand blacks voted the Greeley ticket, and "more and more negroes vote Democratic all the time." I notice that among the grievances of the blacks mentioned in discussions of the so-called insurrection, is one that they are disfranchised if they do not pay their poll and road taxes. This is perfectly true, and, I think, perfectly just. Poll and road tax is all that the greater part of them pay toward the support of the Government; and if they evade this, they do not deserve to vote. The same law applies to the whites.

In the Georgia Congressional delegation there is not now a single Republican. One reason for this is, that in some cases the party nominates men who can not get the support of honest Republicans. One such man I was told of, who was repudiated by the honest Republicans of his district, but was no sooner beaten than he proceeded to Washington and set up a claim to all the Federal patronage of the district. Nor are claims of this kind always disallowed at Washington. For instance, not long ago a man was appointed collector of internal revenue in a Georgia district who, according to general Republican testimony, had been a Ku-klux in Ku-klux times, and who actually could not take the office because he then stood charged with offering a bribe.

One of the most prominent Federal officers in the State, a native and a zealous Republican, and bitter opponent of the Democratic party, said to me, "I don't know that there is any Republican party in the State. The negroes will not vote in general, because they have no white vote back of them. The blacks are almost totally disfranchised by their neglect to pay their taxes. At least two -thirds of the colored voters are thus disfranchised. Then, again, in some communities -where there are large negro majorities half a dozen black demagogues insist on running for the same office, and then Democrats run in between them. Wherever independent tickets have been put up in counties the supporters of these strove for the negro vote, and in such cases the election was always peaceable and full, because there two parties were anxious for this vote. I do not think that for a year or two past there has been much cheating in wages; the people have learned to do better."

Georgia has been longer and more continuously than any other cotton State, since the war, under the rule of the Democratic party. Bullock, the Republican governor, chosen at the adoption of the constitution, in 1868, for a term of four years, abandoned his office and the State in October, 1871; Smith, Democrat, was elected to fill his unexpired term; was re-elected in 1872, and is still governor. The Legislature, which is elected every two years, was Republican by a small majority in 1868; but the body which assembled in November, 1871, was strongly Democratic, and both houses, and all the executive officers, have been Democratic ever since.

It follows that, since the winter of 1871, the State government has been entirely in Democratic hands; and the county governments have also, with but few exceptions, fallen under the same control. The Legislature has been overwhelmingly Democratic in both branches.

It would be strange, considering the circumstances and the party strength, if the ruling party had been always wise; but it must be said that they have done very few wicked or very foolish things. They have been fortunate in the possession of a few wise and Conservative men, with courage enough to make their sentiments known. For instance, in the last Legislature a stupid old Bourbon introduced a bill to make a breach of contract by a negro a penal offense. But Mr. Furlow, a strong Democrat, but a sensible man, rose at once, and declared that he would oppose such a measure as long as he lived; that, in his experience, if you pay a negro and treat him honestly, he will work fairly and stick to his contract. Furlow is a popular man, and has the courage of his opinions; and the result was that, in a house of one hundred and thirty members, only twelve votes were cast for the bill.

In like manner, the Toombs men, who are the Bourbons in Georgia, have tried, on different occasions, to get a constitutional convention, but have always failed, the constitution being a sufficiently good instrument. So, too, in his last message, Governor Smith, who has conducted himself so well in the "insurrection" business, urged the Legislature to stop the appropriation of eight thousand dollars per annum for the colored university; and the superintendent of public instruction supported him, believing, as he told me, that a normal school for colored teachers was more necessary than a university. But, in spite of a foolish prejudice against the teachers in the university, the Legislature refused to do the governor's bidding.

It is but just to add that, if the dread of "social equality" were likely to die out, this would be skillfully prevented by some leading Republicans, chief of whom is the Northern Methodist Bishop Haven, who has on several occasions openly declared himself in favor of "social equality," and who appears to me to have quite a genius for keeping alive a subject which naturally stirs up rancorous feelings, and which is best left to settle itself.

The prostration of the Republican party has given the Democrats such great power that they are now on the verge of a quarrel among themselves. In two Congressional districts, in 1874, Democrats ran against Democrats; in many counties independent candidates were put forward, and, where the Republicans were wise enough to support them, were elected. There are at this time eight or ten candidates for governor. By-the-way, Governor Smith is a candidate for re-election, and, in view of this fact, his firm and just course during the "insurrection" excitement shows that he at least believes that the white people, whose votes he would like to get, are in favor of justice to the negroes.

Georgia has some able and many influential public men. Unfortunately for the Republicans, they are all in the Democratic party. Governor Brown, who is reputed the ablest and most popular man in the State, was a Republican in 1868; but he is one no longer. He is a man of moderate views, a lover of justice. Of Mr. Stephens I need not speak. He is deeply respected by all Georgians, who forgive him all his vagaries, and will support him for whatever place he desires, conscious that he will serve them honestly. General Toombs is a man of but little influence. He has a small and decreasing following, composed of a few extremists.

Mr. Ben Hill, who is a member of the next Congress, Is spoken of in Georgia as a prodigy, and as certain to make a career in Congress. He is a ready speaker, and has spoken, in his time, on both sides of several important public questions. There are other notable men, but those I have named are the leaders of opinion.

"When the Democrats are so likely to split, especially on the nomination for governor, I suppose the Republicans will stand ready to support an independent Democrat," I said to a leading Republican.

He replied, "That is not so certain. It is more probable that some Republican will be selfish enough to demand a nomination for himself, will get it with the help of the negro, and will, of course, be beaten. The fact is," he added, "you can see that there is no room here for a Republican party such as exists, composed of a few ambitious leaders and a mass of ignorant blacks. It is a nuisance."

He was right. Such a party is a danger to the community; and I can not help but admire the self-control of the Democrats, who, with such overwhelming majorities in the Legislature, have committed so few follies. Their management has not always been wise ; and in the parts of the State remote from railroads, there has been maltreatment of blacks which was scandalous, and which the press did not properly report. Such things are getting rare, as I was assured by Republicans who were well informed. But it seemed to me that both the press and many of the public men of the State are foolishly timid in rebuking both folly and wrong. They have not sufficient confidence in the people.

It was laughable to me to see how timidly a part of the press and some of the prominent public men supported a movement in Atlanta to celebrate last Fourth of July, and to see, nevertheless, in what crowds the people turned out in the city, and came in from the country to join in the celebration when it was finally determined on.

I ought to add, on the authority of several Federal office-holders, all earnest Republicans, that the bar of the State, in matters where justice to the colored people is concerned, is not chargeable with neglect or cowardice. They assured me positively that lawyers all over the State, from the highest to the least, were always ready to defend a negro in a court of justice, if called on. The conduct of the recent conspiracy trials shows this to be true.

The difficulty in Georgia is that black and white, Republican and Democratic, demagogues unite in maintaining the color-line in politics. The bad Democrat does not object, for it enables him to control the State. The bad Republican likes it, for it makes him a martyr, and gives him what he longs for — a Federal office — or at least the excuse for demanding one. Governor Smith spoke wisely when he said to me that only when the color-line was broken could the politics of the State be settled, and this would bring absolute security to the negro. There is no doubt, too, that the Civil Rights Bill and the Force Bill, and all the other efforts made to maintain in the South a spurious Republican party, such as giving many of the Federal offices to men who have no real hold or influence in their

State — all these things have only tended to band the white voters together in a more and more inflexible opposition to the Federal administration, and to band the ignorant blacks together, and subject them to the rule of demagogues, leaving the moderate men of both sides without their just voice or influence.

THE END